VISUAL QUICKSTART GUIDE

LIGHTWAVE 3D 8

FOR WINDOWS AND MACINTOSH

Arthur Howe and Brian E. Marshall

 Peachpit Press

Visual QuickStart Guide
LightWave 3D 8 for Windows and Macintosh
Arthur Howe and Brian E. Marshall

Peachpit Press

1249 Eighth Street
Berkeley, CA 94710
510/524-2178
800/283-9444
510/524-2221 (fax)
Find us on the World Wide Web at: www.peachpit.com
To report errors, send a note to errata@peachpit.com
Peachpit Press is a division of Pearson Education

Copyright © 2004 by Arthur Howe and Brian E. Marshall

Editors: Elise Walter
Copyeditor: Nancy Reinhardt
Tech Editor: Rich Hurrey
Production Coordinators: Jake McFarland, Andrei Pasternak
Compositors: Jerry Ballew, Gloria Schruick
Indexers: Julie Bess, Lisa Stumpf
Cover Design: The Visual Group
Cover Production: George Mattingly / GMD

ISBN 0-321-23295-X

9 8 7 6 5 4 3 2 1

Printed and bound in the United States of America

Dedication

Arthur Howe

To my wife, Teri; my daughter, Kaitlin; and my son, Jarred for putting up with me while I locked myself away in the office to write. Without their love, support, and understanding this book would not have been possible.

Brian E. Marshall

To my friends and family for putting up with me while I wrote this book.

Acknowledgments

Art and Brian would especially like to thank the following:

Elise Walter, for exceptional editing, putting up with grumpy authors, and guiding us down the previously unexplored road of writing a book.

Victor Gavenda, for approaching us about doing a LightWave 3D book. Without you, this book wouldn't exist!

Marjorie Baer, for pulling this all together and making sure that things got started.

Richard Hurrey, for his awesome tech editing, making sure that we knew what we were talking about, and for both his encouragement and friendship.

Nancy Reinhardt, for her hawk-eyed copyediting.

Jake McFarland and Andrei Pasternak, production coordinators, for their tireless efforts to make our screenshots look good; Julie Bess and Lisa Stumpf, for indexing the book; and Jerry Ballew and Gloria Schruick, for laying it all out so nicely.

Our partners at H_2MW Consultants, for understanding while we juggled writing this book and working.

The LightWave development team, for their dedication over the years to creating a great 3D application, without which we might be working at a fast-food joint instead of doing something we love.

In addition, Brian would like to thank Skip, for giving him a nice, warm place in California to write during the extremely cold months in New England.

TABLE OF CONTENTS

	Introduction	**ix**
Chapter 1	**Getting Started**	**1**
	The Layout Interface	2
	The Modeler Interface	4
	Changing the LightWave Interface	6
	Changing Keyboard Shortcuts	10
	The Layout Scene Editor	12
	The Hub	13
	Working with Files	15
	Importing and Exporting Object File Formats	18
	Working with Content Directories	19
Chapter 2	**Touring the Viewports**	**23**
	Overview	24
	Changing the Viewport	33
	Configuring the Grid	35
	Customizing OpenGL in Layout	37
	General Display Options	39
Chapter 3	**Creating Geometry**	**43**
	Setting Up Modeler	44
	Using Points and Polygons	47
	Point Information	56
	Primitives	59
	Text and Fonts	63
	Organic Modeling	66
	Skelegons	77
Chapter 4	**Editing Geometry**	**81**
	Modeling with Layers	82
	Selection Methods	86
	Clipboard Actions	90
	Adjusting Geometry	91
	Edge Tools	106
	Extending Geometry	111
	Boolean Operations	116

Chapter 5   **Vertex Maps**   **121**
UV Texture Maps 122
Weight Maps 132
Morph Maps 141
Color Maps 144

Chapter 6   **Beginning Animation**   **147**
Working in 3D Space 148
Using the Basic Animation Tools 155
Working with Time 158
Working with Keyframes 163
Previewing Your Animation 167

Chapter 7   **Objects and Bones**   **171**
Introducing Objects 172
Using Custom Objects 174
Working with Subdivision Surfaces 181
Deforming Your Geometry 183
Using Displacement Tools 187
Morphing Objects 189
Working with Bones 198
Adding Skelegons 206

Chapter 8   **Lighting**   **207**
Lights and Lighting Effects 208
Adding Lights 209
Adjusting Light Parameters 216
Creating Shadows 220
Lighting Special Effects 225
Using Global Illumination 228

Chapter 9   **Cameras**   **231**
Camera Management 232
Customizing the Lens 239
Using Anti-Aliasing 242
Depth of Field 245
Rendering Motion 247

Chapter 10   Advanced Animation Tools   249

Keyframe Automation 250

Managing Keyframes 254

Using Channel Modifiers 268

Targeting Items in Layout 271

Parenting Items in Layout 272

Working with Inverse Kinematics 276

Using the Motion Options 285

Working with Motion Modifiers 287

Working with Coordinate Systems 288

Chapter 11   Creating Special Effects   293

Changing the Backdrop 294

Creating Particle Effects 299

Using Fog in Your Scenes 305

Making Your Objects Glow 308

Applying Image Filters 310

Using HyperVoxels 311

Chapter 12   Surfaces and Textures   321

Creating Surfaces in Modeler 322

Working with Surfaces 325

Basic Surface Attributes 327

Creating a Texture 334

Animating Surface Attributes 350

Viper 353

Presets 355

Chapter 13   Rendering Your Scene   357

Considering Render Time 358

Configuring the Renderer 360

Exploring Render Modes 366

Using Ray Trace Options 369

Using Object Render Options 371

Working with High Dynamic Range Imagery . . 376

Index   379

TABLE OF CONTENTS

INTRODUCTION

Welcome to *LightWave 3D 8: Visual QuickStart Guide.*

LightWave is a high-end 3D modeling, animation, and rendering program. There are many applications for LightWave, ranging from graphics for print to special effects for motion pictures. Whether you want to create a sinking *Titanic* or character models for a video game, LightWave makes it easy by offering a comprehensive set of animation and modeling tools. Not to mention that the unrivaled photorealistic output capabilities of its renderer are considered by many to be the industry standard.

This book introduces you to LightWave 3D's interface and feature set. You'll find that for such a powerful 3D application, LightWave is relatively easy to learn. Its intuitive tool layout helps beginners get up and running quickly, while providing enough depth and configurability to satisfy the experienced animator who needs a little more control. Chapters 3 through 5 cover the Modeler application, where you'll build objects and scenes, and Chapters 6 through 13 cover Layout, where you'll do all your animating, surfacing, lighting, and rendering. The exercises are designed to give you an understanding of how one of the most popular 3D applications in the industry is used—follow along carefully, and maybe one day we'll see your work on the big screen.

Who Is This Book For?

Whether you're a beginner wanting to learn the basic concepts of 3D animation or you're currently using another 3D application and want to learn LightWave, this book is for you. We do assume you're already familiar and comfortable with using computers and other graphics applications, but you don't have to have prior 3D experience, though that would make learning LightWave easier. If you go through the exercises in this book front to back, you'll end up with a solid foundation in the use of LightWave, including how to build 3D models, scenes, surfaces, and textures and how to output your work for yourself and others to see. If you want to learn something specific, though, you can treat this book as a reference guide, look up what you need to know, and jump right in. In a *Visual QuickStart Guide*, we don't necessarily expect you to read the book cover to cover, so feel free to skip around and let the pictures guide you through the techniques.

Although this book touches upon some of LightWave's advanced features such as the particle system, the volumetric renderer, and high-dynamic-range imagery (HDRI), after you finish with this book, you'll be ready to explore them in more depth. You'll also be ready to explore some of the features we don't cover in this book, namely LightWave's extremely powerful Spreadsheet Scene Manager, soft-body dynamics, and the Motion-Mixer nonlinear animation tool. You can find information and tutorials regarding the use of these tools in the LightWave 3D User's Manual or on the Web (see the "Additional Resources" section of this Introduction).

Many people discover that they prefer one particular part of the process, whether it's modeling, animating, or surfacing and lighting. As you work through the exercises in this book, try to identify which part of it you enjoy the most and focus your time there once you start doing work of your own. You never know, it may turn into a career, or you may be happy with simply pursuing it as a hobby.

What You'll Need

You will need to have a copy of LightWave 3D for Windows or Macintosh already installed on your computer. Refer to the LightWave 3D User's Manual for instructions on installing the application.

LightWave is resource-intensive, so please check the system requirements on the product box or on NewTek's LightWave 3D Web site (www.lightwave3d.com) and make sure that your system meets the minimum requirements. We recommend that you upgrade your machine to include as much RAM as you can install and invest in a good OpenGL accelerator. LightWave can also take advantage of, but does not require, a three-button mouse.

Supported Operating Systems

This book covers LightWave 3D 8 for both Windows and Macintosh. LightWave will run on Windows 98 or later (Windows 2000 or XP Pro is recommended) and in Mac OS X.

As you can see from **Figures i.1** and **i.2**, the interface is identical in the two platforms. In fact, the only real difference is that if you're using a single-button mouse on a Mac, when an exercise says to right-click, you'll need to hold down the Command key and click. Otherwise, there's no functional difference between the Mac and Windows versions.

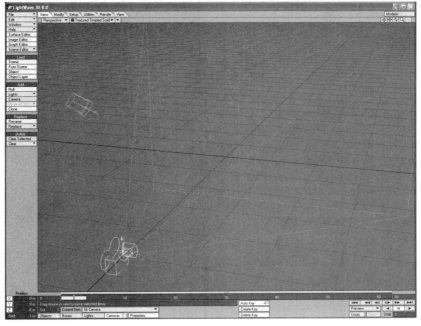

Figure i.1 The LightWave interface in Windows . . .

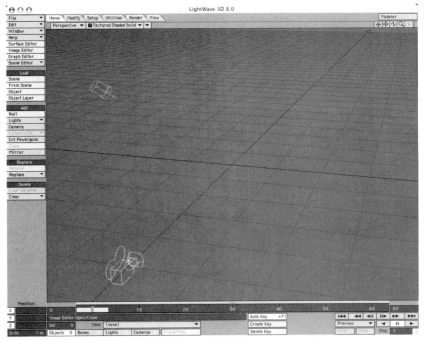

Figure i.2 . . . is nearly identical to the interface of the Macintosh version.

Companion Web Site

At the companion Web site for this book (www.h2mw.com/lw-vqs), you can download example files, check for updates, and report errata. You'll also find some sample color images, because a black-and-white book simply can't do justice to the colored tool indicators in this 3D program. In fact, if you're having trouble seeing the details in any of the images in this book, check the companion site—we may have anticipated the problem and posted a color version.

Additional Resources

There are a number of places on the Internet that offer information, discussion boards, and tutorials on the use of LightWave. In fact, one of the strongest points about LightWave is its devoted user community: On the message boards, you'll find professionals who work on high-profile projects conversing with and helping beginning LightWave users. A whole section of NewTek's Web site is dedicated to displaying user-created art. The user community is a great resource, so don't be afraid to log on and chat with your fellow LightWavers. Other sites of interest are www.flay.com, which has a plug-in database you can search to find free, shareware, and commercial tool plug-ins for LightWave, and www.luxology.net, which is an excellent resource for tutorials and LightWave knowledge. *Keyframe Magazine* and *NewTek Pro* are two publications dedicated to NewTek products that offer extensive coverage and tutorials for LightWave.

GETTING STARTED

LightWave 3D is broken up into two main components: Layout, where all animation, lighting, rendering, and the majority of surfacing are done; and Modeler, where you create your 3D objects, assign vertex maps, and define their surfaces. Before you jump into using Layout and Modeler, you really need to familiarize yourself with the interface of each. Although their general layouts are the same, their tasks are not, so you'll find some important differences.

This chapter will guide you through the Layout and Modeler interfaces and introduce you to working with the Hub, a third component that acts as a data conduit between the other two.

The Layout Interface

Let's look first at the Layout interface (**Figure 1.1**).

◆ **Toolbar:** The toolbar holds Layout's animation tools. The tools are grouped by function, making them easier to find. Notice that if a keyboard shortcut is available for a particular tool, it's displayed on the tool's button (**Figure 1.2**).

◆ **Tabs:** Clicking a tab changes the tools displayed in the toolbar. As you click through them, notice that the upper buttons down to Presets don't change, so these commonly used tools and editors are always available no matter what you're working on.

◆ **OpenGL Viewport:** This is where you'll work with your 3D scene, manipulating items and generating previews of your work. Chapter 2, "Touring the Viewports," covers the OpenGL Viewports of both Layout and Modeler in depth.

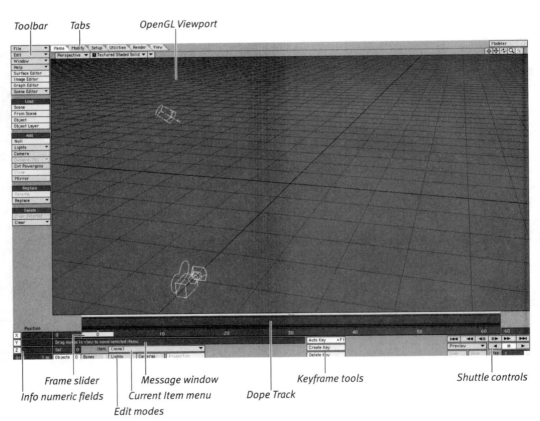

Figure 1.1 In the Layout interface, you animate and surface items, light your scene, and render final images.

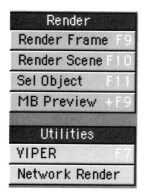

Figure 1.2 To learn the keyboard shortcut for a particular tool, simply look for the white letters on most buttons in the toolbar.

◆ **Shuttle controls:** These let you play back a scene in forward or reverse or step through it a frame at a time.

◆ **Keyframe tools:** These buttons toggle automatic keyframing and open the Create Motion Key and Delete Motion Key dialogs.

◆ **Current Item menu:** This pull-down menu displays the name of the currently selected item. Click it to show the list of items that are selectable in the current edit mode.

◆ **Message window:** This field always displays the name of the tool you're currently working with, and it also shows messages from Layout.

◆ **Edit modes:** These buttons control which edit mode you're currently using. If you click Objects, you'll be able to manipulate any objects in your scene, click Lights to manipulate any of the lights, and so on. If you click an item in the Layout Viewport of a different type than the current edit mode, the edit mode automatically changes so that you can immediately begin working with the selected item.

◆ **Frame slider:** Use the frame slider to control time for your animation in Layout, setting its overall duration, picking start and end times, and choosing which frame is currently displayed.

◆ **Dope Track:** Use the Dope Track to manipulate keyframes in time.

◆ **Info numeric fields:** This box changes according to which tool you're currently using, continually updating to show relevant data. For example, if you're moving something with the Move tool, it displays the item's position, and if you're rotating something with the Rotate tool, it displays the item's angle. This info box also doubles as a numeric input field, where you can type in new values for the different axes.

The Modeler Interface

Now let's look at the Modeler interface (**Figure 1.3**).

◆ **Toolbar:** As in Layout, the toolbar holds most of Modeler's tools.

◆ **Tabs:** As in Layout, clicking the different tabs changes the options available below Presets in the toolbar.

◆ **OpenGL Viewports:** You'll do your modeling and object manipulation in the Viewports, just like in Layout. Modeler defaults to four Viewports, whereas Layout defaults to one. You can configure the number and layout of these Viewports in either application (see Chapter 2).

◆ **Current object menu:** This always shows the name of the object you're currently working on, which will be "Unnamed" until you save the object with a name. Also, if you've modified the current object and haven't saved it yet, you'll see an asterisk next to the name (**Figure 1.4**). Click the menu to see the list of other objects currently available for editing.

◆ **Layer bank:** These buttons represent the layers of your object. Click the top half of a button to make that layer active for editing. Click the bottom half of a button to display that layer in the background for reference. The purple arrow buttons to the left of the layer bank let you to step through the available layer banks for

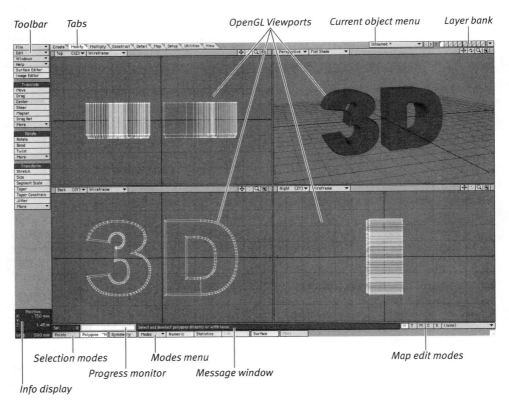

Figure 1.3 In the Modeler interface, you create and edit objects and also create surface groups.

Figure 1.4 Whenever you change an object, the "not yet saved" asterisk appears. It's good practice to save frequently.

Mouse Button Menus

Both Layout and Modeler use mouse button menus to speed up access to many functions. To open the mouse button menus, hold down Ctrl + Shift and press a mouse button (**Figure 1.5**). There's a menu for each of the three buttons on your mouse. (Note: Mac users with a single-button mouse will have access to only one additional mouse button menu. The second is accessed by holding Cmd + Ctrl + Shift when clicking.)

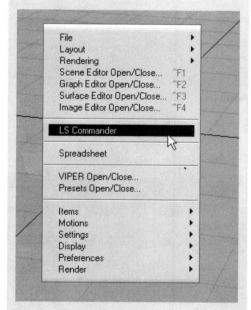

Figure 1.5 The left mouse button menu in Layout. These menus provide fast access to some of the more common functions. They're also configurable.

the current object. By default, the layer bank displays layers 1 through 10, but an object can have as many layers as you wish. Stepping through the layer banks gives you access to all of them.

- ◆ **VMap edit modes:** These buttons switch between the vertex-map ("VMap" for short) edit modes. All vertex maps of the selected type (weight, texture, or morph) are listed in the current VMap pull-down menu just to the right of the buttons.

- ◆ **Editing commands:** These buttons allow you to perform standard editing operations such as copy, paste, and undo.

- ◆ **Modes menu:** The menu lets you choose an origin for the modeling operation. For example, if you select Action Center: Mouse, and then rotate an object with the Rotate tool, it will rotate around the current location of your mouse pointer.

- ◆ **Selection modes:** As with the edit modes in Layout, these buttons control which selection mode you're currently using, and thus what item type you can work with. You can press Spacebar to cycle quickly through the available editing tools.

- ◆ **Progress monitor:** This shows the status of the current operation. You generally won't see it change unless you're performing a complex operation on a lot of geometry.

- ◆ **Message window:** This field displays simple instructions for using the currently selected tool, as well as status messages from Modeler.

- ◆ **Info display:** Like the info numeric fields in Layout, this box changes according to which tool you're currently using, continually updating to show relevant data. In Modeler, however, it does not offer numeric input fields for changing the values of the different axes.

THE MODELER INTERFACE

Changing the LightWave Interface

Layout and Modeler both allow you to rearrange menus and buttons in the interface and change contextual menus and keyboard shortcuts. This powerful feature lets you customize the interface for your own work style. You can create a version of each work space that displays only the tools you commonly use, and reduce the number of menu levels you need to go through.

To change the Layout interface:

1. From the Edit pull-down menu in the toolbar, choose Edit Menu Layout (**Figure 1.6**). (You can access the panel from the same menu in Modeler.)

   The Configure Menus panel opens (**Figure 1.7**).

2. In the Menu hierarchical list, click the arrow next to Items underneath Main Menu to display the list of toolbar entries for the Items tab (**Figure 1.8**).

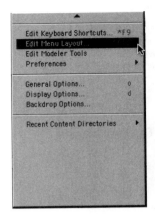

Figure 1.6 Use the Edit pull-down menu in either Layout or Modeler to access many of their configuration options.

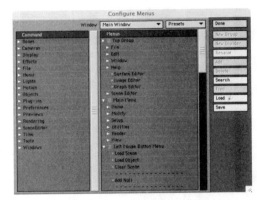

Figure 1.7 In the Configure Menus panel, you can modify how the buttons and menus in the interface are laid out.

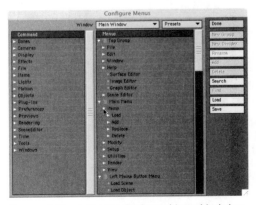

Figure 1.8 The right pane displays a hierarchical view of the current menu layout.

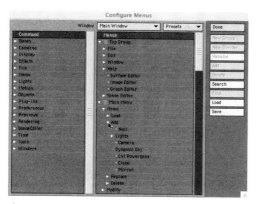

Figure 1.9 The expansion arrows indicate that the list entry is a menu or group heading in the interface.

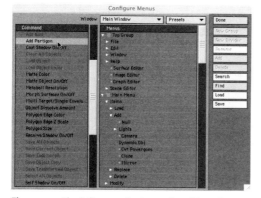

Figure 1.10 The left pane displays a list of functions that can be placed in the interface. Items that are already assigned are grayed out.

3. Click the arrow next to Add to display the entries for the Add subgroup (**Figure 1.9**).

4. In the Command hierarchical list, click the arrow next to Objects to display the list of available Object tools, and then scroll down until you see Add Partigon (**Figure 1.10**).

continues on next page

CHANGING THE LIGHTWAVE INTERFACE

5. Drag Add Partigon into the right pane, positioning the light blue placement indicator under Null (**Figure 1.11**).

An Add Partigon button appears beneath the Null button in the Add subgroup of the toolbar (**Figure 1.12**).

The Configure Menus panel has two hierarchical lists. The Command list on the left displays the currently available tools, and the Menu list on the right represents the current layout of the menus. Items that are dimmed in the left list already appear in one of the existing menus.

In the Menu list, you'll see headings for Top Group, Main Menu, Left Mouse Button Menu, and so on. The entries under these headings are the menus for that particular part of the interface. The Top Group is special because anything placed under this heading will always be displayed at the top of the toolbar no matter what tab you're in.

You'll also notice that some entries have an arrow next to them, some have a dot, and others have nothing. Entries with arrows are menu headings, those with dots are menu items or buttons, and those with nothing are groups. In addition to changing the layout of existing menus, you can create your own tabs. This is a great way to set up custom tool groups for tasks you perform repeatedly.

To create a new tab:

1. Follow Step 1 of the previous procedure, "To change the Layout interface."

2. Click Main Menu in the right hierarchical list to select it.

3. Click the New Group button (**Figure 1.13**). This adds a new entry under the Main Menu heading and adds a tab called New Group to the main interface (**Figure 1.14**).

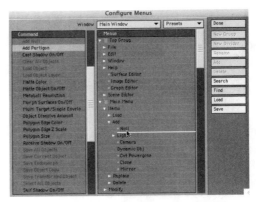

Figure 1.11 To place a button, simply drag it to the group or menu you'd like it to join in the interface.

Figure 1.12 Your new button. Configuring the LightWave interface is a great way to improve your workflow by placing the tools you commonly use in easy reach.

Figure 1.13 The New Group button creates a New Group heading or menu.

Figure 1.14 Because you created a new group under the Main Menu heading, you get a new tab in the interface.

CHANGING THE LIGHTWAVE INTERFACE

Figure 1.15 You can name your tabs anything you want.

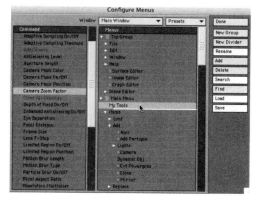

Figure 1.16 The indented placement indicator tells Layout to place this button within the menu.

Figure 1.17 Your new My Tools tab now contains the Zoom Factor button.

Figure 1.18 It's easy to revert to the default menu layout if you ever want to start over.

4. Click the New Group entry in the Menus list on the right of the Configure Menus panel.

5. Click the Rename button and type My Tools in the Rename Group dialog; then press [Enter] or click OK (**Figure 1.15**).

6. Click the arrow next to Cameras in the Command list on the left to show all the available Camera tools.

7. Drag Camera Zoom Factor into the right pane so that the light blue placement indicator is indented underneath the My Tools entry (**Figure 1.16**).

8. Select the My Tools tab.

You should now see a Zoom Factor button in the toolbar (**Figure 1.17**).

✔ Tip

■ You'll notice that we had you position the light blue placement indicator underneath the new My Tools group entry and make sure that it was indented. When the placement indicator is indented, it tells the Configure Menus panel to make this button part of the group or menu it's positioned under.

The exercises in this book assume you're using the default menu setup, so let's return the interface to its default state.

To reset the interface to the default:

1. Follow Step 1 of the procedure "To change the Layout interface."

2. From the Presets pull-down menu at the top right of the Configure Menus panel, choose Default (**Figure 1.18**).

✔ Tip

■ Although you cannot add your own menu presets, you can save your menu configuration using the Save button in the Configure Menus panel. You can then load them in at a later time using the Load button.

Changing Keyboard Shortcuts

As we mentioned, you can also customize the keyboard shortcuts for the various tools and editors. Not everything has a keyboard shortcut by default, so you may want to add a shortcut for a tool that you frequently use, to speed up your work. You may also find it is easier to remember the shortcut for a tool if you reassign it to a key that makes more sense to you. The Configure Keys panel is virtually identical in layout and operation to the Configure Menus panel.

To create a keyboard shortcut:

1. From the Edit pull-down menu in the toolbar, choose Edit Keyboard Shortcuts. (You can access the panel from the same menu in Modeler.)

    This opens the Configure Keys panel (**Figure 1.19**).

2. Click the arrow next to Cameras in the Command hierarchical list on the left to display the list of available tools related to Cameras.

3. Drag Add Camera into the Key Command list on the right so that its light blue placement indicator is located above the "c" entry, to assign it to that key (**Figure 1.20**).

Figure 1.19 Open the Configure Keys panel in much the same way you opened the Configure Menus panel.

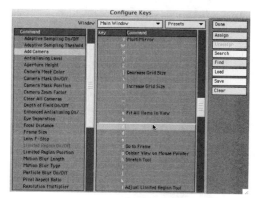

Figure 1.20 To assign a command to a keyboard shortcut, simply drag it so that the placement indicator is above the key you want it assigned to.

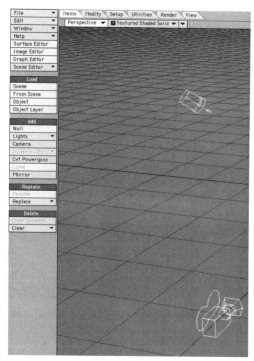

Figure 1.21 Click the Items tab to gain access to new toolbar options, including the Load tool group.

Figure 1.22 As with the defaults, any keyboard shortcuts you create will be displayed on the tool buttons and next to the menu entries.

4. Click the Done button to close the Configure Keys panel.

5. Click the Items tab to display new options in the toolbar (**Figure 1.21**).

6. Look at the Add tool group in the toolbar.

   The Camera entry now has "c" displayed next to it, showing you its keyboard shortcut (**Figure 1.22**).

✔ Tip

■ As with the menus, the exercises in this book assume you're using the default keyboard shortcuts. So select Default from the Presets menu in the Configure Keys panel to reset them back to the defaults when you're done experimenting.

The Layout Scene Editor

The Scene Editor is an overview of the items in your scene, so you can imagine how important it will be to your work. To open it, select Open from the Scene Editor pull-down menu in the toolbar, or press [Ctrl]+[F1] (**Figure 1.23**).

The Item list, in the Items tab, gives you an overview of every item in your scene. Each item type has a different icon associated with it: a box for objects, a bone for bones, a light for lights, and a camera for cameras. Clicking the channel expander symbol next to an item displays what channels are currently associated with that item and an overview of their keyframe information in the timeline view.

Click in the check mark column next to each item to toggle the item's visibility. The column with the eye icon displays each item's current render level, which you can change by clicking in this column and selecting a new render level from the menu that pops up. (See Chapter 2 for more about render levels.) The column with the lock icon indicates whether or not the item is locked, preventing it from being edited.

One of the most important features of the Item list is that is shows parent/child relationships of items in the scene. If an item has an expansion arrow to its left, that indicates the item has children. Clicking the arrow will expand the list to display the children items. You can also drag items in the list to quickly parent and unparent them. (For more about parenting items, see Chapter 10, "Advanced Animation Tools.")

You can shift or scale an item's entire motion by clicking it in the dope sheet view to change its timing. Click directly on a motion in the timeline view and drag to shift it forward or backward in time. Click and drag on the handles at either end to scale the motion's timing.

The operation of the Scene Editor in scaling key frames and modifying item, channel, and surface properties is considered an advanced topic, and is beyond the scope of this book. Please consult the LightWave 3D documentation for detailed information on the operation of the Scene Editor.

Figure 1.23 The Scene Editor is a central location for info about the items in your scene. You can get a quick overview of all your items and their relationships to other items, and also use the dope sheet view to quickly make general changes to an item's motion.

Figure 1.24 Load an object to send it to Layout.

Figure 1.25 The Hub pull-down menu allows you to quickly send information between Layout and Modeler. Once the object is in both, the Hub will update them as you switch back and forth.

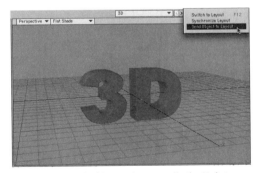

Figure 1.26 Send Object to Layout tells the Hub to load the current object into Layout.

The Hub

The Hub is a background component of LightWave that allows Layout and Modeler to communicate with one another. The simplest way to explain it is that when you create an object in Modeler and save it, you can then have Modeler hand the object to the Hub, which in turn hands it to Layout. Similarly, if you load a scene into Layout and then switch to Modeler, the Hub automatically takes the objects from the scene and loads them into Modeler. Surface attributes and changes to the geometry are automatically updated between Layout and Modeler as you switch from one to the other. However, Modeler will not automatically send a new object to Layout—you must explicitly tell it to do so.

To send an object to Layout:

1. From the File pull-down menu in the tool-bar, select Load Object (**Figure 1.24**).

2. When the Open File dialog appears, select an object from the Objects directory of LightWave 3D content, and click OK to load the object.

3. From the Hub pull-down menu at the top right of the interface (**Figure 1.25**), select Send Object to Layout (**Figure 1.26**).

   If Layout is already running, focus will shift to Layout with your object loaded. If Layout is not running, Modeler will launch Layout and then send the object to it.

✔ Tip

■ You can only send an object to Layout if it exists on disc. The command is dimmed when you're working with new objects that have not yet been saved.

THE HUB

Configuring the Hub

In addition to serving as a data conduit, the Hub will also save configuration changes for Layout and Modeler, and can have them automatically save their current data to temporary files should they unexpectedly quit. Nothing is worse than spending a good deal of time on an object or scene, forgetting to save as you progress, and then losing it all if the application unexpectedly closes.

In Windows, the Hub runs as a system tray application (**Figure 1.27**), and on the Macintosh, it runs as any other application does, opening a window when launched. In Windows, right-click the Hub icon in the system tray and choose Properties from the pull-down menu to open the Hub's Properties dialog (**Figure 1.28**). On the Macintosh, you'll need to switch to the Hub and change its properties from there (**Figure 1.29**).

Click the arrow next to Options to see what's available. Click the Automatic Shutdown option to tell the Hub how long to wait after the applications have closed before shutting itself down. Click the Automatic Save or Automatic Project Save options to tell the Hub how often to have Modeler and Layout, respectively, automatically save their current data.

Figure 1.27 The Hub is a system tray application under Windows.

Figure 1.28 In the Properties dialog, you can configure the time intervals for Automatic Shutdown and Automatic Save.

Figure 1.29 Mac users need to change the properties directly from the Hub's interface. Windows users can access the interface by double-clicking the Hub icon in the system tray.

THE HUB

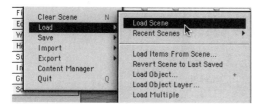

Figure 1.30 The File > Load submenu contains all your scene-loading options.

Figure 1.31 Simply select the file you want to open in the Load Scene dialog.

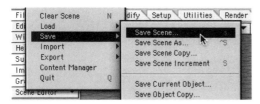

Figure 1.32 The File > Save submenu contains all your scene-saving options.

Figure 1.33 In the Save Scene As dialog, give your scene file a name, and navigate to the directory where you want to save it.

Working with Files

Throughout your 3D work, you'll be creating object and scene files that you save to disc and load back into LightWave. So you'd better know how to perform these operations.

To open a scene file in Layout:

1. In the Items tab, click Scene under the Load tool group in the toolbar, or press Ctrl+o (**Figure 1.30**).

2. When the Load Scene dialog opens, navigate to the desired LightWave scene file, select it, and press Enter or click Open (**Figure 1.31**).

To save a scene file in Layout:

1. From the File pull-down menu in the toolbar, select Save > Save Scene or press s (**Figure 1.32**).

2. If this is a new scene file, when the Save Scene As dialog appears, navigate to the desired save location, give your scene file an appropriate name, and press Enter or click Save (**Figure 1.33**).

   or

   If this is an existing scene file, Layout will ask if you want to overwrite the current scene file. Click Yes to overwrite, or No to open the Save Scene As dialog and save the scene to a new file.

✔ Tip

■ If you want to save a new version of your scene file with a different name, use the Save Scene As option or press Shift+s.

WORKING WITH FILES

15

To open an object file in Layout:

1. In the Items tab, click Object under the Load tool group in the toolbar or press ⊞ (**Figure 1.34**).

2. When the Load Object dialog box appears, navigate to the desired LightWave object file, select it, and press ⟨Enter⟩ or click Load.

To open an object file in Modeler:

1. From the File pull-down menu in the toolbar, select Load Object or press ⟨Ctrl⟩+⟨o⟩.

2. When the Load Object dialog box appears, navigate to the desired LightWave object file, select it, and press ⟨Enter⟩ or click Load.

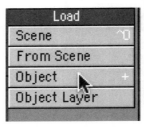

Figure 1.34 Load objects from the Load tool group.

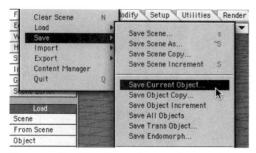

Figure 1.35 The File > Save submenu also contains your options for object saving.

Layout and Modeler each handle object saving differently. In Modeler, you're creating geometry, so you have the option to specify an object filename when you create a new object. Layout uses only existing objects, so it automatically saves over the existing copy of the currently selected object.

To save an object file in Layout:

◆ From the File pull-down menu, select Save > Save Current Object (**Figure 1.35**).

✔ Tips

■ You generally only save an object from within Layout after modifying one of its surface attributes. If you change a surface attribute in Layout and forget to save the object, whatever changes you made will be lost the next time you load the object or a scene that contains the object.

■ If you want to save a copy of the current object with a different name, use the Save Object Copy command.

To save an object file in Modeler:

1. From the File pull-down menu in the toolbar, select Save Object or press ⒮.

2. If this is a new object file, when the Save Object As dialog appears, give your object file an appropriate name, navigate to the desired save location, and press ⒠nter or click Save.

   or

   If this is an existing object, Modeler will simply save over the existing object file.

✔ Tip

■ If you want to save a version of the current object with a different name, use Save Object As or press Ctrl+⒮.

Importing and Exporting Object File Formats

Layout and Modeler can both load object files created in other 3D applications, giving them a great deal of flexibility. To load an object created in another application, simply load it as you would any other object file.

Modeler can also export to a variety of different 3D object file formats. This is useful if you're working with colleagues who use another 3D application.

To export an object to a different format:

1. Load or create an object file in Modeler. (See Chapter 3, "Creating Geometry," to learn how to do this.)

2. From the File pull-down menu in the toolbar, select Export, and then the format you'd like to save to.

   We chose Export 3DS for our example (**Figure 1.36**).

3. When the Save File dialog appears, give the object file an appropriate name and navigate to the desired save location.

4. Press (Enter) or click Save, and a new dialog will open, showing you options for the chosen file type (**Figure 1.37**).

5. After you have chosen the export settings, press (Enter) or click OK to complete the file export.

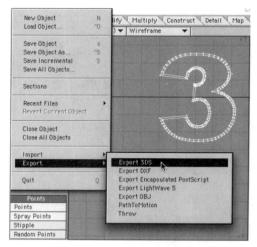

Figure 1.36 You can access the object export features from the File > Export submenu.

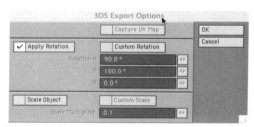

Figure 1.37 Some file formats are configurable, and exporting to them will give you a panel of options.

Working with Content Directories

The content directory is a great way to organize your work. Many users create a new content directory for each project, to keep all object, image, and scene files related to the project in one location. This makes them easier to find and manage. Whether you choose to work with multiple content directories or a single content directory is entirely up to you.

Every LightWave content directory must have at least three subdirectories named "Objects," "Images," and "Scenes," where each of these different file types are stored. When loading and saving files, Layout and Modeler open the dialog in the base directory for the selected file type. For example, when you load an object in Modeler, the Load Object dialog opens in the Objects directory of the current content directory.

Depending on your project, you may also have a Motions directory where you save item motion files or particle and soft-body simulation data. Some users also like to create Render and Preview directories where they save finished frames or animation tests. The key is to keep all files associated with a project in a single, easy-to-find location.

Content directories become even more useful when you're working with scenes. When you save a scene, the references to all the files related to the scene are saved using relative paths. This means Layout writes `Objects/MyObject.lwo` as the file reference in the actual scene file, as opposed to the absolute path `C:/MyContent/Objects/MyObject.lwo`. The same applies to saving references to image files that are used on object surfaces. The advantage to this is that you can move your content directory to a different hard disk, a different computer altogether, or even move the Objects, Images, and Scenes directories to another content directory, and Layout will still be able to find all the files related to the scene, so long as you tell it where the new content directory is. This is a handy feature that allows multiple users to work with the same content over a network.

You will encounter scenes and object files from other users that contain absolute paths. If you accidentally load an object or image from outside the current content directory and then save the object or scene, the file will contain absolute paths. When you next load the scene or object file, Layout and Modeler will prompt you to manually locate any files that they can't find. It's a good idea to identify these files as you're prompted for them, and then move them to the appropriate place in your content directory, reload the scene, and save it with the updated relative path information. This will prevent the problem from occurring again should you move the content to another location.

By default, both Layout and Modeler are configured to look in the directory where you installed LightWave 3D. This is also where the license-free content included with the application is installed. Let's take a look at how to change the current content directory.

To change the content directory in Layout:

1. Click the Display tab to display new options in the toolbar.

2. Click General Options in the toolbar, or press [o] to open the General Options tab of Layout's Preferences panel (**Figure 1.38**).

3. Click Content Directory to open the directory browser (**Figure 1.39**).

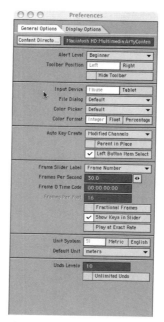

Figure 1.38 In the General Options tab, you can configure your Layout work space, including where to locate the current content directory.

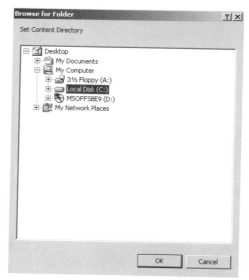

Figure 1.39 The directory browser provides a fast, convenient way to select a directory without having to wade through a lot of files.

Figure 1.40 Select your content directory, and click OK.

4. Navigate to the desired content directory, select it, and press [Enter] or click OK (Choose on the Mac) to set the content directory (**Figure 1.40**).

To change the content directory in Modeler:

1. From the Modeler pull-down menu in the toolbar, select Options > General Options (**Figure 1.41**) or press [o] to open the General Options dialog (**Figure 1.42**).

2. Repeat Steps 3 and 4 of the previous procedure, "To change the content directory in Layout."

Figure 1.41 You can configure Modeler's work space by selecting General Options in the Options submenu of the Modeler menu.

Figure 1.42 Set the content directory in the General Options dialog.

WORKING WITH CONTENT DIRECTORIES

TOURING THE VIEWPORTS

Your main tools when working in LightWave 3D are the Viewports in both Layout and Modeler. As you create your objects and scenes, you not only see them in the Viewports, but you also can manipulate them in the Viewports with your mouse. Each Viewport shows a grid, in whatever units of measurement you choose. The origin, or center of the grid, is located at 0 on all three of the movement axes (X, Y, and Z). Because they're such fundamental tools, it's important to understand how the Viewports and the grid function, as well as how best to tailor them to your needs.

In this chapter, we'll give you a guided tour of the Layout and Modeler Viewports. You'll learn how to use different drawing modes, change measurement units in the grid, and customize display options and configurations for specific tasks. With only a few exceptions, all of these features apply to both Layout and Modeler.

Chapter 2

Overview

You'll spend a lot of your time adjusting the Viewports and modifying how they display information, so take a moment to familiarize yourself with the different Viewport features and controls (**Figure 2.1**).

View types

The view-type pull-down menu lets you specify which view you would like to use for the corresponding Viewport. Most of the different views are available in both Layout (**Figure 2.2**) and Modeler (**Figure 2.3**).

All of the following view types are common to both Layout and Modeler:

◆ **Top:** This is a two-dimensional view looking down the negative Y axis at the X and Z axes.

◆ **Bottom:** This is a two-dimensional view looking up the positive Y axis at the X and Z axes.

◆ **Back:** This is a two-dimensional view looking down the negative Z axis at the X and Y axes.

◆ **Front:** This is a two-dimensional view looking up the positive Z axis at the X and Y axes.

◆ **Right:** This is a two-dimensional view looking down the negative X axis at the Y and Z axes.

◆ **Left:** This is a two-dimensional view looking up the positive X axis at the Y and Z axes.

◆ **Perspective:** This is a three-dimensional view showing your scene on all three axes.

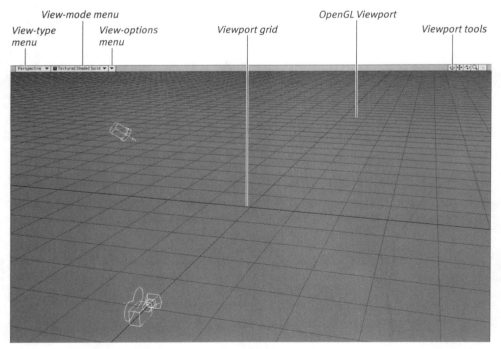

View-type menu
View-mode menu
View-options menu
Viewport grid
OpenGL Viewport
Viewport tools

Perspective | Textured Shaded Solid

Figure 2.1 The Viewports look the same in Layout and Modeler, but their options differ.

Figure 2.2 These view types are available in Layout.

Figure 2.3 These view types are available in Modeler.

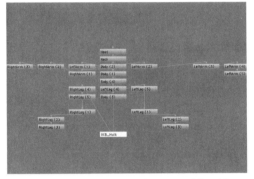

Figure 2.4 The Schematic view is a powerful tool for managing the items in your scene.

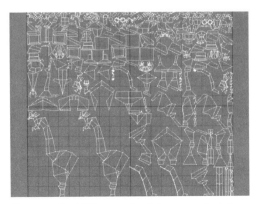

Figure 2.5 The UV Texture view lets you manipulate the values of an object's UV texture map.

The following view types are available only in Layout:

◆ **Light:** This is a three-dimensional view from the viewpoint of the currently selected light. It's useful for when you're trying to narrow a light's focus to a specific portion of your scene.

◆ **Camera:** This is a three-dimensional view from the viewpoint of the currently selected camera. This is an important view because it shows you what will be in your rendered scene. You'll spend a lot of time in the Camera view as you animate, light, surface, and add special effects to your scene.

◆ **Schematic:** This is a node-based schematic, showing all the items in the scene in relation to one another (**Figure 2.4**). For more information on the Schematic view and its use, please refer to the LightWave 3D User's Manual.

This view type is available only in Modeler:

◆ **UV Texture:** This view shows the UV map for an object (**Figure 2.5**). The UV Texture view is covered more in Chapter 5, "Vertex Maps."

OVERVIEW

Drawing modes

Each Viewport also has a drawing-mode pull-down menu where you can specify how LightWave displays information there. Each option is tailored to different uses (**Figures 2.6** and **2.7**).

The only drawing mode shared by both Layout and Modeler is the Maximum Render Level. This option lets you specify how objects are rendered in the Viewport. Each of the render modes is available in both Layout and Modeler, except where noted:

◆ **Bounding Box:** This Layout-only render level displays an object as its bounding box (**Figure 2.8**).

◆ **Vertices:** This Layout-only render level displays only the points in the object (**Figure 2.9**).

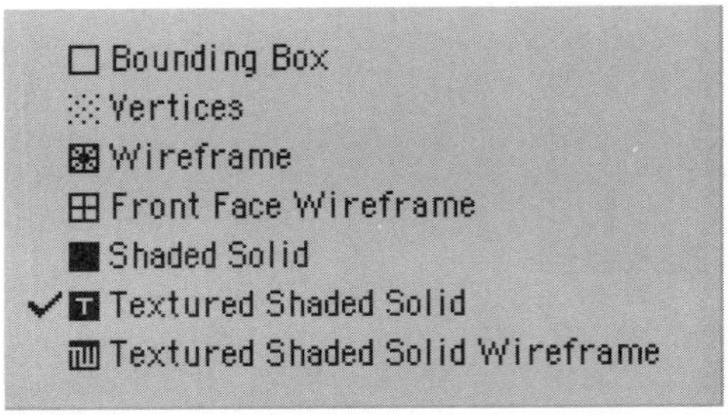

□ Bounding Box
⋮⋮ Vertices
▦ Wireframe
⊞ Front Face Wireframe
■ Shaded Solid
✓Ⓣ Textured Shaded Solid
▥ Textured Shaded Solid Wireframe

Figure 2.6 These drawing modes are available in Layout.

Wireframe
Color Wireframe
Hidden Line
Sketch
Wireframe Shade
Flat Shade
Smooth Shade
Weight Shade
Texture
Textured Wire

Figure 2.7 These drawing modes are available in Modeler.

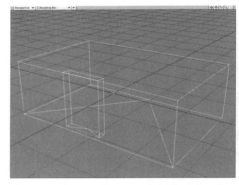

Figure 2.8 The Bounding Box mode displays only the bounding boxes of the objects in your scene.

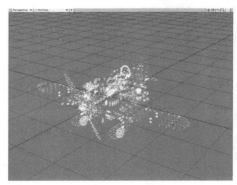

Figure 2.9 The Vertices mode displays only the points of the objects in your scene.

OVERVIEW

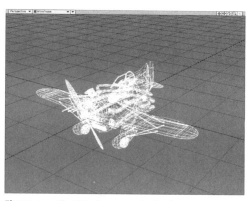

Figure 2.10 The Wireframe mode displays your objects as cages.

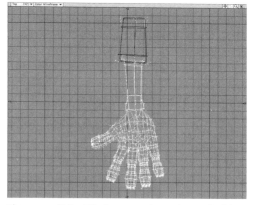

Figure 2.11 Color Wireframe mode can be used with the Sketch Color of polygons to clearly differentiate portions of an object.

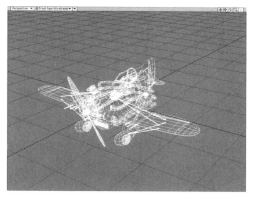

Figure 2.12 The Front Face Wireframe mode is similar to a solid shaded view, but with the object cage.

◆ **Wireframe:** This render level displays the object as a wireframe (**Figure 2.10**). In Wireframe mode, the polygons are transparent, meaning that you can see through the polygons facing the camera to the polygons facing away from the camera.

◆ **Color Wireframe:** This Modeler-only render level displays the geometry of the object using a colored wireframe (**Figure 2.11**). The colors are defined by the Sketch Color assigned to the polygons.

◆ **Front Face Wireframe:** This render level, and the corresponding Hidden Line in Modeler, displays your object as a wireframe, but with only the polygons facing the camera showing (**Figure 2.12**).

continues on next page

◆ **Sketch:** This Modeler-only render level displays a shaded wireframe of the geometry, using the specified sketch color for each polygon (**Figure 2.13**).

◆ **Wireframe Shade:** This Modeler-only render level is similar to Sketch, but uses each polygon's base surface color instead of the designated sketch color (**Figure 2.14**).

◆ **Flat Shade:** This Modeler-only render level displays the geometry using the base surface color, but without smoothing (**Figure 2.15**).

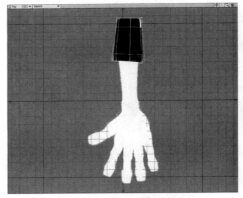

Figure 2.13 Like Color Wireframe mode, Sketch mode can be used to designate different groups of polygons within an object.

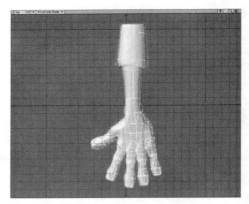

Figure 2.14 Wireframe Shade mode displays a shaded object but with the polygon edges outlined.

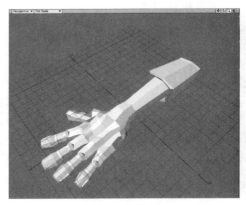

Figure 2.15 Flat Shade mode displays your objects as unsmoothed surfaces.

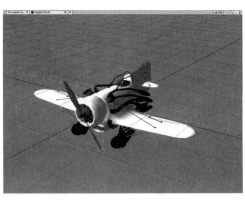

Figure 2.16 The Shaded Solid mode displays your objects as smoothed surfaces.

Figure 2.17 Textured Shaded Solid mode is used to view color textures on an object's surfaces.

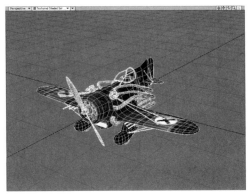

Figure 2.18 Textured Shaded Solid Wireframe mode is used to view the color textures on an object's surfaces with the wireframe overlayed.

◆ **Shaded Solid:** This render level, and the corresponding Smooth Shade in Modeler, displays the geometry using the base surface color and any smoothing that has been applied (**Figure 2.16**).

◆ **Textured Shaded Solid:** This render level, and the corresponding Texture in Modeler, displays the geometry using the base surface color, smoothing, and color texture maps (**Figure 2.17**).

◆ **Textured Shaded Solid Wireframe:** This render level, and the corresponding Textured Wire in Modeler, displays geometry in the same fashion as Textured Shaded Solid, drawing the object's wireframe on top (**Figure 2.18**).

continues on next page

OVERVIEW

- **Weight Shade:** This Modeler-only render level displays your object shaded according to vertex weights, using red for positive weight values and blue for negative weight values (**Figure 2.19**).

- **Bone Weight Shade:** This Layout-only drawing mode shades objects that contain bones to indicate how they influence the geometry, using each bone's wireframe color to highlight its area of influence. You can also select a bone directly to highlight the area that it influences (**Figure 2.20**). This mode is great for fine-tuning (see Chapter 7, "Objects and Bones").

- **Bone X-Ray:** This Layout-only drawing mode displays all the bones in objects through the surface when using a shaded drawing mode, making it easier to select them for animation (**Figure 2.21**).

✔ Tips

- To view objects in Modeler as only vertices, uncheck the Show Surfaces option in the Display Options panel. You can optimize how textures are displayed in the Viewports by modifying the OpenGL Textures option in the Display Options panel for Layout or Modeler.

- In Layout, you can specify the render level of each object using the Scene Editor. Turning off OpenGL for items you aren't currently working with greatly reduces the processing power required to update the Layout Viewport, so you'll see your changes more quickly.

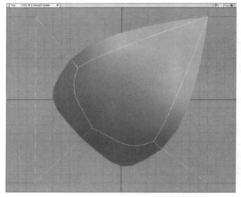

Figure 2.19 Weight Shade mode shows which points in an object contain weight values and how the weights affect the geometry.

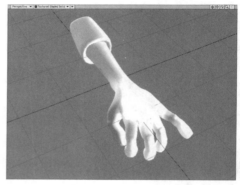

Figure 2.20 The Bone Weight Shade mode is handy for determining which bones affect which portions of your object.

Figure 2.21 Bone X-Ray mode works just like an X-ray machine, allowing you to see the bones inside Shaded Solid objects.

OVERVIEW

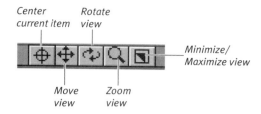

Figure 2.22 The Viewport tools are located at the upper right of every Viewport.

Viewport tools

At the top-right corner of every Viewport is a set of tools that you can use to move, rotate, and zoom the corresponding Viewport (**Figure 2.22**). It's important to note that not all of the manipulators are available in every view type. If a tool is not available for use, it's dimmed.

◆ **Center current item:** Click this Layout-only option to center the currently selected item(s) in the Viewport. The similarly named command in the Layout view-mode menu does the same thing.

◆ **Move view:** Click and drag this button to move the Viewport along the X and Z axes. Right-click and drag this button to move the Viewport along the Y axis. The Set View Position command in the Layout drawing mode pull-down menu allows you to do this numerically.

◆ **Rotate view:** Click and drag this button to rotate the Viewport on the Heading and Pitch axes. Right-click and drag this button to rotate the Viewport on the Bank axis. The Set View Rotation command in the Layout drawing mode pull-down menu allows you to do this numerically.

◆ **Zoom view:** Click and drag this button to zoom the current view. The Set View Zoom command in the Layout drawing mode pull-down menu allows you to do this numerically.

◆ **Minimize/Maximize view:** When working with multiple viewports, clicking this button expands the selected view to fill the entire workspace or returns it to its original size.

continues on next page

OVERVIEW

You saw the remainder of these menu items in Figure 2.6, but they are really tools that you can use to manipulate the view in your Layout Viewport.

◆ **Reset View Position:** This option resets the Viewport to the default position.

◆ **Reset View Rotation:** This option resets the Viewport to the default rotation.

◆ **Reset View Zoom:** This option resets the Viewport to the default magnification factor.

To move the view:

1. Click the move view button.

2. Drag forward and backward to move the view along the Z axis.

3. Drag left and right to move the view along the X axis.

4. Right-click the move view button.

5. Drag forward and backward to move the view along the Y axis.

To rotate the view:

1. Click the rotate view button.

2. Drag forward and backward to rotate the view on the Pitch axis.

3. Drag left and right to rotate the view on the Heading axis.

4. Right-click the rotate view button.

5. Drag left and right to rotate the view on the Bank axis.

To zoom the view:

1. Click the zoom view button.

2. Drag forward and backward to zoom the view in and out.

✔ **Tip**

■ You can also manipulate the Viewports by holding [Alt] (move), [Ctrl]+[Alt] (zoom) or [Shift]+[Alt] (rotate) while pressing the left mouse button and dragging.

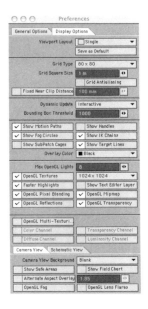

Figure 2.23 In the Display Options tab of Layout's Preferences panel, you configure how the Viewports present information and draw objects in the scene.

Figure 2.24 You can change the number and layout of Viewports in Layout.

Changing the Viewport

You may have noticed that Layout defaults to a single Viewport, whereas Modeler defaults to four. You can change this to match your work style. We'll show you how.

To change the Viewport in Layout:

1. Choose Display Options from the Edit pull-down menu in the toolbar, or press d to open the Display Options tab of Layout's Preferences panel (**Figure 2.23**).

2. From the Viewport Layout pull-down menu, choose a different layout. For example, we chose Quad (**Figure 2.24**). Your Viewport layout has now changed (**Figure 2.25**).

✔ Tip

■ If you prefer a particular layout, choose it from the Viewport Layout pull-down menu, and then click the Make Default button directly below it. This tells Layout to use this Viewport configuration every time you start a new scene or first launch the application.

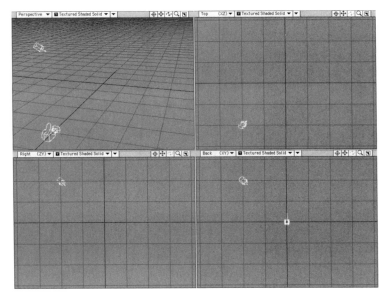

Figure 2.25 You can specify the number (up to four) and layout of the Viewports.

To change the Viewport in Modeler:

1. Choose Display options from the Edit pull-down menu in the toolbar, or press [d] to open the Display Options panel (**Figure 2.26**).

2. From the Layout pull-down menu, choose a different Viewport layout. For example, we chose 2 Left, 1 Right (**Figure 2.27**).

   Your Viewport layout is now different (**Figure 2.28**).

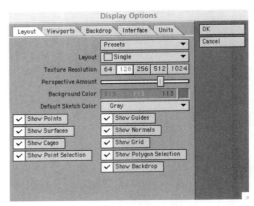

Figure 2.26 In the Display Options panel, you can adjust how Modeler's Viewports draw objects.

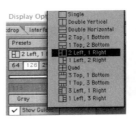

Figure 2.27 Changing the number and layout of the Viewports in Modeler is just as simple as it is in Layout.

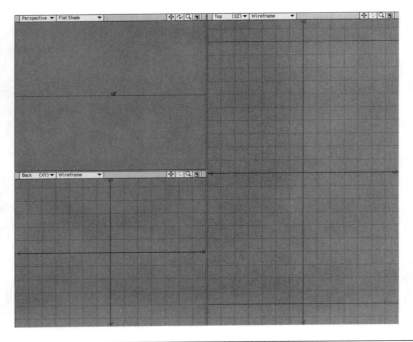

Figure 2.28 Unlike in Layout, when you change the layout of the Viewports in Modeler, that becomes the default until you change it again.

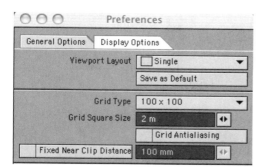

Figure 2.29 Changing the grid size is useful when you're trying to match the scale of an object.

Position	
X	-2 m
Y	2 m
Z	-2 m
Grid:	2 m

Figure 2.30 Layout continuously updates the current grid-size information, so you don't have to open the Preferences panel to check it.

Configuring the Grid

The following exercises will go over how to adjust some of the basic grid-display properties for the Viewports. Many artists like to create scenes at "scale," where the items and motions in the scene correspond to similar situations in the real world. The scale of the scene is determined by the size of each grid square, so if you are working with tiny objects, you might want a fairly small grid size, whereas if you are going to be working with large objects, you might increase that value. For instance, for a scene with a flea hopping across a table, you might set your grid size to 5 millimeters so that the distance and the speed at which the flea travels will be true to life. On the other hand, for a scene where a space fighter attacks a cruiser, you might set your grid size to 5 kilometers so that the size and speed of the fighter's attack runs seem realistic.

To change the grid size in Layout:

1. Click the Display tab, and then click View Options or press ⒹＤ to open the Display Options tab of Layout's Preferences panel.

2. In the Grid Square Size field, type a new value, or use the arrow buttons to raise or lower the current value. For example, we entered 2m (**Figure 2.29**).

The Viewport updates to reflect the change, and the Grid field, located below the info numeric fields, updates as well (**Figure 2.30**).

✔ Tips

■ The keyboard shortcuts for decreasing and increasing the grid size are Ⓕ[and Ⓖ], respectively.

■ The distance the mouse moves an item is relative to the current grid size. The smaller the grid, the smaller the distance you move your items when dragging the mouse. This is useful when you need to fine tune the positions of items.

CONFIGURING THE GRID

To change the grid size in Modeler:

1. Press ⌐,⌐ to decrease the grid size.

2. Press ⌐.⌐ to increase the grid size.

3. As you make the changes, the Grid field (located below the info display) updates to reflect them (**Figure 2.31**).

In Modeler, the grid is infinite, so you can never see its edge. No matter how far you zoom in or zoom out, it is always displayed as a reference. Layout, on the other hand, allows you to see and animate off of the grid's edges. Layout's default grid is 10×10, and it's broken into sections, starting from the origin, so there are 10 grid squares in every direction (**Figure 2.32**). If you like, you can increase the grid in increments of 10, up to the maximum 100×100 grid.

To change the grid type in Layout:

1. Select the Display tab, and then click View Options or press ⌐d⌐ to open the Display Options tab of Layout's Preferences panel.

2. From the Grid Type pull-down menu, select a new size. For example, we chose 40×40 (**Figure 2.33**).

   The grid in your Viewport(s) updates to reflect the change (**Figure 2.34**).

Figure 2.31 The only way to modify the grid size in Modeler is by using the period and comma keys.

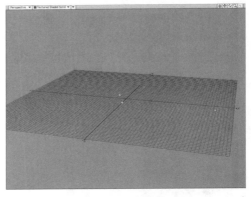

Figure 2.32 By default, the grid in Layout is presented in four sections.

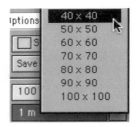

Figure 2.33 You can set the grid as high as 100 grid squares in each direction.

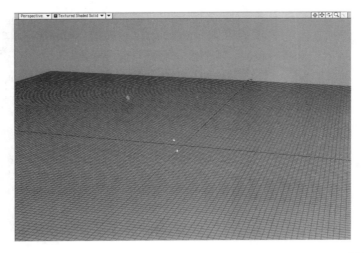

Figure 2.34 When you run out of grid space, add some more.

CONFIGURING THE GRID

Figure 2.35 Use the OpenGL options to modify how the Viewports handle certain OpenGL-specific tasks.

Customizing OpenGL in Layout

The Viewports in both Layout and Modeler use OpenGL to display your items. To change how they do this, you can modify one of the OpenGL-specific options. The majority of these options are in Layout, so we'll focus our attention there.

The OpenGL options are in the Display Options tab of Layout's Preferences panel. Let's take a quick look at what's available (**Figure 2.35**).

◆ **Max OpenGL Lights:** This option tells the Viewports how many lights to take into account when displaying shading in OpenGL. For instance, if you have two lights illuminating an object and this value is set to 1, then only the first light in the scene is used to light the object in the Viewports. The second light is ignored for display purposes. The maximum number of lights that can be displayed in the OpenGL Viewport is 8.

◆ **OpenGL Textures:** This option overrides the Textured Shaded Solid view type. If you deselect this option, your surface textures are not displayed in the Viewports.

◆ **OpenGL Texture Resolution:** You can specify a display resolution for textures in this pull-down menu. Displaying OpenGL textures uses memory, which can slow down the responsiveness of the Viewports. If your scene has a lot of textures and the Viewports are sluggish, try lowering this value; Layout then decreases the display resolution for larger textures. This is the only OpenGL-related option that is also available in Modeler's Display Options panel.

continues on next page

- **Show Texture Editor Layer:** This option affects surfaces with multiple texture layers. The Viewports can display only one texture per surface at a time, so by default they use the first texture associated with the surface. When this box is checked, Layout displays the texture layer that you're currently working with in the Texture Editor for a given surface. This is useful for positioning, rotating, and sizing textures in real time.

- **OpenGL Pixel Blending:** This option is great for when you want low-resolution, smooth textures for maximum Viewport response. When Layout reduces the resolution of images for display, it can create blocky artifacts (**Figure 2.36**). With OpenGL Pixel Blending checked, Layout interpolates between the pixels, in effect smoothing them, for a cleaner display (**Figure 2.37**). The lower the image resolution, the more pixel blending is applied, and the softer the image will become. Our example uses an OpenGL Texture Resolution setting of 128 × 128.

  Which OpenGL options work and how much they impact the performance of the display depends on the OpenGL hardware in the computer. If the applications seem sluggish when you are manipulating items, try turning off some of the OpenGL options.

- **Faster Highlights:** This option tells Layout to use a simple calculation for surface specularity in the Viewports. This can increase the Viewports' responsiveness if there are multiple items with specular surfaces.

- **OpenGL Reflections:** This option tells Layout to simulate and display the reflections for surfaces with a reflectivity value greater than 0.

- **OpenGL Transparency:** This option tells Layout to display any transparent surfaces using their transparency values. Modeler reads this setting from Layout through the Hub and uses the same stippling enabled in Layout.

Figure 2.36 Reducing the resolution of an image in OpenGL for quicker display can make the image blocky.

Figure 2.37 Use Pixel Blending to smooth out the appearance of a lower-resolution OpenGL image, although it can blur the image as well.

Figure 2.38 In Layout's Display Options tab, you can configure some of the basic Viewport display properties.

Figure 2.39 Dynamic Update has three options so you can optimize the responsiveness of the Viewpoints for large scenes.

General Display Options

There are a number of global display options for both Layout and Modeler that you can use to modify how information is presented in the Viewports.

Layout display options

Here are the general display options for Layout, which you can find in the Display Options tab of Layout's Preferences panel (**Figure 2.38**).

◆ **Dynamic Update:** This option determines when changes made in the various Properties panels take effect in the Layout Viewports. There are three settings for this option (**Figure 2.39**):

▲ **Off:** This option tells Layout to wait until the user closes the Properties panel before updating the Viewports.

▲ **Delayed:** This option tells Layout to update the Viewports when the user releases the mouse button after modifying a value.

▲ **Interactive:** This option tells Layout to immediately update the Viewports as the user modifies the value.

continues on next page

GENERAL DISPLAY OPTIONS

◆ **Bounding Box Threshold:** This option determines the maximum number of polygons that will be displayed as the user manipulates the Viewports or items in the scene.

For example, if you have two objects in a scene with 1,000 polygons each (2,000 polygons total), and the Bounding Box Threshold is set to 1,000, then the first object in the scene is drawn using the current view mode, and the second object is drawn as only a bounding box when you interact with either object or the Viewport (**Figure 2.40**). If you set the Bounding Box Threshold to 2,000, then both objects are displayed using the current view mode as you manipulate them or the Viewport (**Figure 2.41**). The Bounding Box Threshold gives priority to the currently selected item(s) when determining which polygons to display. This is an excellent way to optimize the responsiveness of the application. Experiment a bit with different values on large scenes to find out which setting works best for your system.

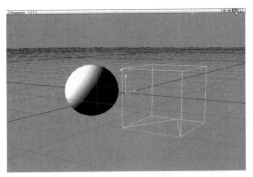

Figure 2.40 A low Bounding Box Threshold allows only the specified number of polygons in the scene to be drawn during item and Viewport manipulation, which can speed up Viewport updates.

Figure 2.41 A higher Bounding Box Threshold value makes more of your items refresh as you manipulate them, but can slow down the responsiveness of the Viewports.

◆ **Show Motion Paths:** Check this box so that when you select items, their motion paths are displayed in the Viewports.

Guides are basically the vertex normal of the SubD surface control point. Check this box to display subdivision surface control points in the Viewports.

◆ **Show Handles:** This option determines whether or not tool handles are displayed in the Viewports.

◆ **Show Fog Circles:** This option determines whether circles representing the near and far distance values for fog are drawn in the Viewports.

◆ **Show IK Chains:** Check this box to display IK Chain indicators in the Viewports.

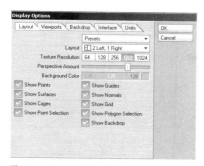

Figure 2.42 You'll find the general display options for Modeler in the Layout tab of the Display Options panel.

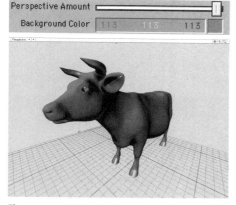

Figures 2.43 Setting the Perspective Amount slider to the far right creates a wide-angle lens effect in all active Perspective Viewports.

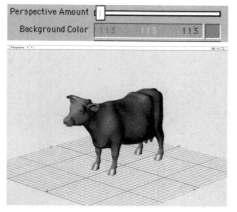

Figures 2.44 Setting the Perspective Amount slider to the far left flattens all active Perspective Viewports, for a two-dimensional effect.

◆ **Show SubPatch Cages:** This option determines whether or not the cage representing the base object of a subdivision surface object is displayed.

◆ **Show Target Lines:** This option determines whether or not target indicators are drawn in the Viewports from the targeting object to the target.

◆ **Overlay Color:** This option determines what color is used when drawing camera overlays in the Viewports.

Modeler display options

You can find the general display options for Modeler in the Layout tab of the Display Options panel (**Figure 2.42**).

◆ **Texture Resolution:** As in Layout, this option sets the resolution at which OpenGL textures are displayed in the Viewports.

◆ **Perspective Amount:** You can use this slider to adjust the amount of perspective shown in any active Perspective Viewports. You can go from a wide-angle effect (**Figure 2.43**) to an almost two-dimensional view (**Figure 2.44**).

◆ **Background Color:** This option lets you choose the background color used in all of the Viewports.

◆ **Show Points:** Check this box to make points visible in the Viewports.

◆ **Show Guides:** Check this box to display subdivision surface control points in the Viewports.

◆ **Show Surfaces:** Check this box to make polygons visible in the Viewports.

continues on next page

GENERAL DISPLAY OPTIONS

- **Show Normals:** Check this box to make polygon surface normals visible in the Viewports.

- **Show Cages:** Check this box to display the cage for a subdivision surface object.

- **Show Grid:** Deselect this box to disable the grid, leaving you with a blank Viewport.

- **Show Point Selection:** Deselect this box to disable the highlighting of selected points.

- **Show Polygon Selection:** Deselect this box to disable the highlighting of selected polygons.

- **Show Backdrop:** Check this box to display reference images in the Viewports.

CREATING GEOMETRY

3

The LightWave installation CD contains tons of objects, images, and scenes for you to play around with. The supplied objects cover a wide range of items—everything from a simple potted plant to very intricate spaceships. They're all completely royalty-free (which means they can be used freely, at no cost) and are great to get you up and running quickly. Some of these models are very complex and look great when they're put in a scene. Others are less detailed and should be considered merely as an example or starting point for your own custom objects. However, in order to meet the specific needs of your project, whether it's for you or for a client, you'll probably have to make your own.

Like sculptors, 3D modelers use various tools to create and shape an object from an unrecognizable pile of materials into their own personal artwork. In this chapter, you'll learn how to use Modeler to create the basic building blocks of an object: points and polygons. We'll also look at how to make several basic geometric shapes, including boxes, spheres, cylinders, and text. Finally, we'll tackle some organic modeling using LightWave's splines and SubPatch features.

Setting Up Modeler

As you learned in Chapter 2, "Touring the Viewports," you can change the way that the Viewports look in both Layout and Modeler. Once you have some experience in creating geometry, you'll want to alter Modeler to better fit your own style, changing the number of tabs displayed, making the tools you use most more accessible and putting the tools you use least, or never, out of the way. For the purposes of this book, let's take a moment to change Modeler's initial settings and interface to match what we'll be working with in this book. This will make the examples in this and following chapters match your screen better and they'll make much more sense as you read them.

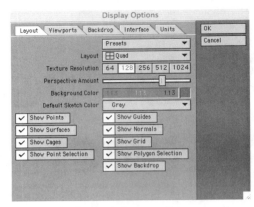

Figure 3.1 The Display Options panel lets you configure the interface to match your working style.

To set up the Modeler interface:

1. Press ⓓ to open the Display Options panel, and select the Layout tab (**Figure 3.1**).

2. From the Layout pull-down menu, choose Quad (**Figure 3.2**).

   This splits Modeler's Viewport into four different modeling views: Top, Back, Right, and Perspective (**Figure 3.3**).

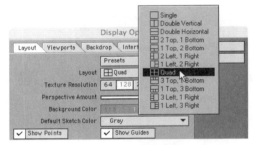

Figure 3.2 Choose Quad from the Layout pull-down menu.

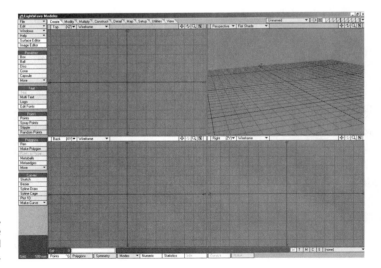

Figure 3.3 By default, Quad view displays the Top, Back, Right, and Perspective views.

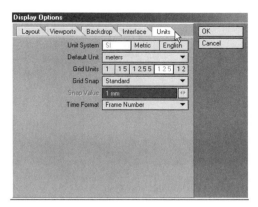

Figure 3.4 The Units tab of the Display Options panel lets you choose Modeler's system of measurement.

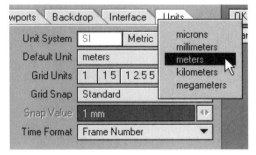

Figure 3.5 Change the system's Default Unit to meters.

3. Select the Units tab to display new options in the panel (**Figure 3.4**).

4. From the Default Unit pull-down menu, choose meters (**Figure 3.5**).

In 3D modeling, scale and proportion are incredibly important, so set this to whatever system of measurement you need or are used to.

5. Close the Display Options panel.

continues on next page

SETTING UP MODELER

6. From the Perspective view's drawing-mode pull-down menu (**Figure 3.6**), choose Wireframe Shade (**Figure 3.7**). This drawing mode best shows what you're building.

✔ Tip

■ LightWave will also create several pull-down menus to display tools that don't fit in a particular toolbar (**Figure 3.8**). You'll have a lot more of these menus if your interface is smaller than the one we're using. So if something isn't there or looks different from our illustrations, be sure to look in these menus for the command.

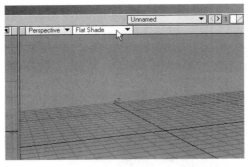

Figure 3.6 This pull-down menu in any of the views lets you select the drawing mode.

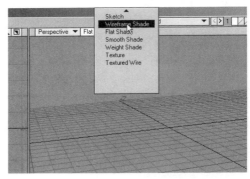

Figure 3.7 Select Wireframe Shade from the drawing mode pull-down menu.

Figure 3.8 The More pull-down menus contain tools and commands that don't fit the interface.

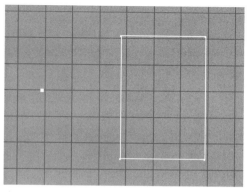

Figure 3.9 A point and a polygon in the Viewport.

Figure 3.10 The Create tab's toolbar displays tools and commands for creating geometry, including the Points tool.

Using Points and Polygons

In school, we're taught that everything is made up of tiny atoms, the basic building blocks of the universe. By putting different types of atoms together into molecules, we can make everything from water (hydrogen and oxygen) to table salt (sodium and chlorine). Everything in nature is built from, and can be broken down into, these very basic parts. Don't worry, we won't be studying atomic structures in 3D modeling, but the example does help illustrate our point.

In LightWave, an object's geometry is made up of points and polygons (**Figure 3.9**). These are the basic building blocks of LightWave's geometric world, and models cannot be built without them. Because points and polygons are so fundamental in creating objects, it's fortunate that they're also easy to create.

Points

A point is simply a location, or set of coordinates, in three-dimensional space. These coordinates define the point's position along the X, Y, and Z axes. Given these values, a single spot in space can be plotted and referenced.

For example, if you create a point with the coordinates 1, 2, 0.5, and your system of measurement is set to meters, these values translate to 1 meter on the X axis, 2 meters on the Y axis, and $\frac{1}{2}$ meter on the Z axis.

LightWave's graphical interface makes point creation simple. Just give Modeler the coordinates of the point to create, measured from the origin (0 on every axis), and you'll get a location, or point in space.

To create a point:

1. In Modeler, click the Create tab to display the tools for creating geometry in the toolbar (**Figure 3.10**).

continues on next page

2. Click Points in the toolbar or press ⊕ to activate the Points tool.

The Points tool's button on the toolbar is highlighted, and remains highlighted until the tool is turned off.

3. Drag the mouse anywhere in the Back view, in the lower-left corner of the screen (**Figure 3.11**).

The info display directly below the toolbar shows the cursor's coordinates as you move the mouse in any of the views (**Figure 3.12**).

4. Click where you want to place the point. Two things happen:

▲ The point is drawn as a yellow dot in the Viewport, directly under the crosshairs of the mouse. It's yellow because the point is automatically selected when created.

▲ Modeler draws large, light-blue crosshairs around the newly created point (**Figure 3.13**). This makes it easier to find which point you actually created if you already had numerous points on the screen. This is just a preview of the point's position, it hasn't actually been created yet. You can still adjust its position by clicking or dragging the point to a new location.

5. Adjust this point's position in either the Top or Left views.

Remember, we're dealing with three-dimensional space, so our point can have a depth coordinate as well.

6. Click Points in the toolbar again or press (Spacebar) to deactivate the current tool. The point is then created.

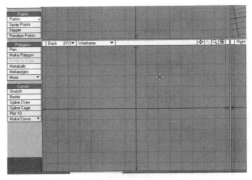

Figure 3.11 Go to the Back view in Modeler.

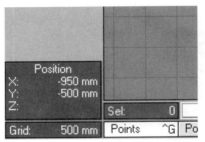

Figure 3.12 The info display provides an interactive report on the current tool.

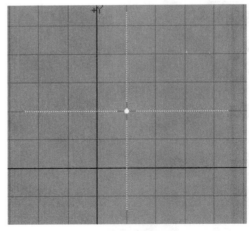

Figure 3.13 The large, light-blue crosshairs indicate where the point will be created.

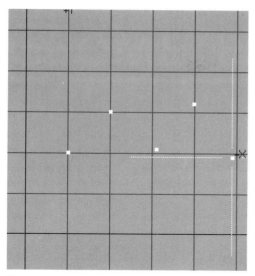

Figure 3.14 You can also make a series of points using the Points tool.

Figure 3.15 The Point tool's Numeric panel lets you type in values.

You'll very rarely ever want to create just a single point; usually you'll create a series of points.

To create a series of points:

1. Follow Steps 1–3 in the previous procedure, "To create a point."

2. Right-click where you want to place a point.

3. Click and drag the point to adjust its position in the three views.

4. Repeat Steps 2 and 3 until you've created all the points you want (**Figure 3.14**).

5. Click Points again or press (Spacebar) to drop the current tool.

If you know the exact position of the point you want to create, you can always use the tool's Numeric panel to enter these values directly.

To use the Point tool's Numeric panel:

1. Follow Steps 1 and 2 in the previous procedure, "To create a series of points."

2. Press (n) to open the tool's Numeric panel (**Figure 3.15**).

3. In the X, Y, and Z fields, enter the coordinates of the point to be created.

   Notice as you enter new values, the point's preview changes to reflect the new coordinates.

4. Click Points again or press (Spacebar) to drop the current tool.

Polygons

Points are nothing more than simple markers in space, extremely important to the big picture, but practically useless by themselves. Their biggest drawback is that they don't really have any surface area. They're just a location; they don't have anything to draw, so we can't see them in our animations. However, connect a few of them together and we have an integral component of computer graphics: the polygon.

In LightWave, a polygon is just a closed shape created by connecting one or more points (**Figure 3.16**). Polygons have a viewable surface area, so they're what actually get drawn when we make images.

There are five different classes of polygon in LightWave (**Figure 3.17**):

◆ **One-point:** These are what's referred to as "particles." They're drawn only as tiny specks on the screen, but are great for sparks or stars.

◆ **Two-point:** These show up as simple lines. Like one-point polygons, two-point polygons don't really have any surface area, but they do have properties that let them get drawn.

◆ **Three-point:** Defined by three vertices, a three-point polygon is drawn as a triangle and is one of the most popular polygon types. Adjust the polygon's three points to change its shape.

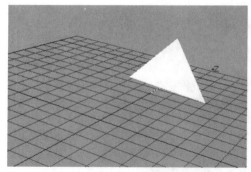

Figure 3.16 A triangle is created when three points are connected to form a polygon.

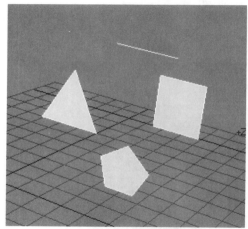

Figure 3.17 The five types of LightWave polygon are one-point, two-point, three-point, four-point, and the N-gon, with more than four points.

Figure 3.18 This four-point polygon is facing us.

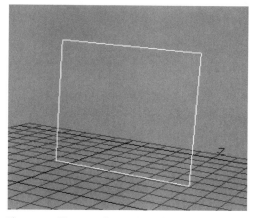

Figure 3.19 The same four-point polygon, now facing away from us.

◆ **Four-point:** A quadrangular (four-sided) surface area, this is the second most popular polygon type. You'll generally create most of the geometry in an object from these and three-point polygons.

◆ **N-gon:** This is any polygon created with more than four points (but less than 1024). It comes in handy when you're creating large, flat surfaces such as floors or other complex platforms. However, due to their complexity, N-gons can often create several surface abnormalities, and they should be used sparingly.

Making polygons is like building a house. Before the plywood goes up, a house is nothing but a framework of wooden beams and two-by-fours. However, after this basic framework is made, the walls and roof can be added, and the building begins to look like a house.

You create a polygon by simply declaring what points will define its shape. However, unlike a sheet of plywood, LightWave's surfaces are like a one-way window, and only one side gets drawn. **Figure 3.18** shows a simple four-point polygon facing us. **Figure 3.19** shows the other side of the same polygon. When you create a polygon, it's important to create it facing the direction you want.

The order in which you select the points of a polygon determines which side will be drawn. You can select the points in either clockwise or counterclockwise order.

To make a polygon:

1. Follow the procedure "To create a series of points" and create four points (**Figure 3.20**).

2. Deselect all points by pressing ⧸.

3. Click the Points button at the bottom of the interface (**Figure 3.21**) or press Ctrl+g to switch Modeler to point-selection mode.

4. Holding down the Shift key, click to select each of the four points in a clockwise direction.

   It's easiest if you start in one corner and just work your way around.

5. Select the Create tab, and with the points selected, click Make Pol in the toolbar or press p to activate the Polygon tool.

   The points are all connected (**Figure 3.22**).

6. Alt-click and drag in the Perspective view to rotate the view (**Figure 3.23**).

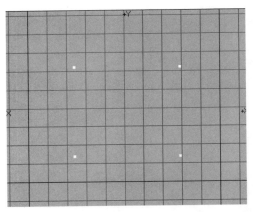

Figure 3.20 Create four points.

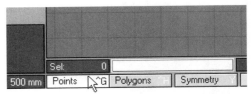

Figure 3.21 At the bottom of the interface, switch Modeler to point-selection mode.

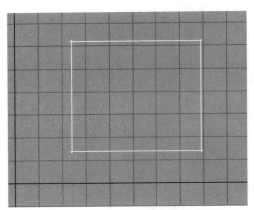

Figure 3.22 All the points are connected, and the polygon is made.

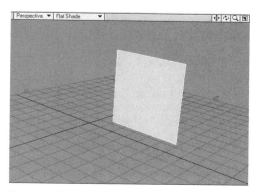

Figure 3.23 Rotate the Perspective view to observe your work.

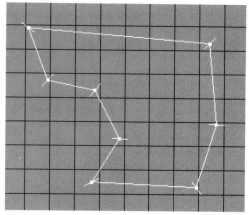

Figure 3.24 You can edit each point in the curve by clicking and dragging its handle.

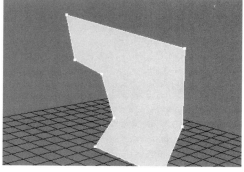

Figure 3.25 Observe your work by rotating the Perspective view.

That's just one way to make a polygon. You can also use LightWave's Pen tool, which lets you draw the polygon as you create its points.

To use the Pen tool:

1. Click the Create tab, then click Pen to activate the Pen tool.

2. Click anywhere in the Back view to create the first point.

3. Click again in any of the other views to create another point.

4. Repeat Step 3 until the shape is complete. Remember to create the polygon in a clockwise direction. Click and drag any point to adjust it (**Figure 3.24**).

5. When you're finished placing the points, press (Enter) to create the polygon.

6. Alt-click and drag in the Perspective view to rotate the view (**Figure 3.25**).

Not every polygon needs to have a unique set of points. They can share points with another polygon. Let's mix together some of the procedures we've learned, to create two polygons that share some points.

To share the points of a polygon:

1. Following the "To use the Pen tool" procedure, create a four-sided polygon (**Figure 3.26**).

2. Follow the steps in "To create a point" to create two points below the polygon you just created (**Figure 3.27**).

3. Switch Modeler to point-selection mode.

4. Press ⌷ to deselect all points.

5. Shift-click the bottom two points from the polygon plus the two independent points, for the four points that will define the second polygon (**Figure 3.28**).

    Keep in mind the point order and which direction you want the polygon to face.

6. With the four points selected, click Make Pol in the toolbar or press ⓟ to create the polygon.

    Now this object has two polygons, each sharing two points with the other (**Figure 3.29**).

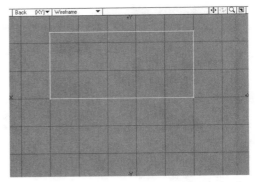

Figure 3.26 A four-sided polygon seen from the back.

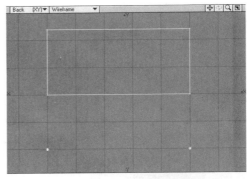

Figure 3.27 Create two extra points below the polygon.

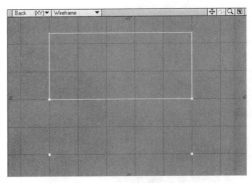

Figure 3.28 Going counterclockwise, select the two new points and the bottom two points of the polygon.

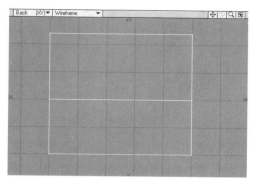

Figure 3.29 A second polygon is created, and it shares two points with the original polygon.

A polygon's normal

We mentioned earlier that the order in which points are selected determines which direction a polygon faces. Sometimes it's difficult to tell simply by looking at the polygon in any of the views, but Modeler provides an easy way to indicate direction: The polygon's *normal* is a dashed line that protrudes from the surface, indicating the direction that the polygon is facing.

To view a normal:

1. Using either of the polygon creation methods described earlier, create a single polygon.

2. Switch Modeler to polygon-selection mode by pressing [Ctrl]+[h].

3. Select the polygon in any of the views (**Figure 3.30**).

The polygon's normal is then displayed.

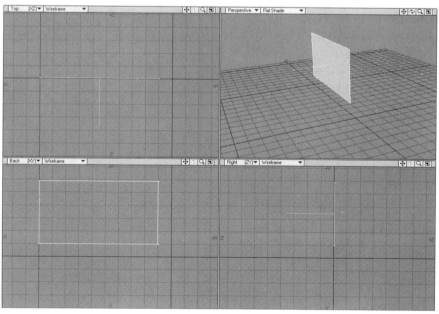

Figure 3.30 The four views better show the created polygon and the normal's direction.

Point Information

Although we've only made very simple polygons up to this point, it should be apparent that the Viewport can very quickly get extremely cluttered. Just imagine twenty thousand polygons in an object (**Figure 3.31**). Now that's cluttered!

Modeler has some pretty cool selection and organization tools that can make an object of this size easier to handle. Two tools, in particular, can really make your job a lot easier: the Info and Statistics panels. Both can help you select and edit the components in a layer.

Point and Polygon Info panels

The Point and Polygon Info panels display an organized list of the components' current values or properties. This lets you know exactly what's going on with every piece of your object. In addition to viewing these values, you can edit several of them directly in the Info panel, for precise adjustments to existing points and polygons.

Which parameters are displayed in each of these panels depends upon what component is currently selected in the Viewport. For example, if you select a group of points and open the Info panel, LightWave displays the Point Info panel (**Figure 3.32**). Select a polygon, and the Polygon Info panel is displayed instead (**Figure 3.33**). The panel is what's known as "context-sensitive." However, at the same time, it's also known as non-modal. This means that while the panel is open, selections in the interface can't be changed until it's closed. Therefore, take special care in selecting which pieces of geometry you want information on before you open the info panel(s).

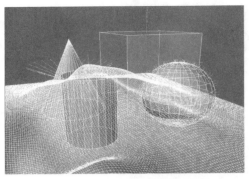

Figure 3.31 Twenty thousand polygons and their normals can really confuse the Viewport.

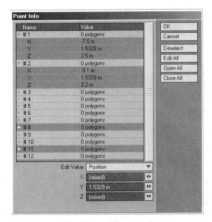

Figure 3.32 The Point Info panel lets you change values of the points.

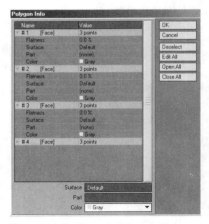

Figure 3.33 The Polygon Info panel lets you change certain values of the polygons.

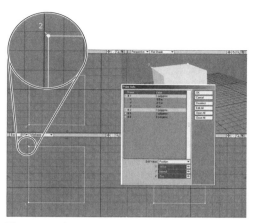

Figure 3.34 The selected points' numbers also appear in each of the views.

Figure 3.35 The panel's number fields let you alter some of the item's values.

The Point Info panel displays such information as the coordinates of the selected point(s) and vertex map data (see Chapter 5, "Vertex Maps"). The Polygon Info panel includes point count, degree of flatness, Surface and Part naming fields, and a wireframe color pull-down menu.

To use the Info panels:

1. Select either points or polygons in your model.

2. Select the Display tab, then click Info in the toolbar or press [i] to display the Point Info or Polygon Info panel.

3. Click a point or polygon in the list of selected items (**Figure 3.34**).

   The light-blue numbers in the views correspond to the numbers in the list.

4. Edit the parameters in the fields below the list (**Figure 3.35**).

5. Close the panel when you're done.

Part Names and Selection Sets

In Modeler, you can assign groups of selected points or polygons to what are known as *parts* and *point-selection sets*. These allow you to quickly select or deselect several components at once by name. For example, if your object has several important points that are a pain to select every time you want to edit them, you can assign them to a selection set. Then the next time you want to select them, you can simply use the Statistics panel.

For points, you'll find the point-selection sets category displayed at the bottom of the list in the Statistics panel. If there's more than one selection set, a pull-down menu allows you to choose which set you want to select.

For polygons, use the Part category, also near the bottom of the list in the Statistics panel. Again, if there's more than one, a pull-down menu lets you choose which part you want to work with.

POINT INFORMATION

Statistics panels

These panels display the statistics of the points and polygons viewable in an object's current layer. The Statistics panels are also context sensitive, but they display different information according to Modeler's current selection mode. **Figures 3.36** and **3.37** show the two states of the panels that we'll be discussing in this chapter, Points and Polygons.

As we mentioned earlier, polygons can have several points in common with each other. When Modeler is in point-selection mode, the Statistics panel will display how many points belong to zero, one, two, three, four, or more polygons at a time. The number of points in each category is displayed in the Number column.

In polygon-selection mode, the panel will display how many polygons in the current layer have one, two, three, four, and more points. Again, the number of polygons in each category is displayed in the Number column. (Categories like SubPatches, Skelegons, Surfaces, and Parts apply to features discussed elsewhere in this book.) Note that you can either select components of your model or have nothing selected for the following procedure.

To use the Statistics panel:

1. Press [w] to open the Statistics panel.

2. To add components to your current selection, click the plus sign (+) in the first column.

3. To remove components from your current selection, click the minus sign (-) in the second column (**Figure 3.38**).

4. Close the Statistics panel.

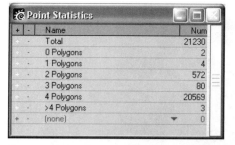

Figure 3.36 The Point Statistics panel displays point information for the layer.

Figure 3.37 The Polygon Statistics panel displays polygon information for the layer.

Figure 3.38 Use the + or – columns to add or remove a category from the selection.

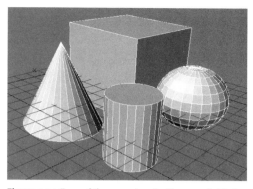

Figure 3.39 Four of the sample primitives available in Modeler.

Figure 3.40 An extremely simple model of a shack, made entirely out of boxes.

Primitives

Making a complex model out of points and polygons can be an incredibly daunting task. Even simple shapes like spheres and cubes can be tedious, and sometimes impossible, to build by hand. If you had to start from scratch and model everything point by point and polygon by polygon, making these shapes would take forever.

Luckily, all the major 3D applications provide some way for you to easily create these geometric shapes. In the 3D world, these spheres, boxes, cylinders, and cones (to name a few) are called *primitives* (**Figure 3.39**).

You may be wondering when you'll ever need these simple shapes, thinking that nothing you'll ever create will be simple enough to warrant using them. Well the fact is, you'll need them all the time.

For example, a building is typically rectangular in shape. So you use a stretched out cube for the basic shape, then add smaller boxes for the trim, windows, and so forth, until you have the start of a shack, made solely of stretched cubes (**Figure 3.40**). This method is the basis for constructing most larger, highly detailed models, too.

We'll start with the easiest of the primitives: the box.

To make a box:

1. Select the Create tab, then click Box in the toolbar or press ⓧ to activate the Box tool.

2. In the Top view, click where you want the top-left corner of the box to be (**Figure 3.41**) and drag the mouse to where you want the bottom-right corner, to define your box (**Figure 3.42**).

3. In the Right view, click the middle light-blue interactive handle of the edge (**Figure 3.43**) and drag it down to give your box a little height.

4. Drag any of the preview's interactive handles to adjust the box.

5. Click Box or press ⓧ again to drop the Box tool or press ⏎Enter⏎ to create the box.

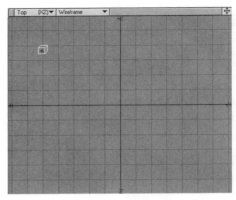

Figure 3.41 Click and hold with the Box tool somewhere in one of the views. This is where the box's top-left corner will be.

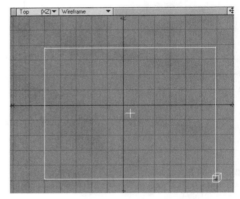

Figure 3.42 Drag the tool across to define the shape of the cube.

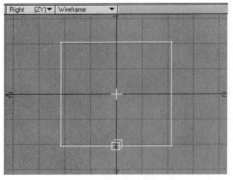

Figure 3.43 Use the Box tool's interactive handles to adjust the dimensions of the box.

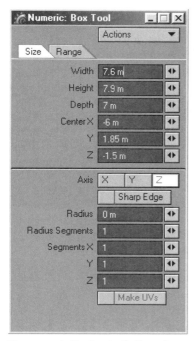

Figure 3.44 In the Box tool's Numeric panel you can directly enter dimensions and other values.

Each primitive has several options that either adjust the amount of detail it has, or alter the technical makeup of the object. These choices can be found in the tool's Numeric panel.

To use a primitive's Numeric panel:

1. Select the Create tab, then click Box or press x.

2. Press n to open the Numeric panel (**Figure 3.44**).

3. Enter the appropriate values in the tool's different fields.

    Each tool in Modeler has different choices and values you can set. Please refer to the LightWave 3D User's Manual for an explanation of each of the primitive's values.

4. Click Box again or press x to drop the Box tool and create the box.

5. Close the Numeric panel.

PRIMITIVES

You've already used the Box tool's interactive handles a bit, but some of the values in the Numeric panel of most primitives can also be set manually.

To create segments interactively:

1. Follow Steps 1–4 in the procedure "To make a box."

2. With the mouse pointer somewhere in the Top view, use the arrow keys (⬆ ⬇ ⬅ ➡) to set the number of horizontal and vertical segments in the box (**Figure 3.45**).

3. Repeat Step 2 for the Back and Side views (**Figure 3.46**).

4. Click Box or press ⓧ again to create the box.

5. Close the Numeric panel.

✔ Tip

■ Some tools have more handles or features than others, but they all have Numeric panels where you can enter values directly. Be sure to also test the Ball, Disc, Cone, Capsule, Platonic (Tetrahedron, Octahedron, Icosahedron, and so on), Super-Quadratic (Ellipsoid and Toroid), and Gemstone tools.

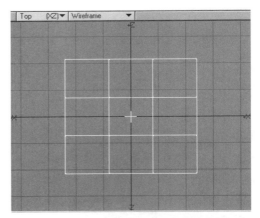

Figure 3.45 Use the keyboard's arrow keys to define the number of segments in the box.

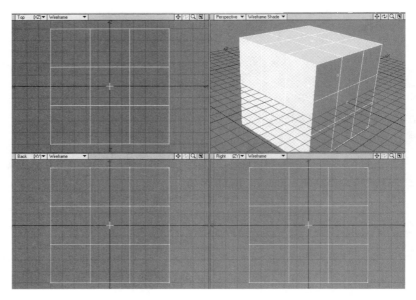

Figure 3.46 The final object should have nine polygons on each side.

Figure 3.47 A typical typewriter style, compared with a script style of lettering.

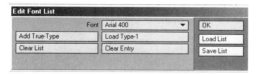

Figure 3.48 In the Edit Font List panel you can load fonts into Modeler.

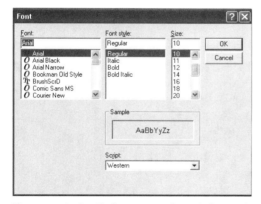

Figure 3.49 In the Windows system-font window, pick the font, its style, and size.

✔ Tip

■ To avoid re-adding each font every time you start Modeler, use the Edit Font List panel's Save List and Load List buttons. To load Type 1 fonts, click Load Type-1 and select the font's file on your hard drive.

Text and Fonts

In computer graphics, text is usually used for titles, captions, diagrams, and credits. Any time you want the viewer to read something, onscreen or in print, you'll need to determine what style of text best fits your message. You can select anything from the impersonal feel of typewritten text to the comfortable feeling of a handwritten message (**Figure 3.47**). It all depends on how you want the viewer to feel about what they're reading.

There are thousands of different styles to choose from, each contained in what's known as a *font*. LightWave makes use of the fonts that are installed on your computer, so you already have several to choose from. Adding more is easy, whether you purchase them or download free fonts from the Web. With the right program, you can even create your own fonts.

When you first launch LightWave, it doesn't have any fonts available (loaded) for you to use. That's because each font you load into LightWave takes up some of your system's memory, so you only want to load the fonts you're going to use. The first step is to add a font to a Modeler session.

To add a font to Modeler:

1. Select the Create tab, then click Edit Fonts to open the Edit Font List panel (**Figure 3.48**).

2. Click Add True-Type to open your system's Font window (**Figure 3.49**).

3. Select a font, font style, and size from the various lists.

4. Click OK to add this font and close the window.

5. Click OK to close the Edit Font List panel.

With the font loaded, you can now create your text, using Modeler's Text tool.

To create text:

1. Select the Create tab and click Text in the toolbar to activate the Text tool w.

2. Click one of the views where you want the text to appear, and a text-insertion cursor appears (**Figure 3.50**).

3. Type your message.

   This creates a template of the text (**Figure 3.51**).

4. Click and drag either of the two sliders to adjust the tool's L-shaped indicator (**Figure 3.52**).

   The vertical bar adjusts the size of the text. The horizontal bar adjusts the kerning (space between each letter).

   Press Tab to cycle through left, right, and center alignments.

5. Click Text again or press Enter to drop the tool and create the text (**Figure 3.53**).

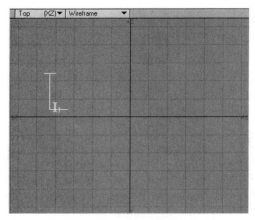

Figure 3.50 Click the Text tool's icon in one of the four views.

Figure 3.51 A preview of the text to be created appears as you type.

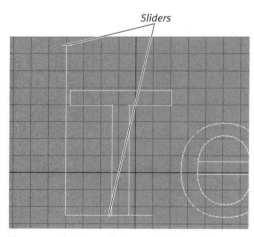

Figure 3.52 The Text tool's interactive sliders let you adjust the size and kerning of the preview.

Figure 3.53 The final text object is created after you drop the Text tool.

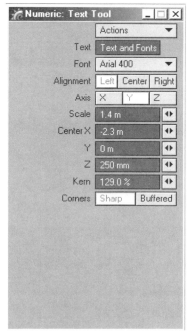

Figure 3.54 You can enter the text options directly in the Text tool's Numeric panel.

As with most of the tools in Modeler, the Text tool's Numeric panel allows you to enter information directly and precisely about the geometry you want to build.

To use the Text tool's Numeric panel:

1. Select the Create tab, then click Text in the toolbar or press [w] to activate the Text tool.

2. Press [n] to open the Numeric panel (**Figure 3.54**).

3. Type your text into the Text field and press [Enter] when you're done.

   The text preview is automatically created in one of the Viewports.

4. Select a font from the Font pull-down menu.

5. Adjust the alignment, axis, scale, position, kerning, and corner values for your text.

   The text is updated with each change.

6. Click Text again or press [Enter] to deactivate the Text tool.

   LightWave creates all the points and polygons needed to make each letter, and arranges them according to the parameters you set, whether in the tool or its Numeric panel.

✔ Tips

- Obviously, when the Text tool is active, anything you type is created as a text object. If you want to use any of LightWave's keyboard shortcuts, press [Esc] first.

- If you plan to use a lot of fonts, it's a good idea to learn more about the thousands of fonts available. A good starting point is the Web site www.1001freefonts.com.

TEXT AND FONTS

Organic Modeling

Points, polygons, and primitives can take you pretty far when you're modeling man-made objects. That's because buildings, furniture, and the like are usually made up of straight edges, sharp corners, or easily defined surfaces.

So how would you make curved or smooth surfaces? Organic objects, such as animals, plants, and people often require different methods of modeling. Although it's possible to create them with what we've learned so far, it's really hard to do. You'd have to gradually drag or shape all the points and polygons that make up the object. The slightest error in the surface could make your object a real eyesore. What you need is a different type of geometry, one that defines organic surfaces better.

There are three methods of modeling you can use to create organic-looking geometry: SubPatches, curves and patches (known as spline patching), and Meta-geometry. We'll cover the two more popular methods, SubPatches and curves and patches, in this book. Meta-geometry has a limited usefulness and is covered well in the LightWave 3D User's Manual.

SubPatches

One of the easiest ways to create organic-looking geometry in LightWave is to create what are commonly known in the industry as *subdivision surfaces*. In LightWave, however, they're called *SubPatches*. And they aren't created, they're converted.

An object's existing polygons are the key to generating SubPatches. Through an extremely simple process, each of the polygons can be converted into a SubPatch.

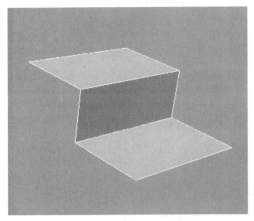

Figure 3.55 Three connected polygons form a very angular step.

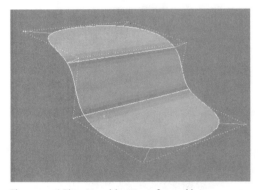

Figure 3.56 The step object transformed into SubPatches.

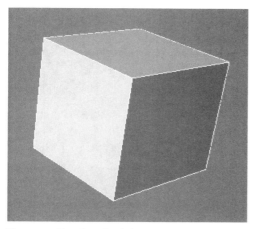

Figure 3.57 Here is a simple box.

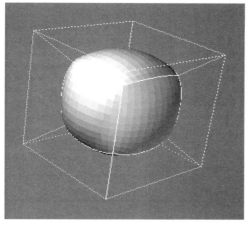

Figure 3.58 This box object has been converted to SubPatches.

Once converted, these newly formed subdivisions gradually smooth out any sharp edges or corners on the object's surface.

In **Figure 3.55**, we have a simple stair-stepped object made up of three polygons, set at 90-degree angles from their two shared edges. After these three polygons are converted to SubPatches, the sharp angles are removed, and the surface is smoothed out (**Figure 3.56**). There are only three SubPatches in this object, one generated for each polygon. No additional geometry was created in the SubPatch conversion process.

It's easy to convert an object's polygons into SubPatches: just press a single key. And it's nearly as simple to work with the SubPatches or convert them back into polygons.

To use SubPatches:

1. Follow the steps in the "To make a box" procedure to create a simple cube (**Figure 3.57**).

2. Select the Construct tab to display different tools in the toolbar, then click SubPatch in the toolbar or press ⌷Tab⌷ to convert all the polygons in this layer into SubPatches (**Figure 3.58**).

continues on next page

ORGANIC MODELING

3. Switch Modeler into point-selection mode.

4. Select a point in the object.

5. Select the Modify tab to display new tools in the toolbar, then click Move in the toolbar or press [t] to activate the Move tool.

6. Drag the point and observe how the SubPatches in the object react (**Figure 3.59**).

7. Press [Shift] to drop the current tool.

8. Press [/] to deselect all points.

9. Click SubPatch or press [Tab] again to convert the SubPatches back into polygons (**Figure 3.60**).

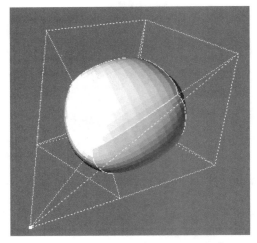

Figure 3.59 The SubPatched object automatically recalculates the smoothing algorithm whenever the geometry is edited.

In the example above, we converted the polygons of a cube, creating a spherical object. You might have been surprised, if you were expecting the SubPatched object to look boxier than it does. Maybe from our description you were expecting only the edges to be smoothed out?

The algorithm used to calculate the smoothing in SubPatches is figured per polygon. So for each of the cube's edges, LightWave can only use two polygons in the algorithm, and the surface is rounded out. Apply this to all the edges in the object, and you get a sphere.

However, there are two ways we can tell SubPatches to be less curved and more boxy. First, the rounding effect of SubPatches is determined by the amount of geometry used to define the surface. The more polygons used in a surface, the more the SubPatch will look like its polygonal predecessor.

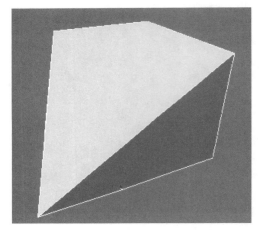

Figure 3.60 Simply press Tab again to convert the SubPatched object back into Polygons.

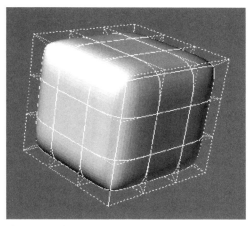

Figure 3.61 The more complicated the mesh, the more the SubPatched object resembles the original shape.

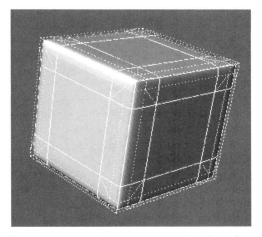

Figure 3.62 Move the segments out to the edges of the box to tighten the smoothing effect even more.

In the previous example, the minimal number of polygons is used to define a surface, so the SubPatch's contour is curvier than if more geometry were used. All that's needed to straighten this surface out a little is more geometry. In fact, you can combine what you've learned in earlier procedures to add geometry and reduce the SubPatch effect. Simply follow the steps in "To create segments interactively" to make a segmented box with nine polygons on each side, and then follow Steps 2–9 in "To use SubPatches" (**Figure 3.61**). There's more geometry defining the shape of the surface, so you'll end up with an object that's much more box-like than before. You can even go one step further by moving the segments' points out toward the edge (**Figure 3.62**) so that the edges are even less round than before.

The second way to control how much smoothing occurs in SubPatches is to use what's called a *vertex map*, or *VMap* for short. This method doesn't require any additional geometry and is much easier to control. To learn how to use this method, see Chapter 5, "Vertex Maps."

✔ Tips

- If you like the shape of an object created by SubPatches, but you want it in polygons, you can freeze it into polygons using the Freeze command (click Freeze in the Construct tab's toolbar or press Ctrl+d).

- Not only can you use the Statistics panel to select polygons that have been converted to SubPatches, you can also use it to select polygons that may violate the three- or four-point polygon rule (see the "SubPatch Pros and Cons" sidebar).

- Control the level of smoothing each patch gets by changing the Patch Divisions amount in the General Options panel.

ORGANIC MODELING

Curves and spline patches

It's incredibly difficult to use SubPatches for exact measurements, precisely matching a shape, or aligning with other geometry. Curves and spline patches solve these problems.

However, this functionality comes with a price. Spline patches are a little more involved and generally more difficult to use than SubPatches. They also require a bit more planning and care to get the exact shape you're looking for. That said, some modelers refuse to use anything but spline patches!

Think of modeling with spline patches like working with papier-mâché. You start with a simple wire mesh, which provides support but more importantly, creates a very crude shape. Then you add material to the wires, filling in the gaps and creating a solid surface. The more wires used to make up this cage, the more detail a surface can have when the paper-goop is added. Spline patches are created much in the same way, minus all the goopy slime.

Unlike SubPatches, spline patches don't use existing geometry or an integrated conversion process to generate their organic shapes. Instead they use a series of new components called *curves* (also known as *splines*) to define the shape of a patch of polygons created in Modeler. The curves are like the wires in a spline patch papier-mâché. When it's all said and done, a spline patch is nothing more than a group of polygons conforming to the shape of some curves.

SubPatch Pros and Cons

As we mentioned, if you move around any of the object's converted geometry, the shape is automatically recomputed, and resmoothed. This amount of feedback makes modeling with SubPatches that much easier. The smoothing combined with this immediate feel can often make editing an object with a fair amount of SubPatches in it seem like playing with clay.

Here are some benefits of using SubPatches:

◆ Creates a "working with clay" environment

◆ Simple to convert to and from polygons

◆ Smoothing algorithm is constantly recomputed as geometry is edited (even in Layout)

◆ SubPatches appear in Layout as they do in Modeler

Although they're incredibly powerful, SubPatches do have a couple of major drawbacks:

◆ The smoothing algorithm only supports three- and four-point polygons. All others generate errors and won't be converted.

◆ The generated surface is difficult to shape exactly. Because so many variables are factored into the conversion process, making a shape match schematics, diagrams, or even other geometry can be difficult.

◆ Exact placement of image maps and UV maps becomes increasingly difficult. See Chapter 12, "Surfaces and Textures," for more on these concepts.

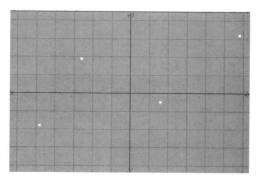

Figure 3.63 Create four points in one of the four views.

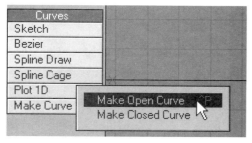

Figure 3.64 Choose Make Open Curve from the Make Curve pull-down menu in the Create tab.

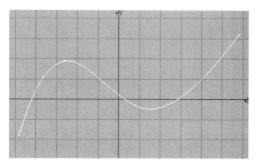

Figure 3.65 A smooth curve is created from the points selected.

There are several different methods and tools you can use to create curves. We'll discuss three of them here.

The first, and least responsive, method is to create them from existing points.

To make a curve from points:

1. Follow the "To create a series of points" procedure earlier in this chapter to create four points, similar to **Figure 3.63**.

2. Click to select the points, in order from left to right.

3. Select the Create tab, then choose Make Open Curve from the Make Curve pull-down menu in the toolbar or press Ctrl+p (**Figure 3.64**).

   The Curve is automatically created (**Figure 3.65**).

The next way to create a curve is by using the Sketch tool. This method is a little more interactive; however, it can be a little harder to control how many points the curve will have. This can become a problem later when you make your spline patch.

To make a curve using the Sketch tool:

1. Click the Create tab, then click Sketch in the toolbar or press ⎡'⎤ to activate the Sketch tool.

2. Press ⎡n⎤ to open the Numeric panel (**Figure 3.66**).

3. Make sure that the Type is set to Curve.

4. With the mouse, draw the same curve you made in the previous procedure (**Figure 3.67**).

✔ Tip

■ Even though the shape you drew matches the one you made before, the number of points created in the generated curve drastically increased. The only remedy for this is an extremely steady hand and an efficient drawing technique. Naturally, this method has limited usefulness.

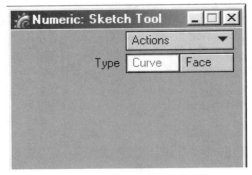

Figure 3.66 Be sure to create curves rather than polygons in the Sketch tool's Numerical panel.

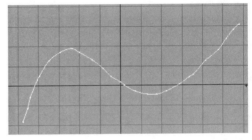

Figure 3.67 The curve generated retains the same basic shape as our previous example, but the number of points created has drastically increased.

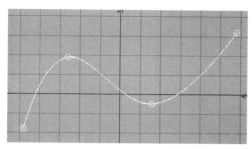

Figure 3.68 Create the same basic shape by clicking four points in the Viewport.

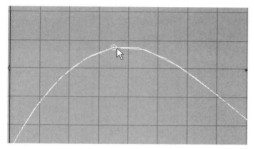

Figure 3.69 The circles around each of the curve's points are editing handles.

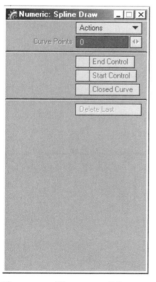

Figure 3.70 Alter some of the Spline Draw tool's options using its Numeric panel.

The third and final way to create a curve is with the Spline Draw tool. This method gives the most feedback, letting you preview the curve before it's built and edit its points until the shape is exactly right.

To make a curve using the Spline Draw tool:

1. Select the Create tab, then click Spline Draw to activate the Spline Draw tool.

2. Click in any view to create the first point.

3. Create three more points by clicking where you want each one.

   Notice that the curve is being created as each point is added, and each point has a light-blue circle around it. This is the point's interactive handle (**Figure 3.68**).

4. Drag one of the circles to change the position of that point (**Figure 3.69**).

5. Press [n] to open the Numeric panel (**Figure 3.70**).

continues on next page

ORGANIC MODELING

6. In the Curve Points field, type a new value or use the mini-slider arrows to increase the value.

7. After you approve of the preview curve, click Spline Draw again to deactivate the tool.

Now the Curve is created (**Figure 3.71**).

✔ Tip

■ Although it's easy control the overall shape of a curve by editing its points, it's more difficult to control the shape of the curve's beginning and ending. To easily manage these troublesome areas you can enable what are known as *Control Points* (see the LightWave 3D User's Manual for more on this option).

Although we consider this newly created geometry a curve, LightWave considers it a non-rendering polygon. This way, curves can be selected and edited with certain polygon tools, as long as Modeler is in polygon-selection mode.

When you select a curve, the first point has a yellow diamond around it (**Figure 3.72**). This indicates the curve's starting point. More about those later.

Now it's time to create a surface out of polygons. A spline patch should use three or four curves to determine its shape. The shape's smoothness is directly proportionate to the number of polygons used to create it. The polygonal dimensions of the spline patch will be determined by the values you choose when the patch is made.

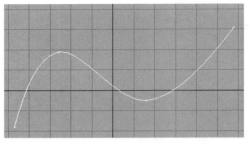

Figure 3.71 The curve generated after using the Spline Draw tool.

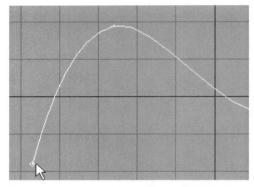

Figure 3.72 Each curve has a beginning, indicated by this diamond.

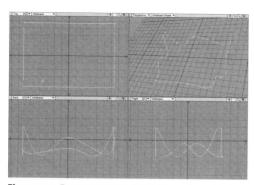

Figure 3.73 Four curves used to define a four-sided patch.

To use the Make Spline Patch command:

1. Using any of the methods outlined earlier, make four curves to define a rectangular shape for your Spline Patch (**Figure 3.73**).

2. Switch Modeler to points-selection mode and select the two points that make up one of the corners of the rectangle.

3. Click the Detail tab, then click Weld or press Ctrl+w to weld the first and last points of the two curves together.

4. Repeat for each of the three remaining corners, until all the curves are connected (**Figure 3.74**).

continues on next page

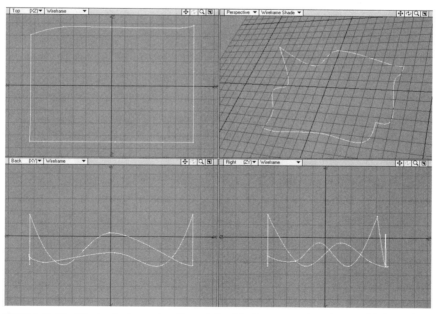

Figure 3.74 All of the beginning and ending points of the four curves have been welded together using the Weld command.

ORGANIC MODELING

5. Switch Modeler into polygon-selection mode.

6. Click each of the curves, counterclockwise, remembering which curve you selected first.

7. Select the Construct tab, then choose Patch in the toolbar or press Ctrl+f to open the Make Spline Patch panel (**Figure 3.75**).

8. In the Perpendicular and Parallel fields, change the values to indicate how many columns and rows of polygons will be created.

   The orientation is based on the first curve you selected.

9. Click the Length button below each field if you want the polygons to be evenly distributed throughout the curve.

   or

   Click the Knots button below each field if you want the polygons placed according to where the points are on the curve.

10. Click OK to close the panel and create the Spline Patch (**Figure 3.76**).

✔ Tip

■ LightWave considers a curve a polygon, so several tools meant for polygons can be used on curves, including Flip, Freeze, Add Points, and Smooth. Check Chapter 4 and the LightWave 3D User's Manual for more information.

Figure 3.75 The Make Spline Patch panel lets you set how many polygons will define your patch, and how they're to be distributed along the curves.

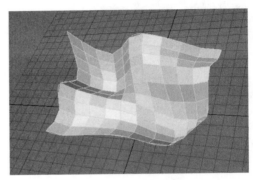

Figure 3.76 The final patch.

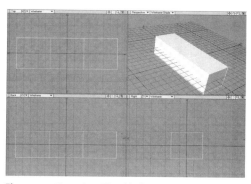

Figure 3.77 Use a box like this for your Skelegons.

Figure 3.78 Click Create Skelegons located on the Setup tab.

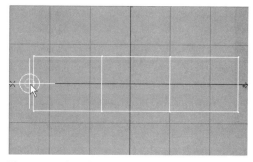

Figure 3.79 Place the beginning of the first Skelegon at the left-most side of the geometry. The target-looking icon indicates the beginning of the Skelegon chain.

Skelegons

Setting up bones in an object can be both tricky and cumbersome. With Layout's somewhat limited toolset, achieving total control over your object's geometry takes experience and a lot of patience. These tools are just not as powerful as those found in Modeler. Unfortunately, Modeler doesn't support bones. How do we solve this? With Skelegons.

Skelegons are a unique type of polygon that assist in creating a model's skeleton. You create the Skelegons in the object, defining its rough position and size, and use Modeler's editing tools to position them exactly where they should be. This geometry is saved within the LightWave object, so after the object is loaded into Layout, the Skelegons can then be converted to bones. This gets us the best of both worlds: the power of bones, with the ease of Modeler's toolset. After you've mastered these techniques, be sure to read Chapter 7 for more on using Skelegons.

To create a series of Skelegons using the Skelegon tool:

1. Create a Box with three segments that looks like **Figure 3.77**.

2. Select the Setup tab, then click Create Skelegons in the toolbar (**Figure 3.78**).

3. Click the left side of the box (**Figure 3.79**).

   This will be the starting point of our first Skelegon.

continues on next page

SKELEGONS

4. Click inside the first segment of the box (**Figure 3.80**).

This defines the position and length of the first Skelegon.

5. Click in the second segment to define the next Skelegon (**Figure 3.81**).

The starting point of each new Skelegon begins where the last one ends.

6. Click in the last segment to create the last Skelegon (**Figure 3.82**).

7. Drag any Skelegon's light-blue circular handle to edit its position.

8. Press (Enter) to drop the current tool.

✔ Tip

■ Now that the Skelegons are created, they can be selected by switching Modeler into polygon-selection mode.

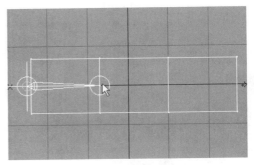

Figure 3.80 The second click defines the end of the first Skelegon.

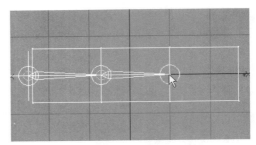

Figure 3.81 The third click defines the end of the second Skelegon.

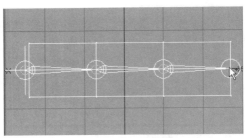

Figure 3.82 The final click defines the end of the third Skelegon.

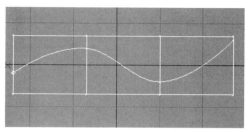

Figure 3.83 Create this spline inside the object.

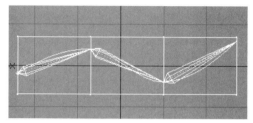

Figure 3.84 The Make Skelegons button creates a bone between each set of points in the curve.

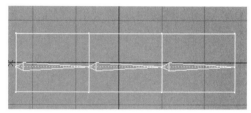

Figure 3.85 Using the Drag tool, straighten out the Skelegons.

Naturally, there's another way to create Skelegons, and that's by using a curve.

To create a series of Skelegons using curves:

1. Create a Box with three segments and a curve that matches the one in **Figure 3.83**.

2. Switch Modeler to polygon-selection mode and click to select the curve.

3. Select the Setup tab, then choose Convert Skelegons from the Skelegon's More pull-down menu.

   A bone is created between each set of points in the curve (**Figure 3.84**).

4. Switch Modeler to point-selection mode.

5. Select the Modify tab, and then click Drag in the toolbar or press Ctrl + t to activate the Drag tool.

6. Straighten out the Skelegons by dragging their shared points (**Figure 3.85**).

7. With the curve selected, press Del to remove it from the model (it's no longer needed).

✔ Tips

■ After the model is saved, you can load this object into Layout and convert the Skelegons into bones. Select the Setup tab and then choose Cvt Skelegons in the toolbar.

■ Use the Skelegon's Numeric panel to name and set VMap parameters for each Skelegon. The LightWave 3D User's Manual covers this subject extensively.

SKELEGONS

One-Way Street

Using Skelegons has one major drawback. Creating bones from Skelegons is a completely one-way conversion. After they're converted to bones in Layout, there's no way to convert them back to Skelegons for Modeler.

This means that you can't simply edit the position of the Skelegons in Modeler and expect the object's bones to automatically be updated in Layout. You'll have to remove the bones and reconvert them from Skelegons. The good news is that Skelegons remain in the object, even after they've been converted, so you don't have to re-create the Skelegons again.

Because Skelegons are a special breed of polygon, the tools used in Modeler to edit polygons can also be used to edit Skelegons. Most of the tools found on the Modify tab's toolbar fall into this category.

The following tools are specific to Skelegons:

◆ **Edit Skelegon:** Reenables the circular handles for editing.

◆ **Rotate Skelegon:** Allows you to preview Skelegons' settings and the effect they have on geometry.

◆ **Split Skelegon:** Splits the Skelegon in half.

◆ **Set Skelegon Weight:** Used with VMaps to set a weight map.

◆ **Rename Skelegon:** Renames the Skelegon.

◆ **Skelegon Tree:** Combines Rename Skelegon and Set Skelegon Weight into a panel that also lets you edit each of the Skelegon's parents.

EDITING GEOMETRY

Unless you plan to only use primitives and text for your animations, you better learn how to edit geometry. In Modeler, you can use a variety of tools to change the location, orientation, and shape of the basic geometry you've already learned to create. By bending, smashing, and twisting your geometry, you can transform your object into whatever your imagination dictates.

The key to editing your geometry efficiently is knowing how each tool works. There may be dozens of ways to shape your geometry into what you want, but you'll learn that some methods are faster and easier than others. Some methods may take you minutes to perform, while others take you hours. In the computer graphics industry, speed and quality are incredibly important to judging your performance. Knowing which tool to use, and when, will come with time and practice.

In this chapter, you learn how to use layers to chop up and organize your objects into smaller, more manageable pieces. You also learn a wide range of methods for selecting exactly the part of an object you want to edit in Modeler. Finally, we introduce you to a large assortment of tools, not only showing you what type of editing is possible in Modeler, but also giving you a greater understanding of how it's performed.

Modeling with Layers

One major aspect of Modeler that we've over-
looked until now is layers. This feature has
evolved from a simple modeling tool to an
organizational necessity. By letting you focus
on a single part of an object at a time, layers
allow you to construct incredibly complex
models from several smaller, well-defined
pieces. This makes even the most daunting
modeling task easier to handle, and often
gives you greater flexibility in Layout.

Figure 4.1 A car model can be very complicated to look at.

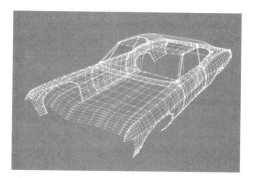

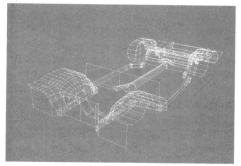

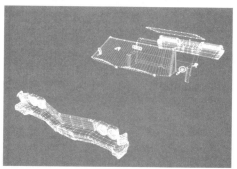

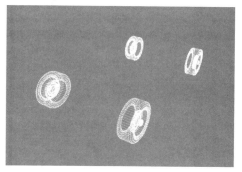

For example, say you were modeling a highly detailed car object. If you constructed all the geometry in a single layer, it would be insanely difficult to manage. You're talking about thousands upon thousands of polygons, some clearly inside and underneath other groups of polygons (**Figure 4.1**). It would be nearly impossible to tell one part of the car from another. However, you could put different parts of the car, like the engine, the seats, and the wheels, in their own separate layers (**Figure 4.2**). This not only makes it easier to model, but easier to edit and to understand visually.

Figure 4.2 If you break its geometry into different layers, the car model is much easier to understand.

Modeler displays the layers of an object in banks, located in the top-right corner of the interface (**Figure 4.3**). Each bank contains ten layers, and each layer has a pair of top and bottom buttons. Click the top button to see the *foreground* layer, used for creating and editing geometry. Click the bottom button, to display the *background* layer, a dark wireframe view of all the geometry in this layer (**Figure 4.4**). Geometry displayed in a background layer is for reference only; it can't be created or edited.

Although a bank contains only ten layers, a LightWave object can have up to 99 different banks. With ten layers to each bank, each object has a possible 990 layers to work with. So it's safe to say that you're unlikely to run out any time soon. You can flip through the various banks using the left and right arrow buttons to the left of the layer buttons, or by pressing Pg Up and Pg Dn on your keyboard.

To use layers:

1. Create a box in the first layer of an object (see Chapter 3, "Creating Geometry").

   By default, the first layer is automatically selected as the active layer when you create an object (**Figure 4.5**).

2. Click the second foreground layer or press 2 to make the second layer of the object active and clear the current geometry from the view (**Figure 4.6**).

3. Create a sphere in the middle of this new layer (**Figure 4.7**).

4. Click the first foreground layer or press 1 to go back to the box you created in Step 1.

5. Shift-click the second foreground layer or press Shift + 2 to select the second foreground layer.

   Now both layers are visible and active (**Figure 4.8**).

Figure 4.3 Access an object's layers with the controls in the upper-right corner of the Modeler interface.

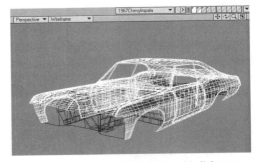

Figure 4.4 The foreground layer is drawn in light gray , and the background layer is drawn in black.

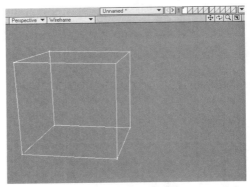

Figure 4.5 The first layer is created when you draw the box in it (shown here in Perspective view).

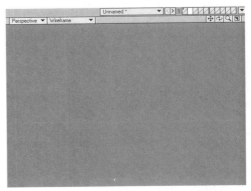

Figure 4.6 The second layer is empty and is now the foreground.

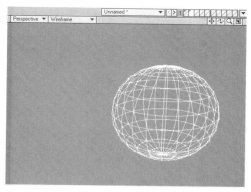

Figure 4.7 Create a sphere in the object's second layer.

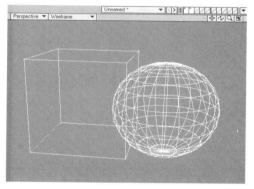

Figure 4.8 Put both the first and second layers in the foreground, and all the geometry is visible.

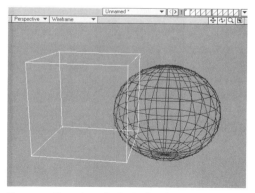

Figure 4.9 Here, the cube in the first layer is in the foreground, and the sphere in the second layer is in the background.

6. Click the third layer or press ③ to deselect both the first and second foreground layers.

7. Click the first foreground layer (or press ①) and the second background layer (or press Alt+②) to display the sphere in the background (**Figure 4.9**).

✔ Tips

- If a layer contains any geometry, a little dot appears on the layer's foreground (top) button.

- In the Layer Browser window, you can name layers and parent them to each other. This comes in handy when loading a multilayered object into Layout. To open the Layer Browser window, choose Layer Browser from the Windows pull-down menu in the toolbar or press Ctrl+F5.

- Use the Pivot command to position a layer's pivot point for use in Layout. You'll find this command in the View tab's toolbar.

- An object whose geometry is in multiple layers acts differently when loaded into Layout. Rather than showing up as a single object, as your objects have done so far, a multilayered object is broken up and each layer is displayed as its own object (**Figure 4.10**). This lets you create very complex mechanical objects with numerous moving parts, all contained within the same object file.

- Use the Save Layers as Object command, located in Modeler's File pull-down menu, to save the currently selected layers as a single-layered object.

Figure 4.10 When a multilayered object is loaded into Layout, each layer is broken out into a separate object.

MODELING WITH LAYERS

85

Selection Methods

In Chapter 3, we showed you how to select points and polygons using Modeler's selection modes. We also showed you how to use both the Info and Statistics panels to select specific types of geometry. These methods are very effective when you're working with simple models, but for more complex objects you need a little more power, or better yet, more selection options.

However, before we can play around with selections, we need to make an object to use.

To create our test object:

1. Select the Create tab to display the tools for creating geometry.

2. Click the Box button or press ⎡x⎤ to activate the Box tool.

3. Drag out a box in both the Top and Back views (**Figure 4.11**).

4. Click Box or press ⎡x⎤ again to finish creating the cube.

5. Click the second layer's top button or press ⎡2⎤ to put the second layer in the foreground.

6. Click the first layer's bottom button or press ⎡Alt⎤+⎡1⎤ to put the first layer in the background.

7. Click Ball in the toolbar or press ⎡o⎤ to activate the Ball tool.

8. Right next to the box you created in step 4, drag out a sphere in both the Top and Back views (**Figure 4.12**).

9. Click Ball or press ⎡o⎤ again to finish creating the sphere.

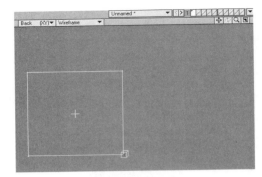

Figure 4.11 Draw a box in the first layer.

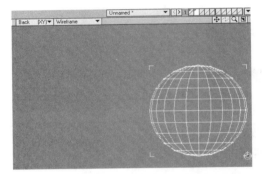

Figure 4.12 Draw a sphere in the second layer.

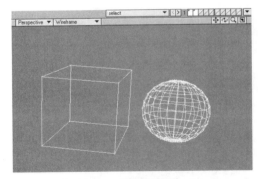

Figure 4.13 Both layers of the select.lwo object are displayed in the foreground.

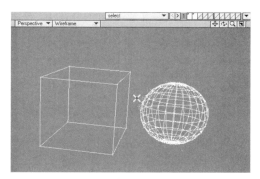

Figure 4.14 Select a few polygons from the sphere.

Figure 4.15 The View tab toolbar handles most of the selection and view commands, including Select Connected.

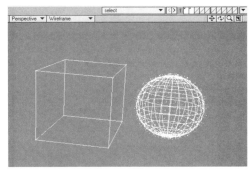

Figure 4.16 Use the Select Connected command, and the rest of the sphere's polygons are selected.

10. From the File pull-down menu, select Save Object.

11. When the Save As dialog appears, name the file `select.lwo`.

Now we'll use this object to demonstrate some of the different commands and functions you can use to help you select exactly what you want. As you learned in the previous chapter, the polygons that the primitives are made from share points with each other. Thus, the polygons are all connected to one another, leaving no holes or gaps. This first selection method takes advantage of this design feature.

To use Select Connected:

1. Load `select.lwo` (**Figure 4.13**).

2. Click the Polygons button at the bottom of the interface or press Ctrl+h to switch Modeler to polygon-selection mode.

3. Click a few polygons in the sphere primitive to select them in any of the views (**Figure 4.14**).

4. Select the View tab to display new options in the toolbar (**Figure 4.15**).

5. Click Connected in the toolbar or press] to select all the connected polygons (**Figure 4.16**).

✔ Tips

■ The Select Connected command also works with points.

■ Remember, by not selecting anything in a layer, you're essentially selecting everything!

SELECTION METHODS

Sometimes it's easier to choose the polygons that you *don't* want selected. When the Viewport is cluttered and specific parts of the object are hard to get to with your mouse, it's faster to only select a couple polygons, then have Modeler invert the selection.

To use Invert Selection:

1. Follow Steps 1–4 in the "To use Select Connected" procedure (**Figure 4.17**).

2. Click Invert in the toolbar or press ⏎ to have Modeler invert the current selection (**Figure 4.18**).

3. Repeat Step 2 to select the original geometry.

✔ Tips

- Use the Expand and Contract commands in the View tab's toolbar to select geometry connected to the currently selected geometry.

- Look in the Point and Polygon Info panels (see Chapter 3) for more selection tools.

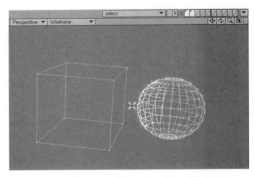

Figure 4.17 Both layers of the select.lwo object we created earlier.

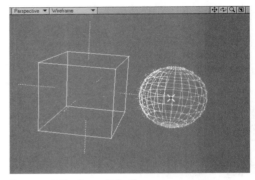

Figure 4.18 The Invert Selection command deselects the selected polygons, and selects the polygons that weren't selected (including the box object in the first layer).

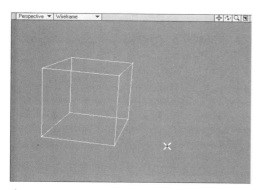

Figure 4.19 The sphere object that was selected is hidden after you click the Hide Sel button.

Sometimes you just want some of the polygons out of the way while you work on other parts of the geometry. Modeler lets you hide groups of polygons (only polygons) from the display and easily unhide them when you're done. Remember that you're merely hiding the polygons, not deleting them. More importantly, even when invisible, these polygons are still connected to the same geometry. So if you hide a polygon and alter the geometry it's connected to, the hidden polygon will be affected. This will be noticeable when you unhide it.

To hide and unhide polygons:

1. Follow all the steps in the "To use Select Connected" procedure.

2. Select the View tab, then click Hide Sel or press ⎯ to hide the sphere primitive (**Figure 4.19**).

3. Click Unhide in the toolbar or press ⧵ to unhide any geometry that was hidden.

✔ Tips

■ Click Volume on the View tab to declare points and polygons inside a selected box.

■ Modeler also has commands that hide unselected polygons, inverts the visibility state (hidden becomes visible and visible becomes hidden), and one that selects the inverted, connected polygons. These are in the View tab's toolbar as well.

Clipboard Actions

Modeler supports most of the common clipboard actions found in other applications, such as cut, copy, and paste. But unlike in a word processor or paint program, Modeler's internal clipboard stores the data locally, so you can't copy geometry to the clipboard and paste it in another application—not even in Layout. Then again, why would you ever want to copy geometry into another (non-3D) program?

Besides the obvious duplication and removal functions, Modeler's clipboard is most useful for moving geometry among the different layers of an object. Simply cut points or polygons from one layer (putting them into the clipboard) and then paste them into another layer. This added level of organization makes it easier to model large objects, one part at a time.

Now we'll use a bit of everything we've learned so far in this chapter.

To use the clipboard with layers:

1. Follow all the steps in the "To use Select Connected" procedure (**Figure 4.20**).

2. Press Ctrl+x to cut or remove the sphere's geometry, putting it in the clipboard. (**Figure 4.21**).

3. Click the object's third layer or press 3.

4. Press Ctrl+p to paste the sphere's geometry from the clipboard and into the third layer (**Figure 4.22**).

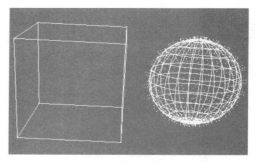

Figure 4.20 The Sphere object is selected.

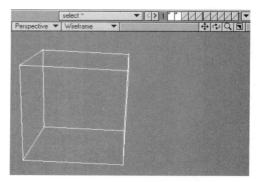

Figure 4.21 Use Cut to remove the Sphere object from the second layer.

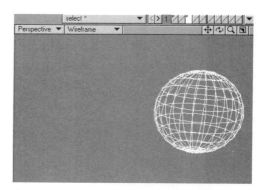

Figure 4.22 Then use Paste to insert the Sphere object into the third layer.

Figure 4.23 The Modify tab's toolbar contains most of the tools you'll use to adjust geometry.

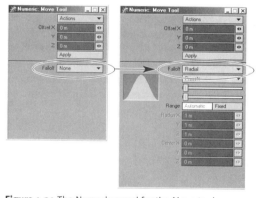

Figure 4.24 The Numeric panel for the Move tool displays the Offset and Falloff settings.

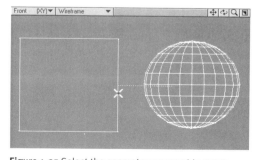

Figure 4.25 Select the geometry you want to move.

Adjusting Geometry

Modeler offers dozens of tools you can use to modify your geometry. Some of them are for minor tweaks, while others drastically reshape the points and polygons in your model. We cover a diverse range of these tools, but we can't possibly cover them all. Each of the tools that comes with LightWave, and all of their options, are well covered in the manual. However, hundreds of additional tools can also be found online at www.flay.com.

We'll cover five different categories of tools: moving, rotating, scaling, polygon-specific, and point-specific. You'll find the first three of these in the Modify tab's toolbar (**Figure 4.23**).

✔ Tip

- With most of the tools outlined in this section, you can gradually adjust the strength of the tool's affect, known as its *falloff,* in each of the tool's Numeric panel (**Figure 4.24**).

Moving geometry

You can move the selected geometry in a layer around a couple different ways. Some of the following tools offer precise editing of little bits, while others are meant for moving larger amounts of geometry. The first method is to use the Move tool.

To use the Move tool:

1. Load select.lwo.

2. Switch Modeler into either polygon-selection ([Ctrl]+[h]) or point-selection ([Ctrl]+[g]) mode.

3. Select the geometry you want to move (**Figure 4.25**). Select nothing if you want to move the whole layer.

continues on next page

ADJUSTING GEOMETRY

4. Select the Modify tab, then click Move in the toolbar or press [t].

5. Drag the geometry to a new position (**Figure 4.26**).

6. Click Move or press [t] again to drop the Move tool.

For editing geometry point by point, you can use the Drag and Snap tools. Both tools allow you to move points one at a time, but Snap makes a dragged point *snap,* or affix itself to nearby points.

To use the Drag or Snap tools:

1. Switch Modeler into either polygon-selection [Ctrl]+[h] or point-selection [Ctrl]+[g] mode.

2. Select the specific points or polygons of the geometry you want to edit.

3. Select the Modify tab, then click Drag in the toolbar or press [Ctrl]+[t] to activate the Drag tool.

or

Select the Modify tab, then click Snap Drag Tool in the Translate section's More pull-down menu located on the toolbar, or press [g] to activate the Snap tool.

4. Drag the individual points to their new locations (**Figure 4.27**).

5. Drop the current tool.

✔ Tip

■ You can also *not* select anything, in which case you'll be able to drag any of the points in the object.

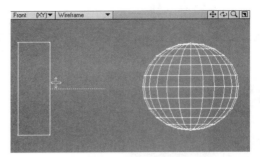

Figure 4.26 Using the Move tool, drag the selected geometry to where you want it.

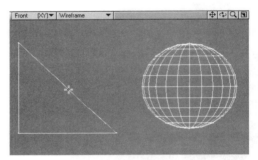

Figure 4.27 Using the Drag tool, click and drag geometry to where you want it.

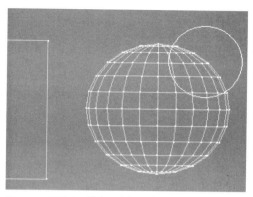

Figure 4.28 Right-click and drag to adjust the radius of the DragNet.

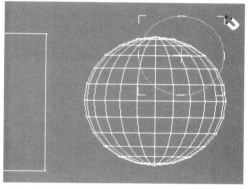

Figure 4.29 Adjust the radius of the Magnet tool by dragging its interactive handles.

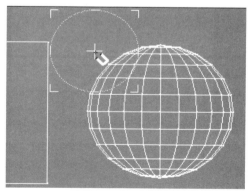

Figure 4.30 Right-click and drag to relocate the center of the tool.

Maybe you want to move points, but you want to do it on a much larger scale. Modeler's DragNet (short for Drag Network) and Magnet tools let you drag all the points in an area that you define. DragNet operates on two dimensions, while Magnet affects points three dimensionally.

To use the DragNet or Magnet tools:

1. Load `select.lwo`.

2. Select the Modify tab, then click DragNet in the toolbar or press ⌷ to activate the Drag Net tool.

   or

   Select the Modify tab, then click Magnet in the toolbar or press ⌷ to activate the Magnet tool.

3. Right-click and drag to adjust the area of influence (**Figure 4.28**).

   Magnet's influence area also has handles you can use to adjust its size (**Figure 4.29**).

4. Right-click and drag the center of the influence area to the area of the geometry you want to modify (**Figure 4.30**).

continues on next page

ADJUSTING GEOMETRY

5. Drag the points around until they're where you want them (**Figure 4.31**).

6. Drop the current tool.

✔ Tip

- Use the Numeric panels for these tools to change how their influence falls off (**Figure 4.32**).

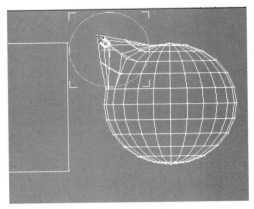

Figure 4.31 Drag the tool to move the geometry included in its area of influence.

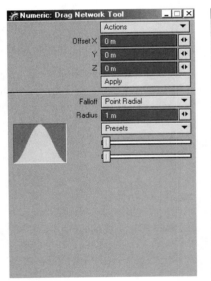
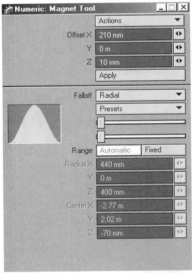

Figure 4.32 The Numeric panels of the DragNet and Magnet tools let you specify an Offset value as well as adjust the Falloff settings.

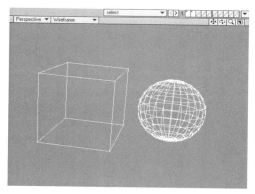

Figure 4.33 The select.lwo object you created in the beginning of this chapter.

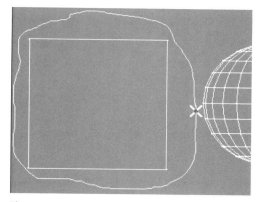

Figure 4.34 Right-click and drag a selection lasso around the cube.

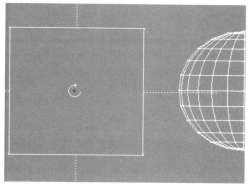

Figure 4.35 In the Back view, click where you want the center of the effect to be.

Rotating geometry

Points and polygons can be rotated using the Rotate tool. The usual method is to first define an axis of rotation, then a center or pivot point for the effect, and finally the angle or amount of rotation. Using these tools you can bend or twist your geometry into all kinds of crazy shapes.

To use the Rotate tool:

1. Load select.lwo (**Figure 4.33**).

2. Switch Modeler to polygon-selection mode by pressing Ctrl+h.

3. Right-click and drag a selection lasso around the cube (**Figure 4.34**).

4. Select the Modify tab, then click Rotate in the toolbar or press y.

5. Move your mouse into the view that corresponds to your rotational axis.

6. Click where you want the center of rotation (**Figure 4.35**).

continues on next page

7. Drag to rotate the geometry (**Figure 4.36**).

8. Drop the current tool.

✔ Tip

- To quickly rotate the selected geometry clockwise by 90 degrees, press $\boxed{r}$; for counterclockwise, press $\boxed{e}$.

Bending geometry

Rather than just rotating the geometry, you can also bend it with the Bend tool. The quality of this effect often depends on how much geometry is used to define the bending part of the object.

To use the Bend tool:

1. Select the Create tab to display new options in the toolbar.

2. Click Box in the toolbar or press $\boxed{x}$ to activate the Box tool.

3. Create a rectangle similar to **Figure 4.37** in the Side or Back view.

4. Use the arrow keys to give it a fair number of vertical segments.

5. Select the Modify tab, and then click Bend in the toolbar or press $\boxed{\sim}$ to activate the Bend tool.

6. Move your cursor into the view corresponding to the axis of the effect; we use the Top view (**Figure 4.38**).

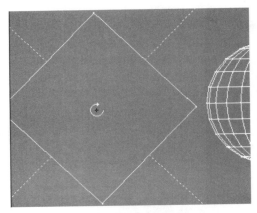

Figure 4.36 Rotate the object by dragging.

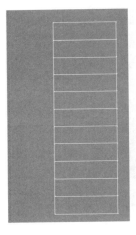

Figure 4.37 Use the Box tool to create this rectangle. Be sure to add plenty of segments to support the shape when it bends.

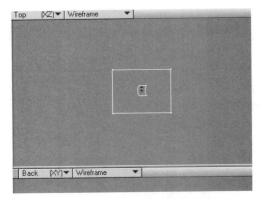

Figure 4.38 Hover the Bend tool's icon in the Top view to determine its axis, and click to place the center of the effect.

ADJUSTING GEOMETRY

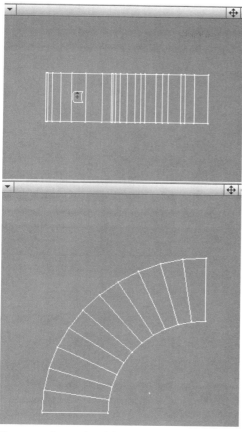

Figure 4.39 Drag to bend the geometry.

7. Click to determine the center of the effect and drag to bend the geometry (**Figure 4.39**).

8. Drop the current tool.

Twisting geometry

You can take bending geometry one step further with the Twist tool. As the name implies, it lets you twist your points and polygons around an axis. The quality of this effect also depends on the amount of geometry used.

To use the Twist tool:

1. Follow Steps 1–3 in the "To use the Bend tool" procedure to create a segmented rectangle.

2. Select the Modify tab, and then click Twist in the toolbar to activate the Twist tool.

3. Click in the view corresponding to the effect's axis to determine the center of the twist; we use the Top view (**Figure 4.40**).

4. Drag to twist the geometry (**Figure 4.41**).

5. Drop the current tool.

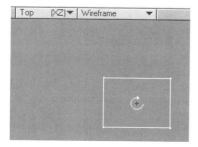

Figure 4.40 We clicked in the Top view here to determine both the axis and center of the effect.

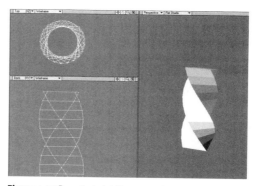

Figure 4.41 Drag to twist the geometry.

Scaling geometry

Modeler's stretch tools affect the size of the selected geometry. Depending on the tool, you can scale different parts of the object by varying amounts and in different ways.

By default, the Size tool increases the overall size of the selected geometry equally in the X, Y, and Z axes. This way, the proportions of the object stay the same, only its scale is altered.

To use the Size tool:

1. Load select.lwo (**Figure 4.42**).

2. Select the Modify tab, and then click Size in the toolbar or press h to activate the Size tool.

3. Drag to adjust the size of the cube (**Figure 4.43**).

4. Drop the Size tool.

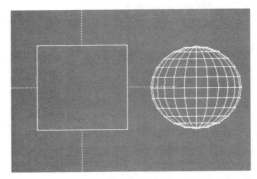

Figure 4.42 Load the select.lwo object, and select the cube.

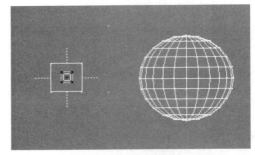

Figure 4.43 Resize the cube by dragging with the Size tool.

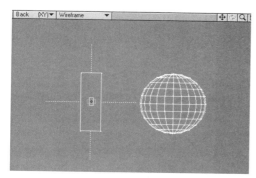

Figure 4.44 Stretch the cube along the Y axis in the Back view.

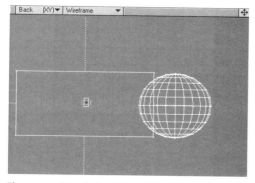

Figure 4.45 Stretch the cube along the X axis in the Back view.

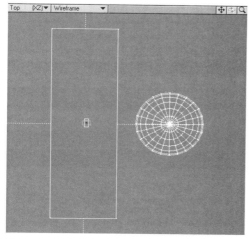

Figure 4.46 Stretch the cube along the Z axis in the Top view.

The Stretch tool works much like the Size tool, but on one axis at a time. You can adjust the amount of stretch per axis, totally independent of the other axes.

To use the Stretch tool:

1. Load select.lwo.

2. Select the Modify tab, and then click Stretch in the toolbar or press h to activate the Stretch tool.

3. Determine the center of the stretch effect by clicking in the view that corresponds to the axis you want to stretch along.

4. Drag upward along the Y axis in the Back view to adjust the height (**Figure 4.44**), left and right along the X axis in the Back view to adjust the width (**Figure 4.45**), or up and down along the Z axis in the Top view to adjust the depth (**Figure 4.46**) of the cube.

5. Drop the Stretch tool.

ADJUSTING GEOMETRY

Tapering geometry

Modeler supplies two tools for tapering (or scaling up or down) one side of your geometry (top/bottom, left/right, or back/front). The TaperConstrain tool scales in all axes equally, like the Size tool. The Taper tool is more like the Stretch tool, affecting each axis independently.

To use the Taper tools:

1. Follow Steps 1–3 in the "To use the Bend tool" procedure to create a segmented rectangle.

2. Select the Modify tab, and then click Taper Constrain in the toolbar.

3. Determine the axis and center of the tapering effect by clicking in the appropriate view (**Figure 4.47**).

4. Drag to taper the geometry (**Figure 4.48**).

5. Drop the Taper Constrain tool.

Spline Guide

The Spline Guide tool creates a user-defined guide that can manipulate geometry according to adjustable curve points. You drag these points to control the amount of a designated effect that is applied to the adjoining geometry. The effects supported by the Spline Guide are Scale, Stretch, Twist, Bend, and Weight Map.

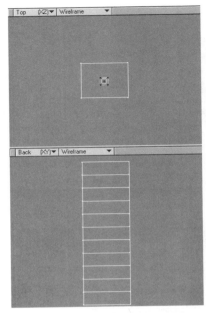

Figure 4.47 Use the Taper Constrain tool in the Top view to determine the axis and click to place the center of the effect.

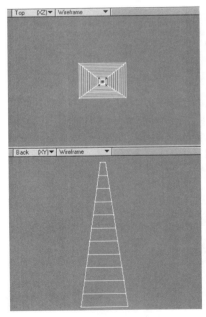

Figure 4.48 Drag to taper the geometry.

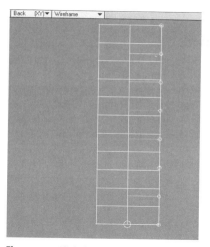

Figure 4.49 Click the geometry in the Back view to make the Spline Guide tool set up the initial guide.

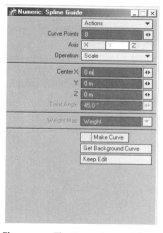

Figure 4.50 The Numeric panel for the Spline Guide tool lets you adjust the number of curve points, plus the axis, operation, center, and curve settings.

Figure 4.51 Change the Curve Points number to increase or decrease the amount of control over the shape.

To use the Spline Guide tool:

1. Follow Steps 1–3 in the "To use the Bend tool" procedure to create a segmented rectangle.

2. Select the Modify tab, and then click the More pull-down menu in the Transform section of the toolbar. Choose Spline Guide from the list to activate the Spline Guide tool.

3. In the Back view, click the geometry to set the tool's initial axis to Y.

   This displays the tool's interactive handles on the geometry (**Figure 4.49**).

4. Press ⓝ to open the tool's Numeric panel (**Figure 4.50**).

5. In the Curve Points field, type or use the arrow button to change the number of edit points in the spline (**Figure 4.51**).

6. From the Operation pull-down menu, select the type of effect the Spline Guide tool will use.

   For this example, we use Stretch (**Figure 4.52**).

continues on next page

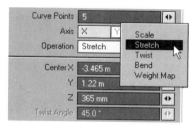

Figure 4.52 Select Stretch from the Operation pull-down menu.

ADJUSTING GEOMETRY

7. Drag to adjust the tool's curve points in any or all of the different views to control the strength of the Stretch effect (**Figure 4.53**).

8. Click Spline Guide again or press [Enter] to drop the Spline Guide tool.

Point-specific tools

Several commands and tools are specifically designed to work only with points, and not polygons. The Merge Points command, for example, combines points that are either directly on top of each other or within a pre-defined range. Typically you would use it to clean up after a particularly messy operation or procedure. Although this command will work on individually selected points, it's far more useful when applied either to large selection areas or to the entire layer.

To merge points:

1. Switch Modeler to point-selection mode.

2. Select the Detail tab to display new options in the toolbar (**Figure 4.54**).

3. Click Merge Points in the toolbar or press [m] to open the Merge Points dialog (**Figure 4.55**).

4. Click Automatic to merge points that are exactly on top of each other.

   or

   Click Fixed to specify a range. Any points that lie within this distance of each other will be merged together.

5. Click OK to perform the merge and close the dialog.

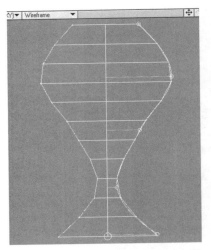

Figure 4.53 Adjust the curve points to modify the geometry.

Figure 4.54 The Detail tab's toolbar lets you edit several aspects of both points and polygons.

Figure 4.55 Choose Automatic to merge points on top of each other or Fixed to specify a range.

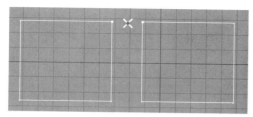

Figure 4.56 Select two or more points of the two polygons.

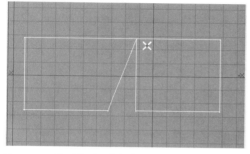

Figure 4.57 Use Weld to join the points together.

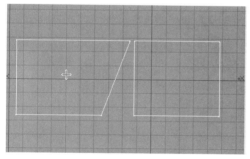

Figure 4.58 Move the polygon to see that the points are no longer welded together.

When you're reducing the complexity of a polygon or simply connecting polygons, use the Weld command to fuse two or more points together. The fused points are now one and the polygons they belonged to now share this single point. The order in which you select the points determines which point is fused to the other. Simply put, the first points selected are fused to the last point selected.

The Unweld command, naturally, does the opposite. It breaks a shared point apart, giving each polygon its own unique point.

To weld and unweld points:

1. Switch Modeler to point-selection mode.

2. Select two or more points in the same layer of an object (**Figure 4.56**).

3. Select the Detail tab to display new options in the toolbar.

4. Click Weld in the toolbar or press Ctrl+w to fuse the selected points (**Figure 4.57**).

5. Click Unweld or press Ctrl+u to separate the points.

6. To see the separated points, drag one of the polygons away from the other (**Figure 4.58**).

Polygon-specific tools

The following tools are designed to work only with polygons. Because polygons are created from points, you may need to select or manipulate points first in order for these commands to work correctly.

You learned in the previous chapter that you can create polygons from one or more points. Needless to say, you won't always create your polygons correctly at first. You may need to correct them by adding or removing points.

To add points to a polygon:

1. Create a four-point polygon (see Chapter 3).

2. Select the Multiply tab, then click Add Points in the toolbar.

3. Click an edge of the polygon to create a point at that location (**Figure 4.59**).

4. Click Add Points again or press (Enter) to drop the tool.

✔ Tip

■ A point added to an edge that is shared by two polygons will actually be added to both of the polygons.

Sometimes when you're cleaning up, or optimizing, your geometry, you'll need to combine two or more polygons into a single one. On the other hand, you might also need to split up a four-sided (or more) polygon into multiple polygons. There's a command for each of these functions.

To split a polygon:

1. Create a four-point polygon in any view. The polygon will remain selected (**Figure 4.60**).

2. Switch Modeler to point-selection mode.

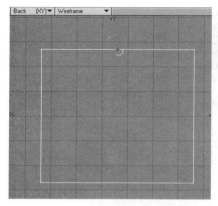

Figure 4.59 Click with the Add Points tool on the edge to add a point to the selected polygon.

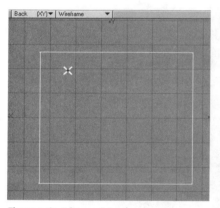

Figure 4.60 A four-point polygon.

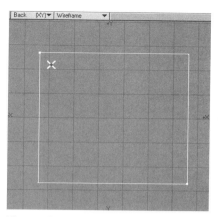

Figure 4.61 Select the two corner points.

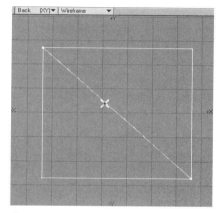

Figure 4.62 Use the Split command to divide the single polygon into two polygons, based on the two points selected.

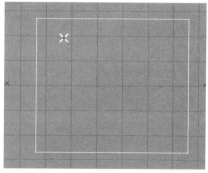

Figure 4.63 Merge the two triangles into a four-point polygon.

3. Select the two points (the corners) that will form the common edge (**Figure 4.61**).

4. Select the Multiply tab, and then click Split in the toolbar or press Ctrl+1. Your rectangle is now two adjacent triangles (**Figure 4.62**).

5. From the File pull-down menu, choose Save Object to open the Save As dialog, and name the object triangles.lwo.

Now merge the two polygons back together again.

To merge two polygons:

1. Load triangles.lwo.

2. Switch Modeler to polygon-selection mode.

3. Select the two polygons.

4. Select the Detail tab, then click Merge Polygons or press z to merge the polygons (**Figure 4.63**).

✔ Tips

■ If the polygon's normal is facing the wrong way (see Chapter 3), use the Flip command in the Detail tab's toolbar to change the polygon's normal to the opposite side.

■ Use the Align command in the Detail tab's toolbar to make all of a surface's normals face the same direction.

■ Use the Knife tool to quickly cut or slice through polygons, essentially slicing them.

ADJUSTING GEOMETRY

105

Edge Tools

Currently, Modeler lets you select groups of points or polygons that make up the geometry in your objects. We use these selections to modify or shape its geometry into the various forms needed to make a more complex model. Simply select the geometry and perform the action. This method is very straightforward. However, something new in LightWave 8.0 is the addition of edge modifying tools.

An *edge* is simply the border of a polygon, defined by two points. Edges can be shared by another polygon, or can simply belong to one (**Figure 4.64**). Although not all tools in Modeler are designed to work with edges, the ones that are offer a greater amount of flexibility when we're making our geometry.

The first of these tools we'll look at is Extender Plus.

To extend an edge of a polygon:

1. Create a rectangle of two four-point polygons in any view (**Figure 4.65**).

2. Select the edges of two of the polygons by selecting the three points that define them (**Figure 4.66**).

3. Select the Multiply tab, and then click Extender Plus in the toolbar.

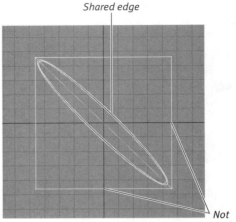

Shared edge

Not shared

Figure 4.64 Polygons can share edges.

Figure 4.65 A rectangle made up of two quadrangles (four-point polygons).

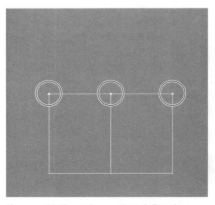

Figure 4.66 These three points define the two edges (one point is shared).

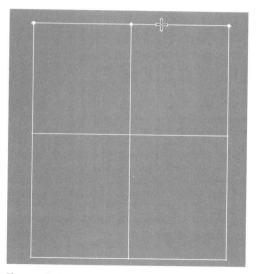

Figure 4.67 Drag to pull the newly created geometry away from the original edge.

4. Select the Modify tab, and then click the Move tool or press `t`.

5. Using the mouse, drag the points in any direction to reveal the new geometry created (**Figure 4.67**).

5. Press `t` or `Spacebar` to drop the Move tool.

Edges can also be added, removed, and reduced with the next set of tools.

To add an edge:

1. Create a four-point polygon (see Chapter 3).

2. With the polygon selected, select the Detail tab and click the Add Edges tool (**Figure 4.68**).

continues on next page

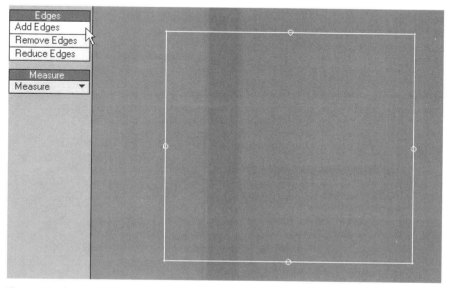

Figure 4.68 The new edge tools can be found on the Detail tab.

EDGE TOOLS

3. Blue handles are drawn in the center of each edge of the polygon. Click on the top and bottom handles to select these edges. The blue bar created is a preview of the edge that will be added (**Figure 4.69**).

4. Click the Add Edges tool again, or press Enter to turn off the tool and create the new edge (**Figure 4.70**).

To reduce an edge:

1. Create two four-point polygons (see Chapter 3) (**Figure 4.71**).

2. With the polygon selected, select the Detail tab and click the Reduce Edges tool.

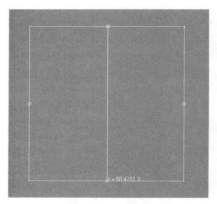

Figure 4.69 When an edge tool is active, blue handles are drawn on each of the selected polygon's edges.

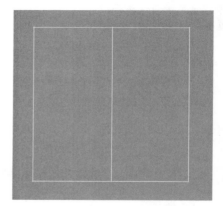

Figure 4.70 The new edge is created.

Figure 4.71 Create two, four-point polygons.

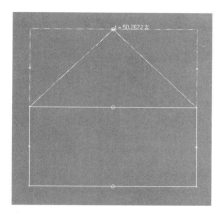

Figure 4.72 Handles are drawn on each of the edges.

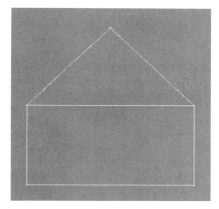

Figure 4.73 The Reduce Edges tool has done its job.

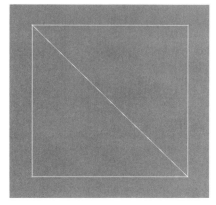

Figure 4.74 Triple the polygon.

3. Handles are drawn in the center of each of the polygon's edges. Click on the top edge's handle (**Figure 4.72**). The blue bar(s) indicate the edge(s) to be affected. The polygon's shape represents what it will look like after the edge is reduced (essentially removed).

4. Click the Reduce Edges tool again, or press Enter to turn off the tool and commit changes to the geometry (**Figure 4.73**).

And finally, what can be created must be able to be removed.

To remove an edge:

1. Create a four-point polygon (see Chapter 3).

2. Select the Multiply tab, and then click the Triple tool or press t to triple the selected polygon (**Figure 4.74**).

continues on next page

3. With the two polygons selected, select the Detail tab, and click on the Remove Edges tool.

4. Handles are drawn in the center of each of the selected polygons' edges (**Figure 4.75**). Click on the diagonal, shared edge with the left mouse button. If the edge can be removed, it will be redrawn as a dashed blue line.

5. Right-click on the same edge to remove it from the shared polygons (**Figure 4.76**). This results in a single, four-point polygon.

6. Click the Remove Edges tool again, or press (Enter) to turn off the tool and commit the changes to the geometry.

✔ Tips

■ In most cases, multiple polygons or edges can be selected and edited at the same time. Results vary, depending on the object's existing geometry.

■ These tools also let you edit the placement of the edited edges before committing to the changes. Slide the blue circles across the created edge before each of the tools are dropped.

■ In some cases, the Reduce and Remove tools will instantly be dropped when the action is performed. To do multiple actions, use the Apply & Clear buttons on their Numeric panels.

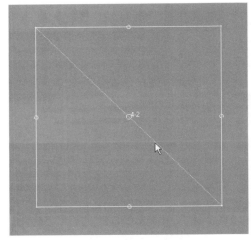

Figure 4.75 Handles are drawn on each of the polygon's edges.

Figure 4.76 The shared edge is removed.

EDGE TOOLS

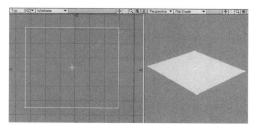

Figure 4.77 Create a four-sided polygon.

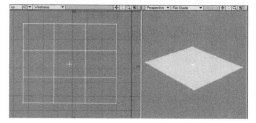

Figure 4.78 Create three vertical and three horizontal segments.

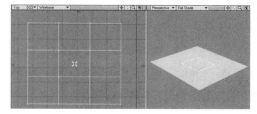

Figure 4.79 Select the center polygon.

Extending Geometry

Modeler has several tools that let you multiply or extend polygons from existing geometry. Modeler's Extrude and Bevel tools both grow geometry from a group of selected polygons.

To extrude polygons:

1. Select the Create tab, and then click Box or press ⟨x⟩.

2. Create a four-sided polygon in the Top view (**Figure 4.77**).

3. Using the arrow keys, create three segments vertically and horizontally (**Figure 4.78**).

4. Switch Modeler to polygon-selection mode.

5. Select the center polygon (**Figure 4.79**).

6. Select the Multiply tab to display new options in the toolbar (**Figure 4.80**).

continues on next page

Figure 4.80 The Multiply tab's toolbar offers new options, including the Extrude tool.

EXTENDING GEOMETRY

111

7. Click Extrude in the toolbar or press e to activate the Extrude tool.

8. Drag the Extrude preview bar out in the Back view (**Figure 4.81**).

9. Drop the Extrude tool.

10. Select the Construct tab, and then click Merge Points in the toolbar or press m to open the Merge Points dialog.

11. Click OK to accept the default values and merge all the points in the layer.

12. Select the Detail tab, and then click Align in the toolbar to make the polygon's normals consistent (**Figure 4.82**).

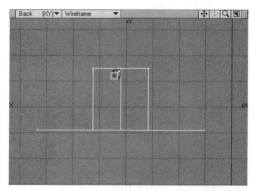

Figure 4.81 Extrude the selected polygon in the Back view.

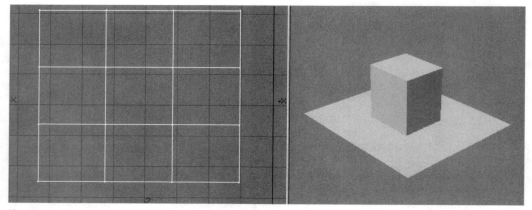

Figure 4.82 Use the Align command to make all the polygons face the same way.

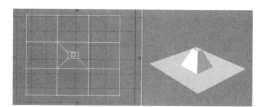

Figure 4.83 Drag to bevel the geometry.

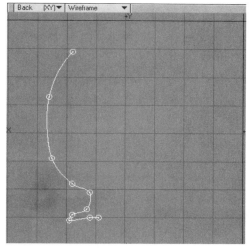

Figure 4.84 Create this curve using the Spline Draw tool.

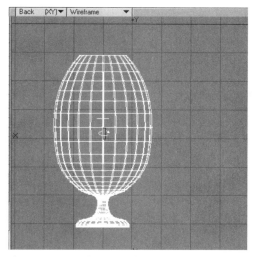

Figure 4.85 Draw the axis in the Back view, and the Lathe operation is automatically performed.

To use the Bevel tool:

1. Follow Steps 1–5 in the "To extrude polygons" procedure.

2. Select the Multiply tab, and then click Bevel in the toolbar or press [b] to activate the Bevel tool.

3. Drag out the beveled geometry (**Figure 4.83**).

4. Click Bevel again or press [Enter] to drop the Bevel tool.

✔ Tip

- You can also bevel edges by using the Edge Bevel tool located on the Multiply tab.

The Lathe tool spins a polygon or curve around an axis, creating a solid object. This is an easy way to create a table leg or a vase.

To use the Lathe tool:

1. Select the Create tab, and then click Spline Draw in the toolbar to activate the Spline Draw tool.

2. Draw a spline curve in the Back view similar to **Figure 4.84**.

3. Select the Multiply tab, and then click Lathe in the toolbar or press [l] to activate the Lathe tool.

4. Click in the Back view and drag to create the axis around which the spline will spin.

   The view updates to preview your lathed object (**Figure 4.85**).

continues on next page

5. Holding down the mouse button, make any adjustments to the axis.

   The previewed object updates as the axis is moved.

6. Drop the Lathe tool.

The Rail Extrude tool uses two layers to create its geometry. A polygon in the foreground layer serves as a profile for the created geometry. A curve in the background layer determines the path of the extrusion. The result is a smooth-flowing rail.

To use the Rail Extrude tool:

1. Press [2] to switch to the second layer of the object.

2. Select the Create tab, and then click Spline Draw in the toolbar to activate the Spline Draw tool.

3. Create a bending spline curve in the Back view similar to **Figure 4.86**, and press [Enter].

4. Press [1] to switch to the first layer of the object.

5. Press [Alt]+[2] to put the second layer into the background.

6. Select the Create tab, and then click Box in the toolbar or press [x] and make a four-sided polygon in the Left view similar to **Figure 4.87**.

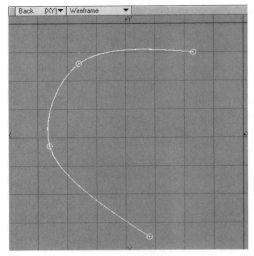

Figure 4.86 Create this curve in the Back view using the Spline Draw tool.

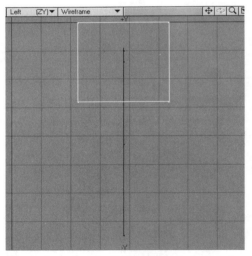

Figure 4.87 Create a four-sided polygon in the Left view using the Box tool.

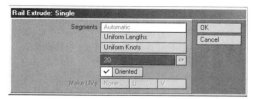

Figure 4.89 Accept the default values in the Rail Extrude dialog.

7. Select the Modify tab, and then click Move in the toolbar or press ⬚t⬚ and drag the polygon so that it lines up with the beginning of the curve (**Figure 4.88**, see bottom).

8. Select the Multiply tab, and then click Rail Extrude in the toolbar or press ⬚Ctrl⬚+⬚r⬚ to open the Rail Extrude dialog (**Figure 4.89**).

9. Click OK to accept the default values and create the rail (**Figure 4.90**).

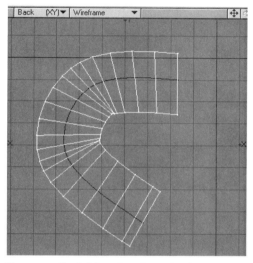

Figure 4.90 The Rail Extrude tool extrudes the foreground shape along the background path.

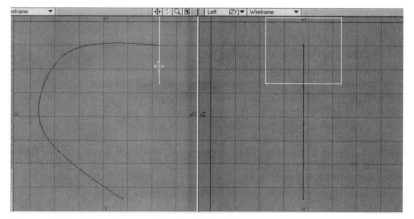

Figure 4.88 Align the polygon with the beginning of the curve.

Boolean Operations

Simply copying and pasting geometry among layers isn't always the best way to join the different parts of your object together. This method often leads to polygons that intersect at strange angles, unwanted gaps in the geometry, and inefficient and messy geometry (**Figure 4.91**). More importantly, such slap-dash methods can produce rendering anomalies.

Naturally, if you're incredibly careful, these unwanted byproducts can be avoided, or at least minimized. You can manually join and merge points and polygons, closing gaps and cleaning up the appearance of the object. But this can be an extremely lengthy process and can affect the quality of the object.

In LightWave, the Boolean operations deal with solid geometry that has volume. That means objects with no breaks or seams in their construction (**Figure 4.92**); they should look like they're modeled from a solid material (**Figure 4.93**). You *can* use geometry that doesn't follow these specifications, but the results of your Boolean operations will most likely be unpredictable.

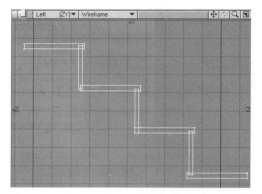

Figure 4.91 This stair-stepped object was sloppily created by smushing the geometry of each rectangle into the others.

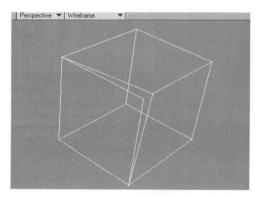

Figure 4.92 This object is not closed. The hole in the geometry will lead to errors when using one of the Boolean operations.

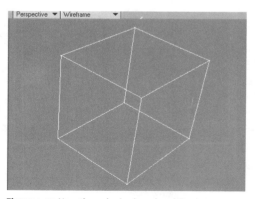

Figure 4.93 Now the cube is closed and Boolean operations will perform correctly.

LightWave's Boolean functions (named for a type of mathematical function) include Union, Intersect, Subtract, and Add. These tools deal with comparing two sets of geometry, one in the foreground and the other in the background layer. Their most common uses are to weld together or carve out geometry from the foreground layer.

◆ **Union:** This joins the foreground and background layers into one object. Polygons that are enveloped by another volume, and therefore would never be seen, are removed from the final geometry (**Figure 4.94**).

◆ **Intersect:** The resulting geometry is the volume that's common to both layers (**Figure 4.95**).

continues on next page

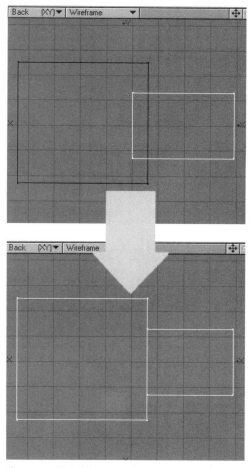

Figure 4.94 The Union operation merges these layers together, removing the geometry inside the larger cube.

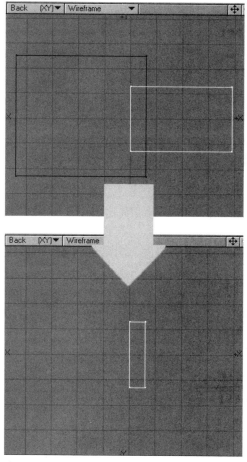

Figure 4.95 The Intersect operation creates an object with only the geometry common to both layers.

BOOLEAN OPERATIONS

◆ **Subtract:** The background object is removed from the foreground object. The surface of the background object is transferred to the new geometry created by the hole (**Figure 4.96**).

◆ **Add:** This is much like copying and pasting geometry from one layer to another. However, new points are created in the foreground object's polygons where the geometry intersects, to make a perfect merge of two layers (**Figure 4.97**).

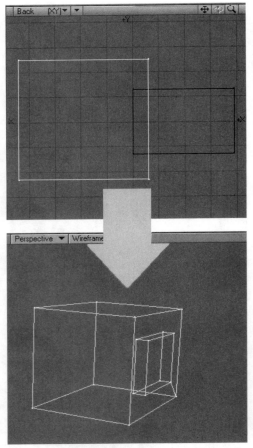

Figure 4.96 The Subtract operation removes the background volume from the foreground volume.

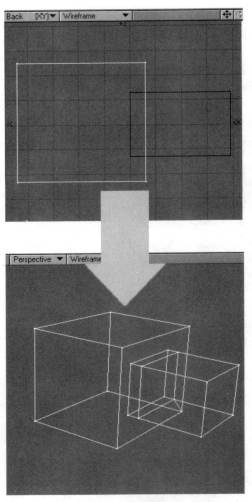

Figure 4.97 The Add operation merges the foreground and background layers together, adding points at the polygons' intersection.

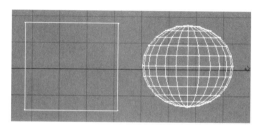

Figure 4.98 The select.lwo object has a cube in the first layer and a sphere in the second layer.

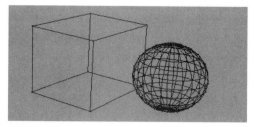

Figure 4.99 The third layer is in the foreground and the first and second layers in the background.

It's important to look over your work after the operation is performed. The Boolean tools are incredibly picky, and will often produce unwanted geometry or errors if they aren't set up correctly.

To use the Boolean operations:

1. Load select.lwo (**Figure 4.98**).

2. Press ③ then (Alt)+① and (Alt)+② to switch to the third layer in Modeler, keeping the first and second layers in the background (**Figure 4.99**).

3. Select the Create tab, and then click Box in the toolbar or press (x) and use the Box tool to create a rectangle that intersects both the box and sphere in layers one and two (**Figure 4.100**).

continues on next page

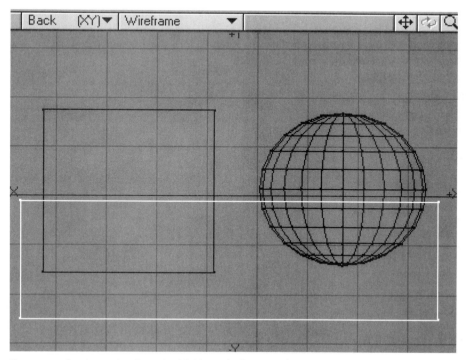

Figure 4.100 Create a rectangle on the third layer, the foreground.

BOOLEAN OPERATIONS

4. Select the View tab, and then click Swap Layers in the toolbar or press ⌐'⌐ to flip-flop the layers, putting layer three in the background and layers one and two in the foreground (**Figure 4.101**).

5. Select the Construct tab, and then click Boolean in the toolbar or press ⌐b⌐ to open the Boolean CSG dialog (**Figure 4.102**).

6. Click one of the Operation buttons, and then click OK to perform the function. We use Subtract in our example.

7. Press ⌐Shift⌐+⌐1⌐ and ⌐Shift⌐+⌐2⌐ to put the first and second layers in the foreground (**Figure 4.103**).

8. Select the Construct tab, and then click Merge Points in the toolbar or press ⌐m⌐ to open the Merge Points dialog.

9. Click OK to accept the default values and clean up the geometry.

✔ Tips

- You often need to use Merge Points after a Boolean operation to clean up the extra points created.

- Use the Drill tools when you're working with two-dimensional objects rather than volumes.

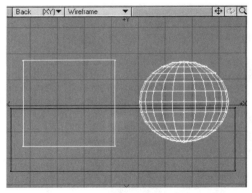

Figure 4.101 The Swap Layers command flip-flops the foreground and background layers.

Figure 4.102 The Boolean CSG window lets you decide what type of Boolean operation to use.

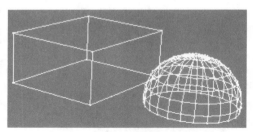

Figure 4.103 After performing one of the Boolean operations, check the geometry to make sure it did what you expected.

VERTEX MAPS

At the very minimum, an object's vertex is defined by its position and rotation within 3D space. This data is stored deep within the object's geometric information found in LightWave's object files. Vertex maps (VMaps) allow the points of an object to hold additional, user-defined values that can be used in the various tools found throughout both Layout and Modeler applications.

Just as you can map texture information onto polygons through the use of surfaces, you can map your custom data onto an object's vertices through vertex maps. These values can then be edited and manipulated using a powerful arsenal of VMap-specific tools found in Modeler.

The user-defined values stored in a VMap are instrumental when you want to use UV mapping, vertex coloring, morphing, and weighting. In order to function correctly, all of these features require that vertices have specific values set. Whether you're determining how a texture will look on a surface, restricting the effect of bones to certain points, or simply applying a "how much" value to a piece of geometry, VMaps allow you to tag this specific information to the vertices.

In this chapter, we'll show you how to create and use the different types of VMaps found in LightWave.

UV Texture Maps

If you play around with surfacing and image mapping enough, you discover that projecting an image along a single axis can be extremely limiting. When surfaces have an irregular shape or cover two or more axes, a projected image can appear to be stretched, distorted, or off-kilter (**Figure 5.1**). In fact, when using standard projections, you may have to create custom images in order for them to be displayed correctly on a surface (**Figure 5.2**).

UV texture maps allow you to pin a specific part of an image to a coordinate on a surface. These coordinates (U and V) determine the image's placement, orientation, and size, resulting in perfect placement of an image map on a model's surface.

Before we start playing with UV mapping, let's make a simple four-sided polygon (quadrangle) to use as an example.

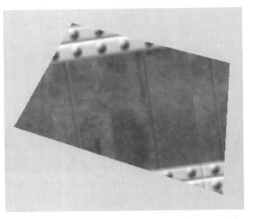

Figure 5.1 Planar projections are very limiting to oddly shaped polygons.

Figure 5.2 Custom images are often made to fit a situation or, better yet, a polygon.

Figure 5.3 Use the Points tool to quickly create a bunch of points and build a polygon.

To create a test polygon:

1. Select the Create tab to display new options in the toolbar.

2. Click Points in the toolbar or press ⊕ to activate the Points tool (**Figure 5.3**).

3. Right-click four new points, going clockwise in the Back view (**Figure 5.4**).

   This determines the polygon's normal (see Chapter 3, "Creating Geometry," for more on normals). As long as you create the points in clockwise order, the polygon's normal will face the correct direction (see the tip on the next page).

4. Press (Enter) to deactivate the Points tool.

continues on next page

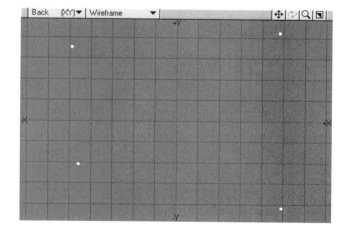

Figure 5.4 These four points will make up our polygon.

UV TEXTURE MAPS

5. Click Make Polygon in the toolbar or press ⓟ to create the polygon (**Figure 5.5**).

6. Click Surface at the bottom of the interface or press ⓠ to open the Change Surface dialog (**Figure 5.6**).

7. From the Name field, type UV and click OK to accept the surface parameters and close the dialog.

✔ Tip

■ If you didn't create the four new points for your polygon in clockwise order, you may find that it's facing the wrong direction and you'll need to backtrack to fix it. First, click the Points button on the bottom of the interface or press Ctrl+ⓖ to switch Modeler to point-selection mode. Then press ⟋ to deselect the points, and Ctrl-click each point in clockwise order to reselect them. Now you can continue from Step 4 in the preceding procedure to create the polygon.

With your test polygon made, you can now make a UV texture map to hold your vertex's custom data. The steps are kind of involved, so in order to make it easier to digest, we've broken the process down into four sets of steps:

◆ Create the UV texture map.

◆ Set up the surface for UV mapping.

◆ Set up the Viewports.

◆ Edit the UV coordinates.

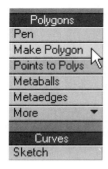

Figure 5.5 Use the Make Polygon command to create a polygon from these four points.

Figure 5.6 The Change Surface dialog lets you set the name and some preliminary surface attributes.

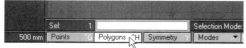

Figure 5.7 Switch Modeler to polygon selection mode.

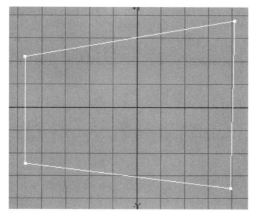

Figure 5.8 Select the four points in clockwise order.

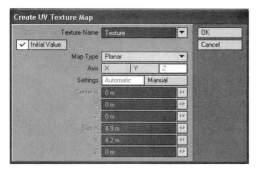

Figure 5.9 The Create UV Texture Map dialog lets you name and quickly assign some values.

Figure 5.10 In the Texture Map menu, LightWave keeps track of which texture VMaps are currently associated with this object.

To create a UV texture map:

1. Follow the previous procedure, "To create a test polygon."

2. Click the Polygons button or press Ctrl+h to switch Modeler to polygon selection mode (**Figure 5.7**).

3. Select the four points of the polygon or just select the polygon itself in the Viewport (**Figure 5.8**).

4. Select the Map tab to display new options in the toolbar, and then click New UV Map to open the Create UV Texture Map dialog (**Figure 5.9**).

   or

   Click the Texture Map button in the bottom-right corner of the interface and choose (new) from the Texture Map pulldown menu to its right (**Figure 5.10**).

5. Use the default name or type your own in the Texture Name field.

6. From the Map Type pull-down menu, choose the projection that Modeler will use to calculate the UV's initial values (for more on projection types, see Chapter 12, "Surfaces and Textures"):

   ▲ **Planar**, **Cylindrical**, and **Spherical** projection types refer to the shape of the surface to be mapped.

   ▲ **Atlas** projections "unwrap" the surface and arrange the UVs in an organized manner.

7. Click X, Y, or Z to choose an axis for the initial projection calculation according to the projection type you set in Step 6.

8. Click OK to close the dialog and create the texture vertex map.

UV TEXTURE MAPS

Now that the UV texture map has been created and assigned to the vertices, we have to set up the model's surface to use the UV map instead of a standard projection.

To set up the surface for UV mapping:

1. Click Surface Editor in the toolbar or press [Ctrl]+[F3] to open the Surface Editor (**Figure 5.11**).

2. In the Surface Name list, select the name of your surface.

3. To the right of the Color field, click the T button to open the Texture Editor (**Figure 5.12**).

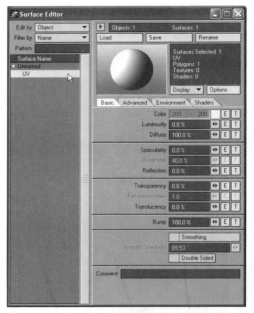

Figure 5.11 Adjust the object's surface parameters using the Surface Editor.

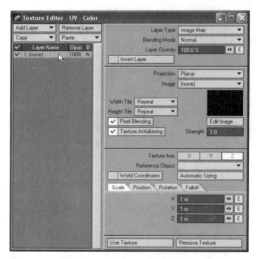

Figure 5.12 The Texture Editor allows you to add texturing details to a surface.

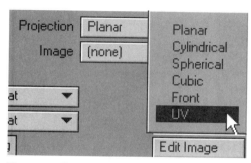

Figure 5.13 Change the Projection type to UV.

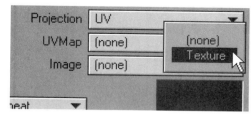

Figure 5.14 Change the UVMap to Texture.

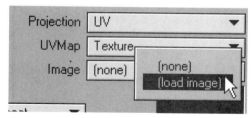

Figure 5.15 Select the image associated with this texture map.

4. From the Projection pull-down menu, choose UV (**Figure 5.13**).

5. From the UVMap pull-down menu, choose the UV map you want to use (**Figure 5.14**).

   This menu contains all the UV vertex maps found for this surface.

6. From the Image pull-down menu, choose or load a new image (**Figure 5.15**).

   This image is loaded into LightWave, and applied to this surface.

UV TEXTURE MAPS

Now that the surface placement is being controlled by UV mapping, you need to set up Modeler's interface so you can view and edit the UV values appropriately. Note: Depending on how you have Modeler configured, some of the following settings may already be correct.

To set up the interface for UV mapping:

1. From the Edit pull-down menu in the toolbar, choose Options > Display Options or press d to open the Display Options panel, and select the Layout tab (**Figure 5.16**).

2. From the Layout pull-down menu, choose Quad (**Figure 5.17**) to switch to Quad Layout mode (**Figure 5.18**).

3. Click OK to close the Display Options window.

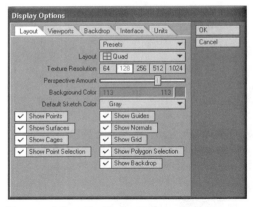

Figure 5.16 Open the Display Options window.

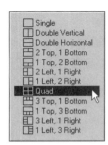

Figure 5.17 Choose Quad from the Layout menu.

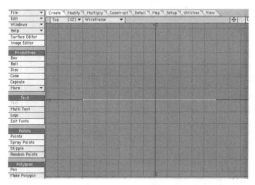

Figure 5.18 In Quad view Modeler shows four views of the object.

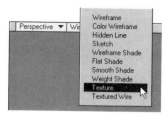

Figure 5.19 Switch the Perspective view's drawing mode to Texture.

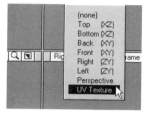

Figure 5.20 Change the bottom-right view to UV Texture.

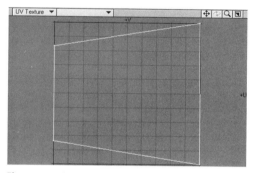

Figure 5.21 The UV coordinates are displayed so you can see and edit the map.

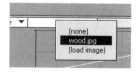

Figure 5.22 Select the image to display.

4. From the Perspective view's drawing mode pull-down menu, choose Texture (**Figure 5.19**).

5. From the Right view's drawing mode pull-down menu, choose UV Texture (**Figure 5.20**).

   This view mode is unique to UV mapping. It displays the UV coordinates (as points and their polygons) in relation to each other and the texture (**Figure 5.21**).

6. From the UV Texture view's pull-down menu, choose the image you set for this texture (**Figure 5.22**).

   The background of the UV Texture view is now the image (**Figure 5.23**)

✔ Tip

- Press [Shift]+[F9] to have Modeler automatically set up the UV Texture view's background image according to the image set in the surface's color texture.

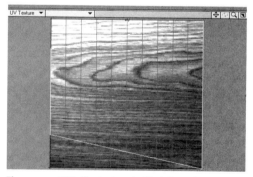

Figure 5.23 With the texture behind the points and polygons, it's pretty easy to see what has to be done.

Now we're ready to start manipulating some UV coordinate data and customize the map.

To edit UV coordinates:

1. Switch Modeler to point selection mode.

2. Select the Modify tab to display new options in the toolbar and then click Drag or press Ctrl+t to activate the Drag tool.

3. Drag the UV coordinates in the UV Texture view (**Figure 5.24**).

   Notice that as you manipulate the points, the texture adjusts itself in the Perspective view (**Figure 5.25**).

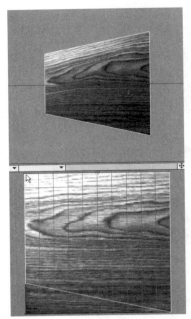

Figure 5.24 Before you edit the top-left point, the texture looks off.

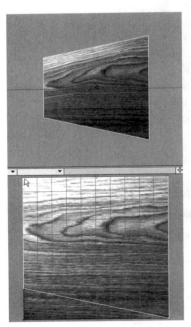

Figure 5.25 After you edit the top-left point, the texture begins to look right.

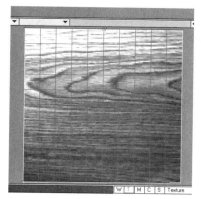

Figure 5.26 Adjust the UV coordinates to have the polygon use the entire image.

Figure 5.27 The final UV product even follows the geometry's irregularities.

4. Align the UV points so that each is in a corner of the texture (**Figure 5.26**).

   Notice that although our polygon is irregular, the image follows the contour of the geometry (**Figure 5.27**).

Discontinuous UVs

With standard UV mapping, polygons that share vertices also share UVs. Unfortunately, this means that when a coordinate for one polygon is adjusted, it may actually affect several polygons. This can be very annoying during complex UV mapping, but you can get around it by using discontinuous UVs.

Simply use the Unweld command on the Detail tab, and you're essentially creating another set of vertices, and thus UVs, that are no longer shared. You can now edit their coordinates independently of the other polygons. When you're done mapping your object, use the Weld command on the Detail tab or the Merge Points command on the Construct tab. Even though the vertices are now shared, the UV mapping is not.

Weight Maps

There are several uses for weight maps in LightWave. They provide a way for users to adjust how some of LightWave's features function and also define what geometry is affected and by how much. Plug-in developers also have access to weight map information, so you can often add custom data to these points for plug-ins to use.

The three types of weight maps we'll be discussing are SubPatch Weights, Bone Weights, and Tool Falloffs.

SubPatch Weights

In the past, artists using LightWave's SubPatch modeling technique had to create additional geometry in order to control the smoothing appearance of this effect (**Figure 5.28**). Since the introduction of the vertex map, you can now set a weight value for the vertex that will determine the amount of smoothing each part of the polygon gets.

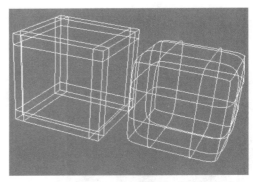

Figure 5.28 Extra geometry was added to the model on the left in order to produce the smooth object on the right.

Figure 5.29 Use this tool to create a box.

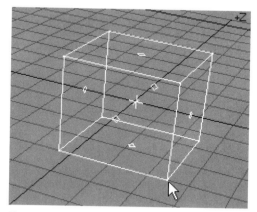

Figure 5.30 Try to make your box look like this.

This vertex map differs from the others in that it doesn't need to be created (it already exists), just modified.

To adjust the SubPatch Weight:

1. Select the Create tab, then click Box in the toolbar or press [x] to activate the Box tool (**Figure 5.29**).

2. Click anywhere in the Viewport and drag the box out in the different views until it resembles the one in **Figure 5.30**.

3. Select the Construct tab to display new options in the toolbar and then click SubPatch (**Figure 5.31**) or press [Tab] to convert the polygons to SubPatches.

4. Click the W button in the lower-right corner of the interface to switch the VMap to Weight Map mode and choose SubPatch Weight from the adjacent pull-down menu (**Figure 5.32**).

continues on next page

Figure 5.31 Convert the polygons into SubPatches.

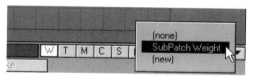

Figure 5.32 Select SubPatch Weight from the menu.

WEIGHT MAPS

133

5. Select the Map tab, then click Weights in the toolbar to activate the Weights tool (**Figure 5.33**).

6. In the Perspective view, click and drag the Weights tool over a vertex you want to adjust.

Drag left for smooth (**Figure 5.34**) and right for sharp (**Figure 5.35**).

7. When you're done, click Weights again to turn the tool off.

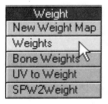

Figure 5.33 Activate the Weights tool.

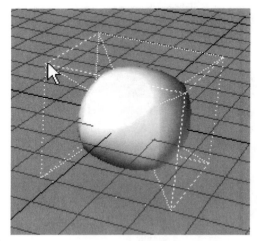

Figure 5.34 This point is now smoothing the object.

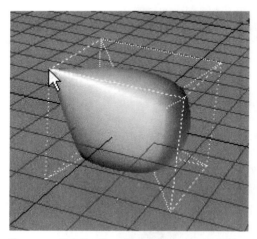

Figure 5.35 Painting the values onto a polygon either tightens or loosens the vertex's influence over the SupPatch effect. This point is now tightening the vertex and the geometry around it.

WEIGHT MAPS

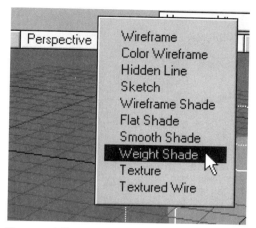

Figure 5.36 Change the drawing mode to Weight Shade.

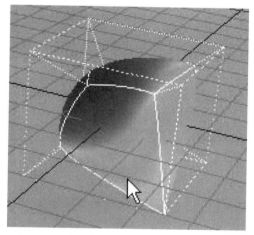

Figure 5.37 In Weight Shade mode, the darker section results in a smoother surface.

Modeler offers you an additional way to see and edit the object's SubPatch values. In any of Modeler's Viewports, you can switch the drawing mode to Weight Shade. Modeler shades the geometry using the color blue for smooth and red for sharp, so you can see exactly what's going on.

To use the Weight Shade mode:

1. Follow the preceding procedure to create and edit a SubPatched object.

2. From the Perspective view's drawing mode pull-down menu, choose Weight Shade (**Figure 5.36**).

   This shades the polygons blue and red, according to the vertices' SubPatch values.

3. Continue to adjust the SubPatch Weight values using the method in the preceding procedure.

   Notice how the colors change as you alter the values. The stronger the color and the more a polygon is shaded, the stronger the influence of the vertex map on the smoothing effect (**Figure 5.37**).

WEIGHT MAPS

Bone Weights

The second type of weight map is used to control a bone's influence on geometry. Rather than depending on a bone's position or falloff setting in Layout, you can use Bone Weights to say that this bone will affect these points by this much. Such fine-tuning gives unparalleled control when using bones within complex geometry. (For more information on using bones, see Chapter 7, "Objects and Bones.")

For example, when animating a character with bones, the arms or fingers often cause problems. A bone will "grab" or influence points it shouldn't, like the chest or nearby fingers. With Bone Weights, you can specify that this bone will affect only the points in this arm or this finger. Points not included in the bone's Bone Weight map won't be affected.

To control bone strengths using weight maps:

1. In Modeler, create or load an object you want to animate in Layout.

2. Switch Modeler to point selection mode.

3. Select the points you want to be restricted to a bone (**Figure 5.38**).

4. Click the W button to switch the VMap to Weight Map mode and choose (new) from the adjacent pull-down window (**Figure 5.39**).

5. When the Create Weight Map dialog appears, type `Bone 1` in the Name field (**Figure 5.40**).

6. Click OK to accept the initial value of 100 percent to assign these points to a single bone.

7. Press ⑤ to open the Save As dialog, setting a directory and filename. The Bone Weight maps are saved within the object file.

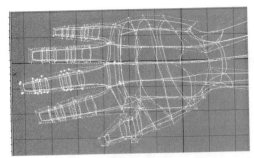

Figure 5.38 Assign these points of the finger to a Bone Weight map.

Figure 5.39 Choose (new) to create a new weight map.

Figure 5.40 Name this weight map Bone 1.

✔ Tip

■ The rest of the setup is done in Layout. To set up your bones in Layout, select the **Bone 1** weight map in the Bone Weight Map pull-down menu in the Bone Properties panel. With this set, the selected bone will only affect these points. In fact, if the names of the Bone and the Bone Weight Map are the same, layout will set them up automatically.

WEIGHT MAPS

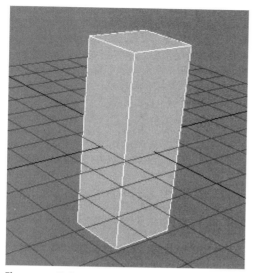

Figure 5.41 Make your box look like this.

Figure 5.42 Use the New Weight Map command to create a new map.

Tool Falloffs

The third type of weight map allows you to control how much a vertex is influenced by certain tools (like Move, Rotate, and Twist). By assigning the Tool Falloff values to a weight map, you can have one part of an object be affected a lot more (or less) than another.

To use a weight map to control a tool's falloff:

1. Select the Create tab, then click Box in the toolbar or press [x].

2. Click anywhere in the Viewport and drag the box out in the different views until it resembles the one in **Figure 5.41**.

3. From the Perspective view's drawing mode pull-down menu, choose Weight Shade.

4. Select the Map tab, then click New Weight Map in the toolbar (**Figure 5.42**) to open the Create Weight Map dialog.

continues on next page

WEIGHT MAPS

137

5. Click OK to accept the default name and initial value (100 percent) for the new weight map.

6. Switch Modeler to point selection mode.

7. Right-click and drag a selection lasso around the bottom points in the Side view (**Figure 5.43**).

8. Click Set Map Value in the toolbar to open the Set Vertex Map Value dialog (**Figure 5.44**).

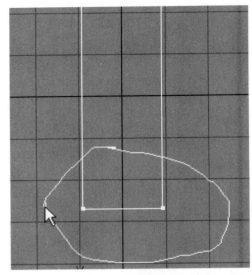

Figure 5.43 Group-select the bottom four points of the model.

Figure 5.44 Set a value of 0 percent in the Set Map Value dialog.

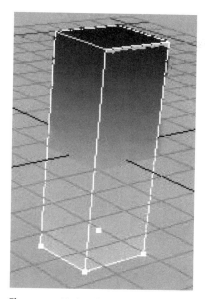

Figure 5.45 Notice the gradient, light to dark, as the values range from 0 to 100 percent.

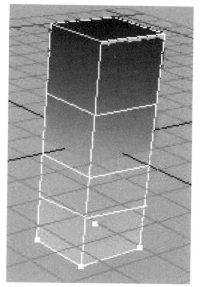

Figure 5.46 Use the Knife tool to cut the box you just made into four sections.

9. In the Value 1 setting, use the numeric field or arrow button to assign a value of 0 percent.

   Notice the gradient blend between the top and bottom of the model in the Perspective view (**Figure 5.45**).

10. Select the Multiply tab, then click Knife in the toolbar to activate the Knife tool.

11. Make three slices through the box.

    Notice that the gradient blend is preserved (**Figure 5.46**).

12. Select the Modify tab, then click Rotate in the toolbar or press $\boxed{y}$ to activate the Rotate tool.

   continues on next page

13. Press ⒩ to open the Numeric dialog (**Figure 5.47**).

14. In the Angle field, type 90.

15. Select the Y axis.

16. From the Falloff pull-down menu, choose the weight map you created in Step 4 (**Figure 5.48**).

Notice that as the shading becomes more intense, the rotation is increased (**Figure 5.49**).

Figure 5.47 Open the Numerical input dialog for the Rotate tool.

Figure 5.48 Select the name of the weight map in the Falloff menu.

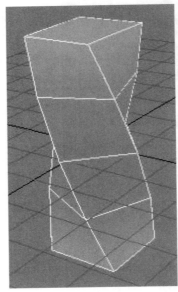

Figure 5.49 Notice how the rotation is nice and gradual.

WEIGHT MAPS

Morph Maps

Morphing has been around in computer graphics for years. It's simply a transformation, animating an object from one shape to another. Several movies in the early '90s made morphing a household name, wowing audiences with special effects like turning people into creatures and transforming faces into each other.

One use of morphing is facial animation. To animate speech, you'd morph from one mouth shape to another. Of course, you'd first have to make a different pose for each English phoneme, and even a short speech would involve hundreds of morphs.

Worse yet, each of the thousands of different face poses would have a specific naming convention and an insanely complex setup. They'd all have to be loaded at the same time and they'd all have to have exactly the same number of points for the morph to work.

Luckily, those days are past. In LightWave, now you do this by stating what the model initially looks like, then what it should look like when it's transformed. Then you tell LightWave how long it takes to get from one shape to another. Morph maps not only give us much more control, but the setup work is drastically reduced and the animation process is much more intuitive.

Instead of loading the different objects for each pose, now all the poses are contained in one object file. That's because morph maps simply record *only* the differences between the original shape and the altered shape, and everything else is the same.

Using the mouth example, say you have a blank face as your initial pose. Now you alter that pose so the mouth is open, making the "oh" sound. This can be pose one. Pose two is the mouth in the "ee" position. Pose three makes the "oo" sound. Nothing changes but the position of the points surrounding the mouth, so that's all that's stored in the morph maps.

Furthermore, you no longer need all the different combinations of objects in order to achieve facial animation. Because morph maps only record the differences between poses, you can set up specific poses to control the mouth positions, others for the eye positions, some for the cheekbones, and so on. Then back in Layout, where the animation takes place, a plug-in known as EndoMorph Mixer lets you blend all of them together using a slider for each of the poses.

Animating a face is way out of the scope of this book, however, so here we'll simply show you how to properly create several morph maps for an object. Then in Chapter 10, "Advanced Animation Tools," we'll talk about how to animate them using the EndoMorph Mixer plug-in.

To create morph maps:

1. Select the Create tab, then click Box in the toolbar or press [x].

2. Click anywhere in the Viewport and drag the box out in the different views until it resembles the one in **Figure 5.50**.

3. Click the M button in the bottom-right corner of the interface and choose (base) from the adjacent pull-down menu (**Figure 5.51**).
   This step sets the base pose that all the other poses will be compared to.

4. Choose (new) from the same menu to open the Create Endomorph dialog (**Figure 5.52**).

5. In the Name field, enter a name like 1 for the endomorph, to indicate which pose you're recording.

Figure 5.50 Make a box like this.

Figure 5.51 First choose (base) to set the base geometry, then choose (new).

Figure 5.52 Use the Create Endomorph dialog to indicate which pose you're recording.

MORPH MAPS

Figure 5.53 Move some of the points around to create a pose.

Figure 5.54 This is Layout's EndoMorph Mixer plug-in.

6. Click OK to close the dialog and create the morph map.

7. Drag some of the points around, creating a pose similar to **Figure 5.53**.

The changes you make to the points are recorded in the morph map.

8. Repeat Steps 4–6 for each pose you want to record, changing the name of the endomorph for each pose.

9. Press (s) to save this object, setting a directory and filename.

Within the object file is the base shape, and all the vertex transformation values stored as morph maps. Now your object is ready to be animated using the EndoMorph Mixer plug-in (**Figure 5.54**).

✔ Tip

■ You can view each pose by simply changing the current morph map in the pull-down menu.

MORPH MAPS

Color Maps

You can set the color of a polygon's surface by selecting the polygon's color in the Surface Editor or by using an image map. Although both methods are very powerful, and can often do the job, color maps let you go one step further.

Instead of coloring an entire polygon, color maps allow you to set a red, green, blue, and alpha (RGBA) value for each individual vertex of a polygon. Each added color is strongest at the vertex to which it was applied, and a blend will occur between two or more points with different colors or color intensities. This is known as *vertex shading*.

Vertex shading makes it easy to add multiple colors to a single polygon (**Figure 5.55**), adding yet another level of detail to your textures. One of the added benefits of vertex shading is that any color applied to the polygon's vertices also affects the polygon's surface. So if vertex shading is added to the vertices of a polygon, and a texture is applied to the surface of that polygon, the added texture will inherit the shading of the polygon as well.

Figure 5.55 Polygons can now have multiple base colors.

Color Maps and Video Games

Due to the very limiting memory restrictions in home video game machines today, artists have to reduce the amount of texture memory used in order to display their worlds and characters. A game's look, speed, special effects, and load times all depend on the artist's ability to use image maps efficiently.

Rather than creating hundreds of custom images, which would take a lot of memory, artists can use vertex maps to add shading to their existing textures. This method can be useful, and is extremely successful in LightWave, for the same reason.

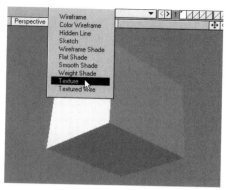

Figure 5.56 Change the Perspective view to Texture drawing mode.

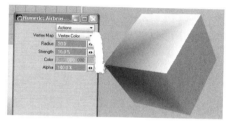

Figure 5.57 Click a vertex and notice how the geometry gets colored.

What's Next?

There are several tools within Modeler to help you with vertex maps, but some are far too complex to cover in this book. Please refer to both the manual and online resources for more information on the following subjects:

◆ **Vertex Paint:** This plug-in is designed to make painting on points easier.

◆ **Texture Guide:** This tool lets you place an image on a surface.

◆ **Multiple UV manipulators:** This lets you do everything concerning all UV-related topics, including Rotate, Spread, Quantize, and Normalize.

To create a Vertex Color Map:

1. Create or open a object that you wish to color.

2. From the Perspective view's drawing mode pull-down menu, choose Smooth Shade or Texture so that you can see the shading (**Figure 5.56**).

3. Select the Map tab, and then click New Color Map in the toolbar or press the C button in the bottom-right corner of the interface, and choose New from the adjacent pull-down menu.

   The Create Vertex Color Map dialog appears.

4. Click OK to accept the default color map settings.

   With no points selected, the color map is created for all the points of the model, and is ready to be colored.

5. Click Airbrush in the toolbar.

6. Press ⓝ to open the Numeric panel.

7. In the Color field, select the color you want to paint with. (This window can stay open while you're working in Modeler.)

8. Ctrl-click to select the points in the model to change the object's surface color (**Figure 5.57**).

9. Repeat Steps 7 and 8 to paint the object different colors.

10. Click Airbrush in the toolbar.

✔ Tip

■ Although vertex shading requires fewer images to be loaded, an object's geometry often needs to be more complex in order to achieve better results.

COLOR MAPS

BEGINNING ANIMATION

Animation can be simply defined, on a technical level, as positional change over a period of time to create the illusion of motion. Therefore, in order to create motion in Layout, you must make positional (or size) changes at different time intervals and create what are known as *keyframes*.

Keyframes are a concept carried over from 2D animation, in which artists create various poses at key frames in the animation of a character or object. Once this process is complete, the steps in between those frames (called *in-betweens* or just *tweens*) are then created by another 2D artist, generally referred to as a *tweener*. Similarly, when performing 3D animation in Layout, you define key item changes and Layout then works as the tweener to create those missing steps.

This chapter, designed to familiarize you with these animation concepts, begins our coverage of the Layout application. You'll learn how to move your items in 3D space, manipulate time, and create the keyframes that will define the motion in your animation.

Working in 3D Space

The first step in 3D animation is moving or resizing your item, but before you can begin pushing things around you need to know how to work in three dimensions. In Layout, each dimension is represented by its own axis along which you can move your item. You can think of the X axis (–X and +X) as left and right, the Y axis (–Y and +Y) as down and up, and the Z axis (–Z and +Z) as backward and forward (**Figure 6.1**).

Layout offers a selection of tools that allow you to manipulate your item along these axes in a multitude of ways. For example, the Rotate tool, which you'll find in the tool-bar (**Figure 6.2**), offers a slight variation on the three axes. Its H axis (heading; –H & +H) is used for "panning" left and right, the P axis (pitch; –P & +P) for "tilting" down and up, and the B axis (bank; –B & +B) for "rolling" left and right (**Figure 6.3**).

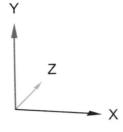

Figure 6.1 These are the three axes along which an item can move.

Figure 6.2 Click Rotate in the toolbar to use the Rotate tool.

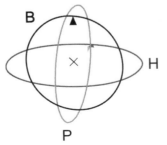

Figure 6.3 An item can rotate or pivot on these three axes.

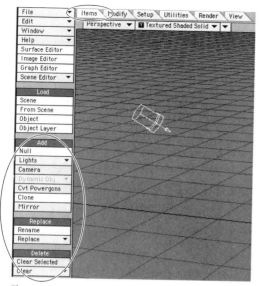

Figure 6.4 The Items tab offers new options, including the Add pull-down menu.

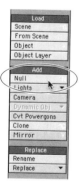

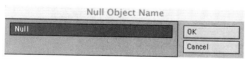

Figure 6.5 Use the Add tool group to load the objects and other items you'll use to create your scenes.

Figure 6.6 Use this dialog to name your Null object.

To manipulate items with the mouse:

1. Select the Items tab to display new options in the toolbar (**Figure 6.4**).

2. From the Add tool group in the toolbar, choose Add Null or press Ctrl+n (**Figure 6.5**).

3. In the Null Object Name dialog that appears, click OK to accept the default name for the Null Object (**Figure 6.6**).

4. Select the Modify tab to access the animation tools.

continues on next page

5. Click Move in the toolbar or press $\boxed{t}$ to activate the Move tool.

In **Figure 6.7**, notice how the Null Object has three colored arrows protruding from it. These represent the axis (red = X, green = Y, blue = Z) that the item can be moved along and also serve as handles, which point in the positive direction of their corresponding axis.

6. Click and drag anywhere in the Layout Viewport.

As you move the mouse forward and backward, notice that the item moves along the Z-axis. When you move the mouse left to right, the item moves along the X-axis (**Figure 6.8**).

7. Right-click and drag anywhere in the Layout Viewport.

Notice that as you move the mouse forward and backward the item moves along the Y axis (**Figure 6.9**).

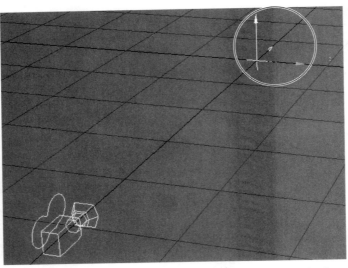

Figure 6.7 Use the Move tool to change your object's position along the three movement axes.

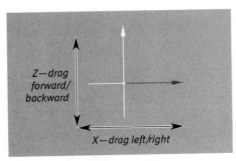

Figure 6.8 When animating with the mouse, use the left button to operate on the X and Z axes.

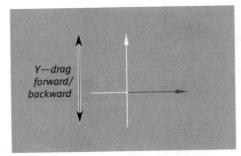

Figure 6.9 Use the right mouse button to operate on the Y axis.

8. Click the Reset tool in the toolbar to return the item to its original position (**Figure 6.10**).

Figure 6.10 The Reset tool is useful for undoing your actions and returning the current items to their initial positions.

9. Click Rotate in the toolbar or press [y] to activate the Rotate tool.

Three colored circles now encompass the Null Object (**Figure 6.11**). These represent the directions (red = H, green = P, blue = B) in which the item may rotate around its center.

10. Click and drag anywhere in the Layout Viewport.

As you move the mouse forward and backward, the item rotates on the P axis, tilting up and down. As you move the mouse left to right, the item rotates on the H axis, panning side to side (**Figure 6.12**).

continues on next page

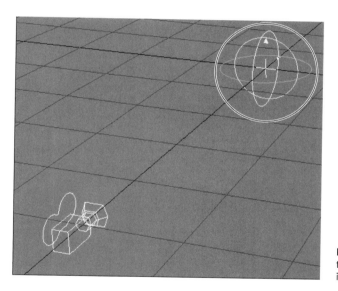

Figure 6.11 Use the Rotate tool to spin the current item around its center, or pivot point.

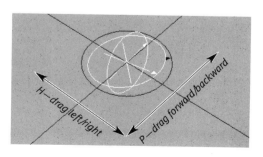

Figure 6.12 Use the left mouse button to modify an item's Heading and Pitch.

WORKING IN 3D SPACE

11. Right-click and drag anywhere in the Layout Viewport.

As you move the mouse left to right, the item rolls from side to side. (**Figure 6.13**).

12. Click Reset to return your item to its original position.

✔ Tips

■ The tool handles are also a visual indicator for the tool you are using. Lines with arrows indicate the movement; lines with blocks at the ends indicate a stretch operation; and the circles represent rotation.

■ The Reset tool is a quick and dirty way to return the currently selected item (or items) to its original position. Even though it only affects the item's position in the current frame, use this feature sparingly, because it can't be undone. Also, Reset can only undo changes for the currently selected tool. For example, if you have the Rotate tool selected, only the item's rotations are reset and any size or position changes you made are untouched.

In addition to freely moving an item about, you can also determine which axes are affected by your dragging. There are two ways to accomplish this, and the first is to use the handles for your selected tool.

To use a tool handle:

1. Select the Modify tab, and then click Move in the toolbar or press ⓣ.

2. Click and drag the red arrow (**Figure 6.14**). No matter how you move the mouse, the item only moves along the X axis.

3. Click Rotate in the toolbar or press ⓨ.

4. Click and drag the blue circle (**Figure 6.15**). Notice that you can move the item only along the selected axis.

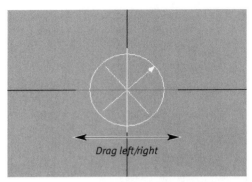

Figure 6.13 Use the right mouse button to modify an item's Bank.

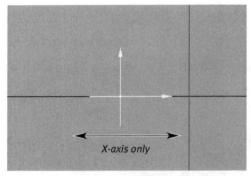

Figure 6.14 When using the tool handles, you can only move the item along a single axis.

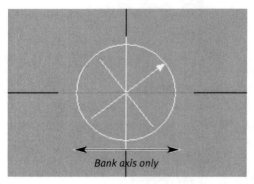

Figure 6.15 When using the tool handles, you can only rotate the item on a single axis.

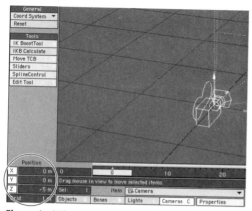

Figure 6.16 The axis toggle buttons are in the lower-left corner, next to the axis input fields.

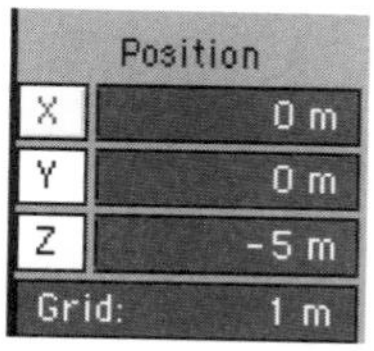

Figure 6.17 Disabling an axis in the info numeric field will prevent you from moving the item along that axis.

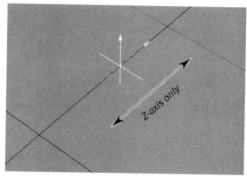

Figure 6.18 With the X axis disabled, moving the mouse left or right has no effect.

The second method is to disable movement along a single axis by clicking the button next to the info numeric field for that axis (**Figure 6.16**).

To disable movement on an axis:

1. Select the Modify tab, and then click Move in the toolbar or press t.

2. In the info numeric fields in the lower-left corner of the screen, click the X button to disable that axis (**Figure 6.17**).

3. Click and drag anywhere in the Layout Viewport.

   The item will move along the Z axis as you move the mouse forward and backward, but nothing happens when you move the mouse left or right (**Figure 6.18**).

4. Click and drag with the right mouse button.

   The item moves freely along the Y-axis.

5. Click Reset to return your item to its original position.

✔ Tips

- Using the axis button is a good way to lock an item after you've finished animating it. This prevents you from accidentally modifying it when working with other items in your scene.

- You'll notice that when you disable an axis for an item, the corresponding tool handle is dimmed in the Layout Viewport and cannot be selected.

There will come a time when you want to move your item to a specific location on a particular axis and the mouse won't be precise enough. A more precise method is to use the info numeric fields.

To use the info numeric fields:

1. Click the Modify tab, then click Move in the toolbar or press [t].

2. Double-click next to the X button in the info numeric field.

   The field becomes highlighted and a cursor appears to the right of the current number (**Figure 6.19**).

3. Press [Enter] to keep the current value, or type a new value and press [Enter].

   For example, if you type 2 in the field, the item will move to the 2 meter position on the X axis in Layout (**Figure 6.20**).

✔ Tips

- To change the values for each axis in succession, press [Tab] to highlight the next field and enter the desired value. Tabbing out of the Z axis field, though, will not highlight the X axis field, it simply accepts the Z value as though you pressed [Enter].

- Layout also allows you to perform simple mathematical operations in all of its numeric input fields. This is especially useful when you need to move or rotate items by some factor of their current position. For example, assume you have an object that is at 537.77 mm on one of the axes and you want to move it to a position that is exactly half that distance. Instead of having to pull out the calculator you could simply type 537.77 mm / 2 into the corresponding numeric input field.

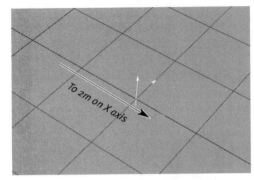

Figure 6.19 Double-click in the input field to highlight the current value.

Figure 6.20 Enter a value of 2 to move the item to 2m on the X axis.

Using the Basic Animation Tools

Now that you understand how to manipulate an item in three dimensions, let's take a look at the tools you'll use.

At the beginning of this chapter, you used the Move and Rotate tools to manipulate your items and Reset to return them to their original positions. But these are only three of the six basic animation tools available in Layout, so now we'll take a look at the other three: Size, Stretch, and Squash.

It's important to note that not all animation tools work for all Layout items (see "Animation Tool Usage"). As with the Move and Rotate tools, almost every tool has a set of handles corresponding to the axes on which they can be used.

The remaining basic animation tools are used to achieve different effects. If you want objects in your scene to grow over a period of time, whether uniformly or along a single axis use the Size or Stretch tools. To animate something being squashed and spread out over an area, use the Squash tool.

Animation Tools

Here's a list of which animation tools work with which Layout items.

◆ **Move:** All items

◆ **Rotate:** All items

◆ **Size:** Objects, Bones, Area lights, and Linear lights

◆ **Stretch:** Objects, Bones, Area lights, and Linear lights

◆ **Squash:** Objects and Bones

◆ **Reset:** All items

To resize an item:

1. Create and load an object into Layout.

2. Select the Modify tab and click Size in the toolbar (**Figure 6.21**) or press $\boxed{h}$ to activate the Size tool.

3. Click and drag anywhere in the Layout Viewport.

   The object grows as you move the mouse to the right (**Figure 6.22**) and shrinks as you move the mouse to the left.

✔ Tip

- The Size tool doesn't have axis handles, because it resizes the object evenly on all axes.

To stretch an item:

1. Create and load an object into Layout.

2. Select the Modify tab and click Stretch in the toolbar (**Figure 6.23**) or press $\boxed{h}$ to activate the Stretch tool.

3. Click and drag anywhere in the Layout Viewport.

   As you move the mouse left and right, the object stretches along the X axis. As you move the mouse forward and backward, the object stretches along the Z axis (**Figure 6.24**).

4. Grab the green tool handle.

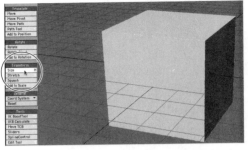

Figure 6.21 Use the Size tool to change the scale of an item uniformly along all axes.

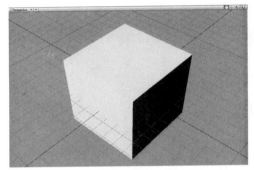

Figure 6.22 Drag left in the Viewport to shrink the item, drag right to enlarge it.

Figure 6.23 Use the Stretch tool to change an item's scale along a single axis.

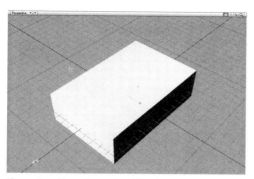

Figure 6.24 Drag forward and backward to stretch the item along the Z axis; drag left and right to stretch the item along the X axis.

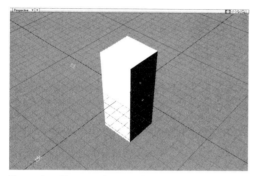

Figure 6.25 You can also use the Stretch tool's handles to limit the stretch effect to a single axis.

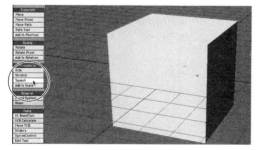

Figure 6.26 The Squash tool maintains the volume of an item as you resize it along one axis, creating a cartoonish flattening and expanding effect.

As you move the mouse up and down, the object grows taller and shorter, stretching along the Y axis (**Figure 6.25**). Moving the mouse left and right has no effect.

The Squash tool acts like a steamroller going over a cartoon character. As your object is squashed, it flattens and spreads out.

To squash an item:

1. Load an object into Layout.

2. Select the Modify tab and click Squash in the toolbar (**Figure 6.26**) to activate the Squash tool.

3. Click and drag the red tool handle to the left.

   The box shrinks on the X axis but grows on the Y and Z axes, as Layout pushes the geometry out along on the unsquashed axes to maintain the volume of the object (**Figure 6.27**).

✔ Tip

■ The Squash tool is the only one that requires you to use the tool handles. This is because you can only use it on a single axis at a time—the effect on the other two axes is calculated automatically. So if you click and drag in the Layout Viewport using the Squash tool, nothing happens.

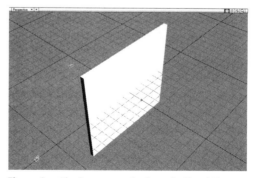

Figure 6.27 The item expands along the Z and Y axes as you squash it on the X axis.

USING THE BASIC ANIMATION TOOLS

157

Working with Time

Let's take a moment to discuss time as it relates to animation. At the beginning of any animation session, you should know what you want to accomplish with the animation and roughly how much time you would like to accomplish it in. All animation is created for output in some medium whether video, film, or computer movie files. And every medium runs at a specific frame rate, or number of frames per second (fps).

NTSC video, the U.S. standard, runs at a rate of 30 fps (the default fps of Layout); PAL video, the standard in most of Europe, runs at 25 fps; and motion pictures are presented at 24 fps. The frame rate for computer movie files varies, depending on the intended viewer application.

After you know your final output medium, the next step is figuring out how long your animation should be. For example, if you're outputting a 10-second animation to video, each second of animation requires 30 frames, so you can calculate that it will require 300 frames. Here's a simple formula you can use to figure out how many frames your animations need:

```
seconds of animation x fps = number of >
frames
```

Alternately, if you have a certain number of frames, you can determine the length of your animation sequence in seconds by applying this formula:

```
number of frames ÷ fps = length in >
seconds
```

Figure 6.28 The frame slider is used to move about in time and also serves as a visual indicator of where you are in your animation.

Figure 6.29 The start frame input field sets the first visible frame in the frame slider track.

Figure 6.30 The end frame value determines the last visible frame in the frame slider track.

Layout represents time with the frame slider located directly below the Layout Viewport. As you can see in **Figure 6.28**, the frame slider sits in a track that contains numbers and ticks. Each tick marks an individual frame and the numbers serve as intermittent guides. In addition, the frame slider itself displays the current frame number of the animation. To make the frame slider even more useful, before you set to work, you need to give it a couple of parameters: your start and end frames.

To set the start and end frames:

1. Double-click in the numeric field directly to the left of the frame slider track (**Figure 6.29**).

   The number highlighted there represents the first visible frame in the current time range and can be set to any whole number.

2. Leave the start value as 0 and press (Enter).

3. Double-click in the numeric field directly to the right of the frame slider (**Figure 6.30**).

   The highlighted number represents the last visible frame in the current time range.

4. Type 90 in the field for a 3-second time range (30 fps multiplied by 3 seconds), and press (Enter) to accept the value. Notice that the frame slider track updates to reflect the new time range.

✔ Tip

■ You must type whole numbers (not fractional numbers like 1.2 or 5.778) in the frame slider.

To change the current frame number:

◆ Click and drag the frame slider. As you move the slider, the time label on its face updates to reflect the currently displayed frame (**Figure 6.31**).

or

1. Press ⸤f⸥ to open the Go to Frame dialog (**Figure 6.32**).

    The current frame is shown by default and the input field is already active.

2. Type the number of the specific frame you want to move to and press ⸤Enter⸥.

    The frame slider jumps to that frame in the track.

At some point during the course of your animation work, you'll want the frame slider to display something other than simple frame numbers. For example if you were working with material from a video project, you might want the frame slider to display timecode. If you were working with film, you might want to use Frame Key-Code. Layout offers a few different slider label options tailored to various media (see the "Frame Slider Time Options" sidebar for an explanation of the different choices).

To change the frame slider label:

1. Select General Options from the Edit menu in the toolbar or press ⸤o⸥.

    The Preferences dialog opens with the General Options panel showing (**Figure 6.33**).

WORKING WITH TIME

Figure 6.31 You can click and drag the frame slider to display a different frame.

Figure 6.32 The Go to Frame dialog is a quick and easy way to jump to a specific frame.

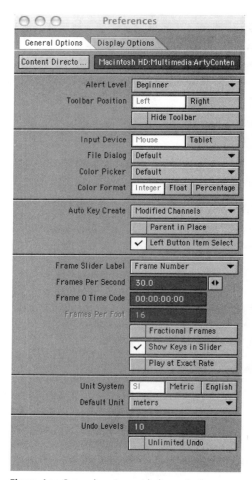

Figure 6.33 Set up how Layout behaves in the General Options panel of Preferences.

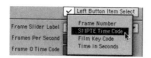

Figure 6.34 Use the Frame Slider Label pop-up menu to set how Layout displays time.

Figure 6.35 Both the frame slider and its track are updated to reflect your label choice.

2. From the Frame Slider Label pull-down menu, choose the units you want displayed.

In our example, we chose SMPTE Timecode (**Figure 6.34**). The frame slider label changes from 0 to read 00:00:00:00 (**Figure 6.35**).

✔ Tip

■ You can also set the start frame timecode value here by typing it into the Frame 0 Time Code input field.

To change the frame rate (fps):

1. Move the frame slider to a particular frame. In our example, we're using frame 24.

2. Select General Options from the Edit menu in the toolbar or press o.

The Preferences dialog opens with the General Options panel showing.

continues on next page

WORKING WITH TIME

Frame Slider Time Options

There are four different label options available for use with the frame slider.

◆ **Frame Number:** This option displays frame numbers, in whole numbers. It's very useful for any medium.

◆ **SMPTE Time Code:** This option displays the standard time code for video, as set forth by the Society of Motion Picture and Television Engineers. It's very useful when you're working on material that will be output to videotape. It's important to note that this option displays only non–drop frame timecode.

◆ **Film Key Code:** This option displays time in feet and frames, in the format 2 +13 (2 feet and 13 frames). It's extremely useful for working on projects destined for output to film. You can specify your film type (35 mm, 16 mm, and so on) by counting how many frames there are per foot of film and entering this value into the Frames Per Foot field in the General Options tab of the Preferences panel.

◆ **Time in Seconds:** This option displays time in seconds. It's useful in any medium.

3. From the Frame Slider Label pull-down menu, choose Time in Seconds.

In **Figure 6.36**, the frame slider now reads "0.800 s"—the 24th frame at 30 fps.

4. Double-click in the Frames Per Second input field and change the value.

In **Figure 6.37**, we changed the value to 24 so the frame slider now reads "1.000 s," meaning that the 24th frame is now recognized as 1 second along.

✔ Tip

■ It is important to note that after you start animating at one frame rate, changing to another frame rate can have adverse effects on the timing of elements in your animation. Try to determine the intended frame rate before beginning your work. Also, if you are working with different frame rates from project to project, try to make a habit of double-checking what the frame rate value is so you don't inadvertently begin working with the wrong setting.

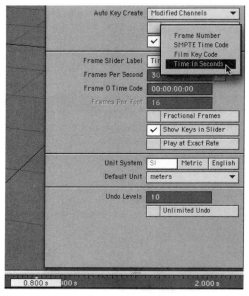

Figure 6.36 When the frame rate is set to 30 fps, frame 24 is equal to 0.8 seconds. Preferences panel contains many useful settings for configuring your animation environment.

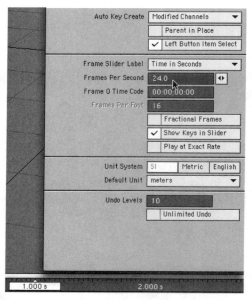

Figure 6.37 If the frame rate is updated to 24 fps, the 24th frame becomes equal to 1 second.

WORKING WITH TIME

Figure 6.38 Click Auto Key to disable the Auto Key functions.

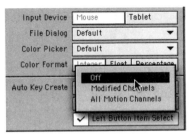

Figure 6.39 Choose Off from the Auto Key Create pop-up menu.

Working with Keyframes

Keyframes are the final piece of the animation puzzle. They mark key positional or size changes at specific points in time that define the animation path of your item. After you set up these initial points, Layout automatically fills in the gaps so that the item moves through them at the appropriate times in a smooth motion path. It's a little like creating a connect-the-dots puzzle for Layout to complete.

In order to fully understand keyframes, it's important to learn how to create and modify them manually. So for this section, disable Layout's Auto Key features, which automatically create and modify keyframes as you manipulate items in Layout's Viewport.

To disable Layout's Auto Key features:

1. Click the Auto Key button just below the frame slider track to disable it (**Figure 6.38**).

2. Press o to open the General Options tab of Preferences.

3. From the Auto Key Create pull-down menu, choose Off (**Figure 6.39**).

4. Close the Preferences window.

Now we'll create a simple animation with the camera, setting keyframes manually.

To manually create keyframes:

1. Click the default camera in the Layout Viewport (**Figure 6.40**).

2. Press ⌐Enter⌐ or click Create Key below the frame slider to open the Create Motion Key dialog (**Figure 6.41**).

3. Click OK or press ⌐Enter⌐ again to accept the current frame number displayed in the Create Key At input field and create a keyframe.

4. Drag the frame slider to frame 30 (**Figure 6.42**).

5. Click the Modify tab, then click Move in the toolbar or press ⌐t⌐.

6. Drag the camera to the upper-right portion of the Layout Viewport (**Figure 6.43**).

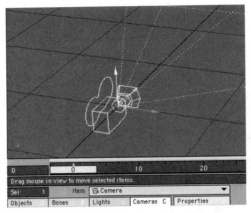

Figure 6.40 Select the Camera by clicking it in the Layout viewport.

Figure 6.41 The Create Motion Key dialog gives you several options for creating a keyframe.

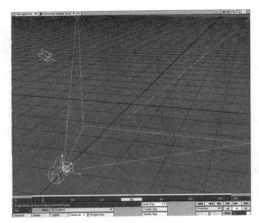

Figure 6.42 Go to frame 30, where you'll create the next key.

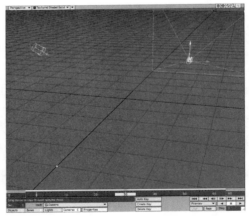

Figure 6.43 Move the Camera to the upper-right corner of the Layout viewport.

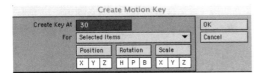

Figure 6.44 By default, the Create Motion Key dialog offers to create a key frame at the current frame.

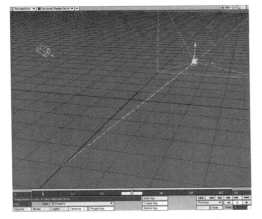

Figure 6.45 Layout updates to display the motion path for the Camera.

Figure 6.46 Go to frame 60 for the last keyframe of the animation.

7. Repeat Steps 2 and 3 to create another keyframe (**Figure 6.44**).

   Notice the line that Layout draws behind the camera. This is the motion path that the camera will move along as it travels between the keyframes (**Figure 6.45**).

8. Drag the frame slider to frame 60 (**Figure 6.46**).

9. Drag the camera to the upper-left portion of the Layout Viewport.

10. Repeat Steps 2 and 3 to create another keyframe.

    Layout connects all the dots and creates a smooth curve for the camera to travel along (**Figure 6.47**).

✔ Tips

- Layout will automatically create a keyframe at frame 0 for each item as it is added to the scene. In the case of the default scene, the default light and default camera both have keyframes at frame 0.

- Layout places yellow markers in the frame slider track to indicate where keyframes are for the currently selected item(s).

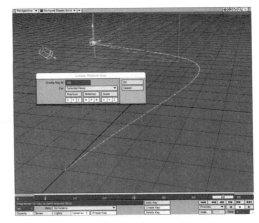

Figure 6.47 Layout displays the smooth arc along which the camera will travel.

Suppose you want the camera to move in a straight line from the keyframe at 0 to the keyframe at 60. You could reposition it at keyframe 30 to lie directly between the two or you could simply delete keyframe 30.

To delete a keyframe:

1. Press [f] to open the Go to Frame dialog (**Figure 6.48**).

2. In the input field, type the frame number of the key you want to delete (30 in our example) and click OK or press [Enter] to jump to frame 30.

3. Make sure the Camera is still selected and press [Del] or click Delete Key below the frame slider to open the Delete Motion Key dialog (**Figure 6.49**).

4. Click OK or press [Enter] to confirm that you want to delete the current keyframe and close the dialog.

The curve is replaced by a straight line from keyframe 0 to keyframe 60 (**Figure 6.50**). (See Chapter 10, "Advanced Animation Tools," for an explanation of Spline Interpolation.)

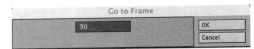

Figure 6.48 Go to the frame where you want to delete a key.

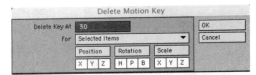

Figure 6.49 Use the Delete Motion Key dialog to remove a keyframe from the animation, whether at the current frame or another frame you specify.

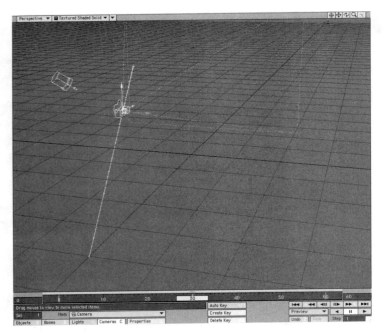

Figure 6.50 Layout updates to display the camera's modified motion path.

WORKING WITH KEYFRAMES

Forward Play

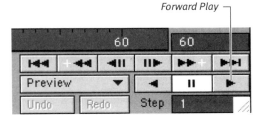

Figure 6.51 Use the shuttle controls on the frame slider in much the same way you'd use the similar-looking buttons on your VCR or DVD player.

Figure 6.52 As with your VCR/DVD player, pushing the play button will play your animation.

Previewing Your Animation

Now that you've created a simple animation, it's time to preview it. One way is to simply drag the time slider to the right with the mouse. This will give you a sense of your item's motion, but it isn't an accurate representation of timing.

Another way is to use the shuttle controls below the frame slider (**Figure 6.51**). The accuracy of the playback speed using this method depends on the speed of your graphics card. Some slower cards won't be able to refresh the Layout Viewport at the appropriate fps, while some faster cards will play the animation back too quickly.

To play your animation with the shuttle controls:

1. Create or load a scene with some animation in it.

2. Click the Forward Play shuttle control in the lower-right corner of the screen.

   The animation begins to play (**Figure 6.52**).

✔ Tip

- In the General Options tab of the Preferences panel, you can limit frame slider playback to the specified fps by checking the Play at Exact Rate check box. This will make the frame slider automatically skip frames to keep up with the specified fps if the animation is playing back too slowly, or slow the frame slider down if it's playing back too quickly.

Another factor in playback speed is the complexity of your animation. The more you have going on, the more calculations Layout has to perform, which will also slow things down. For a complex animation, you'll want to create a preview to get an accurate representation of the timing.

To create an animation preview:

1. Create or load a scene with some animation.

2. From the Preview pull-down menu in the lower-right corner of the screen, choose Make Preview (**Figure 6.53**).

   The Make Preview dialog appears.

3. Click OK or press (Enter) to accept the default values and start generating the preview (**Figure 6.54**).

   When the preview is ready, Layout will automatically open the Preview Playback Controls.

4. Click the play button to preview your animation (**Figure 6.55**).

   Notice that you have the option to loop the preview, play to the end and stop, or step through the frames one at a time, in either forward or reverse.

5. To adjust the preview's playback rate, click any of the numbered buttons (labeled "Frames per second" in Figure 6.55) to the right of the playback controls to change the frame rate.

   For example, if you click the button labeled "3," the animation will start to play back in super-slow-motion at 3 frames per second.

Figure 6.53 The Preview pull-down menu presents you with several options for generating and manipulating previews.

Figure 6.54 Specify the first frame, last frame, and frame step for the portion of the animation you'd like to preview.

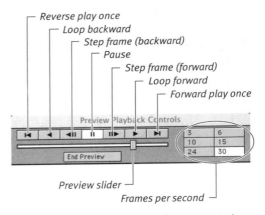

Figure 6.55 When the preview has been generated, a set of playback controls appears automatically.

PREVIEWING YOUR ANIMATION

Figure 6.56 You can drag the preview slider to scrub back and forth through the preview.

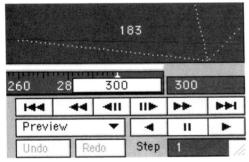

Figure 6.57 Layout displays the current frame number of the preview, so you can note where to make any necessary modifications.

6. Click pause to stop the preview, then click and drag the preview slider to scrub through your animation (**Figure 6.56**).

Layout displays the current frame number in the lower-right corner of the Layout Viewport (**Figure 6.57**).

7. Click End Preview to close the dialog and return control to the Layout interface.

✔ Tips

- Should you decide to end preview generation early, pressing ESC will cancel the operation and retain the portion it has already generated, which can be viewed by selecting "Play Preview" from the preview pulldown menu.

- You can save your previews as AVI or QuickTime movie files. Simply choose Save Preview from the Preview pull-down menu, and Layout will prompt you for a filename and location. Select Preview Options from the Preview pull-down menu to open the dialog where you can choose a file format for saving, as well as specifying a codec.

- By default, the Make Preview dialog will use your current frame slider settings for First Frame, Last Frame, and Frame Step. Change these values if you want to focus on a specific portion of your animation.

OBJECTS AND BONES

7

Earlier in this book you learned how to build objects in Modeler for use in your animations. Objects are the foundation on which you'll build your 3D scenes. No matter how simple or complex your animation, your 3D scene will require 3D objects—whether a ball bouncing on the floor or a complex character walking across a room. Your 3D scene is limited only by your imagination and, of course, what you can build in Modeler.

Another component that works hand in hand with objects is bones. Bones are items that you use to deform the geometry of your objects in much the same way that the bones in your body bend your arms and legs. You can use them to animate a character walking or a blob of gelatin dancing, to stretch the corners of a sheet or just about anything else you can think of where items are pushed, pulled, and stretched.

In this chapter, you'll learn what a Null object is, how to use custom objects, how to perform an object replacement, and how to deform objects using deformation tools and bones.

Introducing Objects

Like Modeler, Layout can work with multi-layered objects. Layout considers each layer a separate object that can be manipulated independent of the other layers, so there's no layer palette to quickly switch between them like in Modeler. Instead, Layout defines different object layers by the names it applies to them.

If you name your individual layers in Modeler they'll load into Layout as <object name>: <layer name>. An object with three layers appears to load three separate objects named <object name>:Layer1, <object name>:Layer2, and <object name>:Layer3. Multilayered objects are a great way to minimize the clutter in your scenes, making them more manageable.

For instance, you can create a car object that's made up of separate layers containing the chassis, wheels, and other moving parts. You could then animate the layers separately, but you'd only have to load one object file. Multilayered objects are a powerful feature, so take the time to understand and take full advantage of them.

✔ Tip

■ Saving an object with the first layer selected will save the entire object, with changes made to all of the layers. Saving an object with any other layer selected will save that layer as a separate object.

Working with Null Objects

Before we get into the nitty-gritty of using your geometry in Layout, let's take a moment to examine Null objects. A Null object is a unique, non-rendering, Layout item that you can use as a placeholder, as a parent for another item, as an inverse kinematics goal, as a custom object, and much more. The possibilities are endless, making Null objects one of the most flexible tools in your animation toolkit.

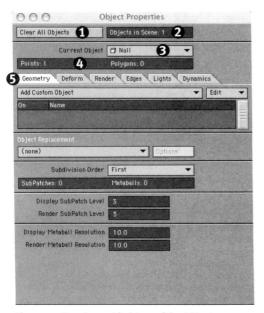

Figure 7.1 Here is a guided tour of the Object Properties panel.

The Object Properties Panel

The Object Properties panel is the information center for the individual objects in your scene. This is where you view information on the object, modify its attributes, and apply object-specific tools. Let's take a quick look at the main panel before jumping into the individual properties tabs (**Figure 7.1**).

The **Clear All Objects** button **(1):** This is a quick way to remove all objects from your scene.

The **Objects in Scene** field **(2)** keeps track of how many objects you currently have loaded into Layout.

The **Current Object** pull-down menu **(3)** displays the name of the currently selected object. Click it to select another object in the scene to modify.

The **Points and Polygons** field **(4)** displays how many points and polygons the current object has.

The **object property** tabs **(5)** each contain different controls. Select a different tab to change the controls shown below it.

The first four controls and fields are always displayed, regardless of which properties tab you're in.

Using Custom Objects

One use for Null objects is creating custom objects, which provide you with visual feedback for many of Layout's tools. You can access custom objects through the Object Properties panel.

To use a custom object:

1. Select the Items tab to display new options in the toolbar and click Null in the Add tool group (**Figure 7.2**).

2. When the Null Object dialog appears, click OK or press [Enter] to accept the default name "Null" (**Figure 7.3**).

   The Null object now appears in the Layout Viewport at the grid's origin—X = 0, Y = 0, Z = 0 (**Figure 7.4**).

3. Click the Item Properties button at the bottom of the screen (**Figure 7.5**) or press [p] to open the Object Properties panel.

Figure 7.2 Select items from the Add tool group to create them in your scene.

Figure 7.3 You can give a Null object any name you like, but it's a good idea to use names that relate to the object's function ("Bend Handle," and the like).

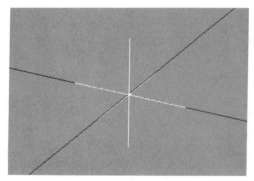

Figure 7.4 A Null object looks somewhat like a jack. It doesn't render with your scene, so it's good as a reference or stand-in for other items in your scene.

Figure 7.5 The Item Properties button opens the Properties panel for the currently selected item.

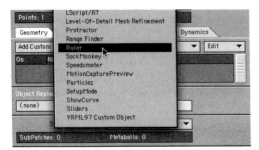

Figure 7.6 Add a ruler in the Geometry tab of the Object Properties panel.

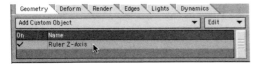

Figure 7.7 You can open the properties panel for a custom object by double-clicking its name in the list.

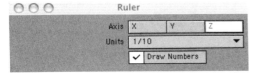

Figure 7.8 In the Ruler Custom Object's properties panel, you can change the settings or leave the default values.

4. Select the Geometry tab in the panel and choose Ruler from the Add Custom Object pull-down menu (**Figure 7.6**).

5. Double-click Ruler Z-Axis in the Custom Object list panel (**Figure 7.7**).

6. When the Ruler properties panel appears, leave the default values shown in **Figure 7.8** and close the panel.

7. From the View pull-down menu in the upper-left corner of the Viewport, choose Right (ZY) to switch views.

8. Select the Modify tab to change the toolbar options.

9. Click Stretch from the Transform tool group in the toolbar to activate the Stretch tool.

10. Drag the Null object around in the Layout Viewport.

    As you drag left and right, you'll see the ruler shrink and grow appropriately, providing a visual aid for distance (**Figure 7.9**).

✔ Tip

■ There are many included custom objects to choose from in LightWave 3D. For a complete list and detailed explanations, please refer to the LightWave 3D User's Manual.

USING CUSTOM OBJECTS

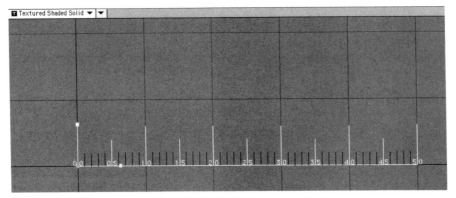

Figure 7.9 Stretching the Ruler custom object will help you measure distances in the Layout Viewport.

Performing object replacement

Sometime in the course of your animation work, you'll want to replace one object with another. A common example is when you've been using a Null object as a placeholder and want to swap it with the actual object.

Other uses include having an object change resolution at a certain distance from the camera or simply having one object change into another over the course of an animation.

To replace an object:

1. Follow Steps 1 and 2 in the first procedure, "To use a custom object."

2. Select the Items tab and choose With Object from the Replace pull-down menu in the Replace tool group of the toolbar (**Figure 7.10**).

3. When the open file dialog appears, select an object to load and click Open (**Figure 7.11**).

   Layout will replace the Null object with the selected object.

To replace an object with a Null object:

1. Load an object into Layout.

2. Select the Items tab and choose With Null from the Replace pull-down in the Replace tool group of the toolbar (**Figure 7.12**).

3. When the Null Object Name dialog appears, click OK or press [Enter] to accept the name of the item that you're replacing (**Figure 7.13**).

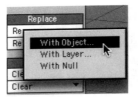

Figure 7.10 Null objects are often used as placeholders and later replaced with an actual object.

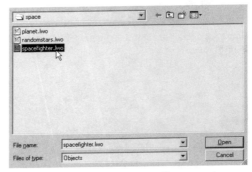

Figure 7.11 Select the object that will assume the Null's position in the scene.

Figure 7.12 Replacing objects with placeholders is also handy. You can focus on the animation of another item without the object getting in the way.

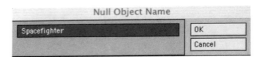

Figure 7.13 When replacing an object with a Null, the Null Object Name dialog defaults to the name of the object you're replacing.

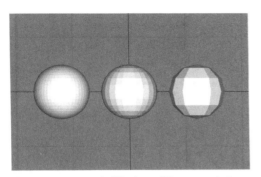

Figure 7.14 Create a ball in three different resolutions to use in our Level of Detail exercise.

As mentioned earlier, you can also replace an object over the course of your animation. This is accomplished using the Object Replacement tools. The most common use for object replacement is Level of Detail, meaning that the closer an item comes to the camera the higher its resolution. You use the Level-Of-Detail Object Replacement tool to switch between different resolutions of the same model.

Using Level of Detail cuts down on the memory overhead of your scene. For instance, you wouldn't want a 500,000-polygon object loaded into memory for the entire duration of a 10-second animation when it's only close enough to the camera for scrutiny for 3 seconds. Instead, you might create 250,000- and 125,000-polygon variations of the object for use at different distances from the camera. As the object comes closer, it's replaced with a higher-resolution variant. We broke the following example into several parts to make it easier to follow.

To use Level-of-Detail:

1. In Modeler, create three spherical objects (see Chapter 3, "Creating Geometry"): one with 48 sides and 24 segments, one with 24 sides and 12 segments, and one with 12 sides and 6 segments. Leave all other values at their default settings (**Figure 7.14**).

2. Save the first ball as LOD-HiRes.lwo, the second as LOD-MedRes.lwo, and the third as LOD-LowRes.lwo.

3. Load LOD-HiRes.lwo into Layout.

continues on next page

4. Press] twice to set the grid size at 1m (**Figure 7.15**)

Position
X
0 m
Y
0 m
Z
0 m
Grid:
1 m

Figure 7.15 The] key is used to increment the Viewport grid size while the [key is used to decrement the Viewport grid size.

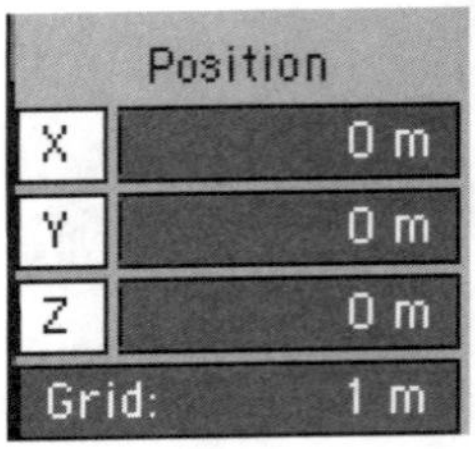

5. Click the Modify tab to display new options in the toolbar, click Move or press m to activate the Move tool, and drag `LOD-HiRes.lwo` to 10m on the Z axis.
6. Press e to create a keyframe.
7. Go to frame 60 of the animation.
8. Drag `LOD-HiRes.lwo` to –2m on the Z axis.

   The motion path moves toward the camera (**Figure 7.16**).
9. Click Item Properties or press p to open the Object Properties panel.

Textured Shaded Solid
0
10
20
30
40
50

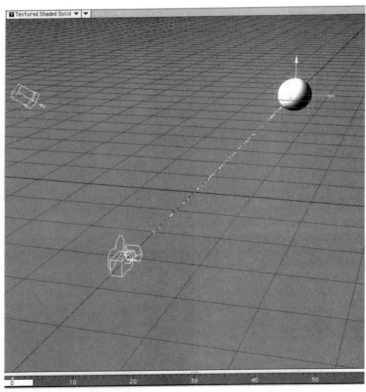

Figure 7.16 Your object's motion path should move from 10m on the Z axis toward the camera.

Figure 7.17 Object Replacement tools are good for swapping objects on the fly during your animation.

Figure 7.18 The Level-Of-Detail Object Replacement properties panel shows the default Base Object.

Figure 7.19 Select the medium-resolution version of the ball you created.

10. Select the Geometry tab and choose Level-Of-Detail Object Replacement from the Object Replacement pull-down menu (**Figure 7.17**).

11. Click the Options button next to the pull-down menu to open the Level-of-Detail Object Replacement properties panel (**Figure 7.18**).

The default Base Object is the one we applied the tool to.

12. In the first Beyond Distance input field, type 4m and press (Enter).

This tells the tool that when your object moves more than 4 meters from the camera you want a different object to be loaded.

13. Click the first Use Object button and in the open file dialog, click LOD-MedRes.lwo (**Figure 7.19**), and press (Enter) or click Open to load the object.

This tells the tool that you want LOD-MedRes.lwo to be loaded whenever the base object moves more than 4 meters from the camera.

14. Type 7m in the second Beyond Distance input field.

This tells the tool that you want a different object loaded when the base object moves more than 7 meters from the camera.

15. Repeat Step 13 to load LOD-LowRes.lwo into the second Use Object field.

This tells the tool to use LOD-LowRes.lwo when the object moves more than 7 meters from the camera.

USING CUSTOM OBJECTS

The results of using the Object Replacement tools are not immediately viewable, so you have to generate a preview or render a test clip.

To generate a preview:

1. From the Preview pull-down menu below the frame slider, choose Make Preview.

2. Press [Enter] to accept the default values.

3. After the preview is generated, click the preview play button in the preview shuttle controls panel.

    As the object gets closer to the camera, it is swapped out with LOD-LowRes.lwo between 10 and 7 meters from the camera (**Figure 7.20**), LOD-MedRes.lwo between 7 and 4 meters from the camera (**Figure 7.21**), and LOD-HiRes.lwo gets reloaded when it moves within 4 meters of the camera (**Figure 7.22**).

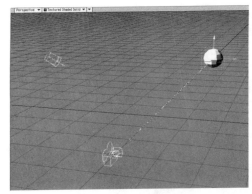

Figure 7.20 When the ball is 7 to 10 meters away, it's replaced with the low-resolution version you created.

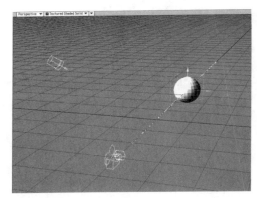

Figure 7.21 When the ball is 4 to 7 meters away, it's replaced with the medium-resolution version you created.

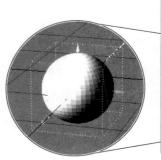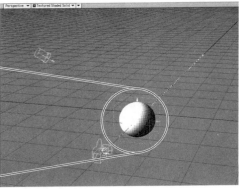

Figure 7.22 When the ball is 0 to 4 meters away, the full-resolution version is used.

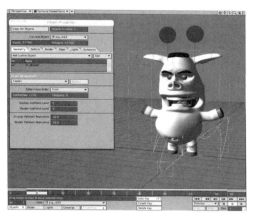

Figure 7.23 Your object will "smooth out" more as you increase the Display SubPatch Level value.

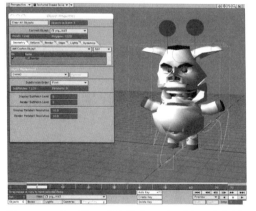

Figure 7.24 A setting of 0 tells Layout not to subdivide the object for display. This can dramatically increase responsiveness in scenes that use many subdivision surface objects.

Working with Subdivision Surfaces

In Chapter 3, you learned that subdivision surfaces are a very powerful modeling tool. Subdivision surface models can also be loaded into Layout for use in your animations. As you may have noticed earlier, subdivision surfaces are computationally intensive, especially when you're working with complex models.

As you can imagine, this adds to the workload of Layout and can affect how interactive your model is when animating. For this reason, Layout provides the option to set the subdivision level of your object for display in the Viewport, as well as to specify a subdivision level to be used when the object is rendered. The Display SubPatch Level determines how many subdivisions Layout performs on the geometry for display in the OpenGL Viewport.

To change the subdivision level of a model:

1. Load a subdivision surface model into Layout.

2. Click Item Properties or press [p] to open the Object Properties panel.

3. Select the Geometry tab and type **5** in the Display SubPatch Level field.

   Your model will be displayed at a higher subpatch resolution (**Figure 7.23**).

4. Type **0** in the Display SubPatch Level field.

   Your model will now be displayed as the base SubPatch cage (**Figure 7.24**).

continues on next page

✔ Tips

- You probably also noticed the other field, labeled Render SubPatch Level. This value determines how many subdivisions Layout performs on the geometry at render time. This allows you to give a model a low subpatch level for animation, to maximize Layout's response time when manipulating it, and to set the SubPatch level for final output to a higher resolution.

- Below the SubPatch Level controls you can see that there are similar controls for Metaballs. These work in the exact same manner as their subdivision surface counterparts, allowing you to specify a Display Metaball Resolution and a Render Metaball Resolution (**Figure 7.25**).

- The total number of SubPatches or Metaballs in the current object is displayed in the info field just above the SubPatch level input fields.

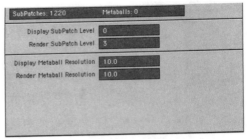

Figure 7.25 You can also specify the display and render resolution of Metaballs.

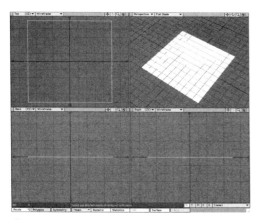

Figure 7.26 Create a box for use in this exercise.

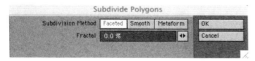

Figure 7.27 Subdividing the box creates more geometry.

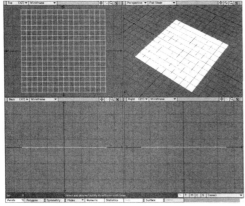

Figure 7.28 In order to create a smooth effect, the displacement tool needs a decent amount of geometry to work with.

Deforming Your Geometry

In order to create certain effects, such as water flowing across a surface, trees swaying in the breeze, or a character's face changing expression, you need to deform your geometry. That is to say, you need to be able to manipulate the points in your object by pushing them around in order to achieve the desired effect. There are no modeling tools in Layout, so you use the Deform tools. Layout's Deform tools rely on manipulating an object's points, so the more points you have in your geometry, the smoother the effect. In the following task, you make a wave move across a surface, using a displacement map.

To use a displacement map:

1. In Modeler, create a box with the following dimensions: width 2m, height 0m, depth 2m, center X 0, center Y 0, center Z 0 (**Figure 7.26**).

2. Click the Multiply tab to display new toolbar options and click Subdivide or press d to open the Subdivide Polygons dialog.

3. Click OK or press Enter to accept the default setting of Faceted next to Subdivision Method (**Figure 7.27**).

4. Repeat Steps 2 and 3 three more times to further subdivide the box (**Figure 7.28**).

5. Press s to save the object as Wave-Box.lwo and send it to Layout.

6. In Layout, select Wave-Box.lwo as the current item.

continues on next page

7. Click Item Properties or press ⓟ to open the Object Properties panel and click the Deform tab to display new tool controls (**Figure 7.29**).

8. Click the T button next to Displacement Map to open the Texture Editor (**Figure 7.30**). (See Chapter 12, "Surfaces and Textures," for more on the Texture Editor.)

9. From the Layer Type pull-down menu, choose Procedural Texture (**Figure 7.31**).

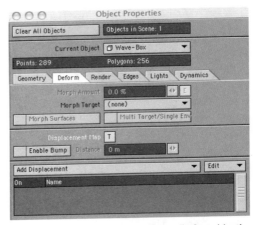

Figure 7.29 The Deform tab contains all of an object's deformation and displacement properties.

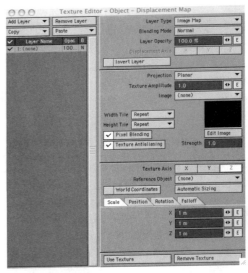

Figure 7.30 Use the Texture Editor's Object-Displacement Map to deform the object using a procedural texture or image map.

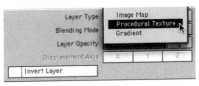

Figure 7.31 Procedural textures are seamless textures that can be used for a variety of effects. Some are animated, others simply reproduce real-world phenomena.

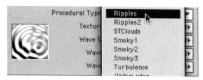

Figure 7.32 Use the Ripples procedural texture to create a rippling water effect.

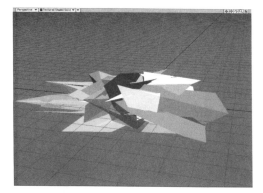

Figure 7.33 The displacement is based on the current grid size. Because your object is 1-meter square and the displacement size is 0.5 meters, the effect is too large and mangles it.

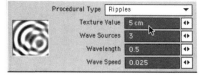

Figure 7.34 The Texture Value field defines the size of the effect.

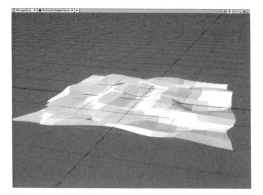

Figure 7.35 With a lower value, the effect area is smaller, making it more manageable.

10. From the Procedural Type pull-down menu, choose Ripples (**Figure 7.32**).

When Layout applies the displacement, you'll see your object become a tangled mess (**Figure 7.33**). This is because the default Texture Value is 0.5 (500mm), which also happens to be our current grid size—so your wave is equal to one full grid square in the Layout view.

11. Type .05 (or 5cm) in the Texture Value input field (**Figure 7.34**).

The ripples are now one-tenth of a grid square, and in better proportion to the object (**Figure 7.35**).

12. Press the frame slider play button to preview the effect.

The effect looks a little blocky, so let's smooth out the surface a bit.

continues on next page

13. Click Surface Editor in the toolbar (**Figure 7.36**) or press `Ctrl`+`F3` to open the Surface Editor.

14. Check the Smoothing check box to activate surface smoothing (**Figure 7.37**).

15. Close the Surface Editor.

Your surface is now smoother, producing a more realistic effect (**Figure 7.38**).

✔ Tips

■ The more points that there are to be manipulated by the deformation, the smoother the effect will be. A common practice is to triple (triangulate) any geometry that will be deformed.

■ Instead of using a pre-subdivided box for the above task, you could have simply made the box a subdivision surface object. You would then use the display and render SubPatch levels to dictate how much resolution the mesh had for the displacement effect. To try it, repeat the above exercise, but this time import the box as a subdivision surface object instead of manually subdividing it. Change the Display SubPatch Level to 6 for a comparable effect.

Figure 7.36 The Surface Editor button is available on every toolbar tab, so you can get to it whenever you need it.

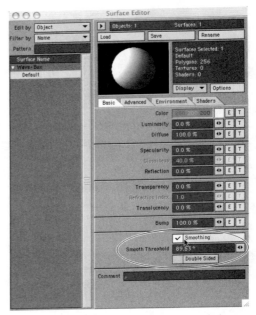

Figure 7.37 The Smoothing option will smooth the edges between polygons on the object's surface.

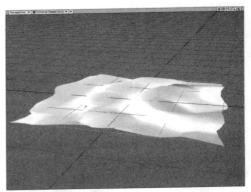

Figure 7.38 The surface of the rippling box is now smooth, producing a more realistic water surface effect.

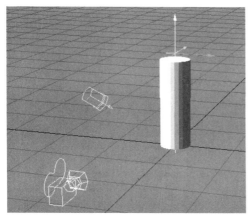

Figure 7.39 Your bend setup should look like this. This is a good example of using Null objects as tool handles.

Figure 7.40 Use displacement tools to deform your geometry.

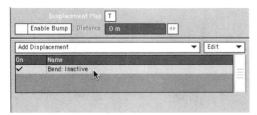

Figure 7.41 You can access a displacement tool's properties panel by double-clicking its name in the list.

Using Displacement Tools

In addition to deforming your objects with displacement maps, you can use a displacement tool, each with a effect. We'll use the bend tool as an example.

To use the bend displacement tool:

1. In Modeler, use the Disc tool to create a cylinder with following dimensions: sides 24, segments 6, bottom 0m, top 3m, centerX 0m, centerY 1.5m, centerZ 0m, radiusX 500mm, radiusY 1.5m, radiusZ 500mm.

2. Save the cylinder as Bendy-Disc.lwo and send it to Layout.

3. Select the Items tab, click Add Null from the Add tool group, and name the Null object Bend-Base.

4. Repeat Step 3 to add another Null object and name it Bend-Handle.
   Select the Modify tab to change your toolbar options.

5. Click Move from the translate tool group in the toolbar or press m and drag Bend-Handle to 3.2m on the Y axis.
   Your scene should look like **Figure 7.39**.

6. Click Bendy-Disc.lwo in the Layout Viewport.

7. Click Item Properties or press p to open the Object Properties panel.

8. Select the Deform tab and choose Deform: Bend from the Add Displacement pull-down menu (**Figure 7.40**).

9. Double-click Bend: Inactive in the displacement tool list panel (**Figure 7.41**) to open the tool's properties.

continues on next page

USING DISPLACEMENT TOOLS

10. From the Effect Base pull-down menu, choose Bend-Base (**Figure 7.42**).

11. From the Effect Handle pull-down menu, chooseBend-Handle (**Figure 7.43**).

12. Leave the Axis set to Y so the effect will occur along the Y axis of the object, and click OK or press (Enter) to accept the settings and close the panel.

13. Click Bend-Handle in the Layout Viewport.

14. Click the red tool handle and move Bend-Handle along the X axis.

As you move the mouse left and right, the Bendy-Disc bends in the direction you move the handle (**Figure 7.44**).

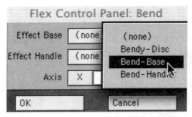

Figure 7.42 Select the point of origin for the effect.

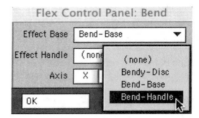

Figure 7.43 Select the handle that you'll use to control the effect.

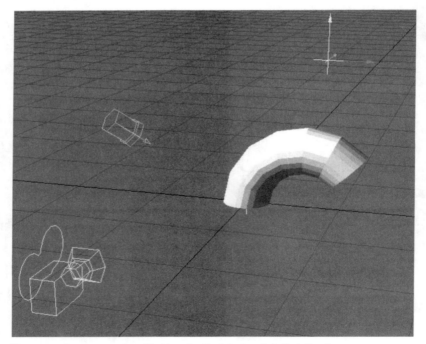

Figure 7.44 As you move the effect handle, the tube bends in that direction.

Morphing Objects

In Chapter 6, "Beginning Animation," you learned that "morphing" is when one object changes into another over time. You've probably seen this effect on television and in films. LightWave allows you to morph one object into another, but there are a couple of strict rules you need to follow for a smooth transition. The first rule is that every object involved in the morph must have the same number of points. The second is that the point order of the objects has to be the same, meaning that the points need to have been created in the same order.

The best way to set up objects for a morph sequence is to start from the original object and use that to create all of the objects it will be morphing into. It's important when doing this to remember not to add any points to the target objects or to delete a point and re-add it elsewhere in the geometry. We broke the following example up into several parts, to make it easier to follow.

To set up the geometry:

1. In Modeler, build a 1-meter square box.

2. Select the Multiply tab, and then click Subdivide or press ⌐d⌐ to open the Subdivide Polygons dialog and click OK or press ⌐Enter⌐ to accept the default settings.

3. Repeat Step 2 two more times to create some more geometry to work with.

4. Press ⌐c⌐ to copy the geometry.

5. Press ⌐2⌐ to switch to the second layer and press ⌐v⌐ to paste the geometry, so you have another copy of the box object.

6. Press ⌐1⌐ to switch back to the first layer.

7. Select the Modify tab to display new options in the toolbar and choose Spherize from the More pull-down menu in the Transform tool group to activate the Spherize effect (**Figure 7.45**).

   Your box turns into a sphere, but now it's enlarged (**Figure 7.46**).

8. From the More pull-down menu in the Transform tool group of the toolbar, choose Absolute Size to shrink your object back to its original size (**Figure 7.47**).

Figure 7.45 The Spherize tool rounds out an object.

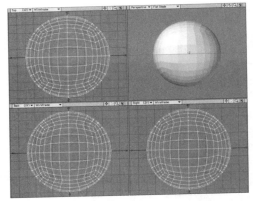

Figure 7.46 Your box is now a ball.

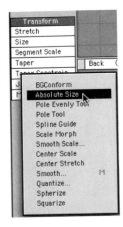

Figure 7.47 The Absolute Size tool allows you to specify a target size for your objects, unlike Modeler's normal Scale tool which works on a relative basis.

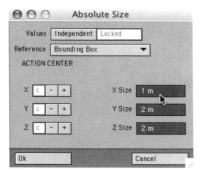

Figure 7.48 Size the ball down to a 1-meter radius.

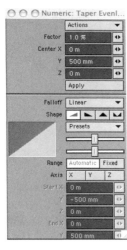

Figure 7.49 Use the numeric panels in Modeler for precise input.

9. In the Absolute Size dialog, click Locked next to Values and enter 1m in the X Size field (**Figure 7.48**).

   That value is used for all three axes.

10. Click OK or press Enter to close the dialog.

   Your sphere is now 1 meter in diameter, to match the size of your box.

11. Press 3 to switch to the third layer, and paste another copy of the box.

12. Click Taper Constrain in the Transform tool group of the toolbar to activate the Taper Evenly tool.

13. Press n to open the Numeric options dialog and apply the tool with the following settings: Factor 1.0%, Center Y 500mm (**Figure 7.49**).

14. Click Apply to taper the box, creating a pyramid shape (**Figure 7.50**).

15. Press s to save the object, name it Morph-Ball.lwo in the Save As dialog that appears, and send it to Layout.

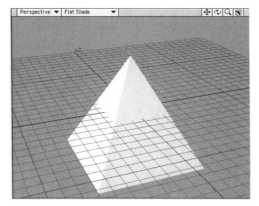

Figure 7.50 Taper the box to create a pyramid object for use in your morph sequence.

MORPHING OBJECTS

Now you need to make the morph target objects invisible so that you don't see them until the ball object morphs into them.

To make the target objects invisible:

1. From the Current Object pull-down menu below the frame slider, choose Morph-Ball:Layer2.

2. Click Item Properties or press [p] to open the Object Properties panel and select the Render tab to access the object's visibility options. (Visibility options will be covered in Chapter 13, "Rendering Your Scene.")

3. Type 100 in the Object Dissolve input field and press [Enter] to make the box invisible (**Figure 7.51**)

4. From the Current Object pull-down menu, choose Morph-Ball:Layer3 to display visibility options for the pyramid object.

5. Repeat Steps 2 and 3 for the pyramid object.

Figure 7.51 The Render tab contains an object's visibility options.

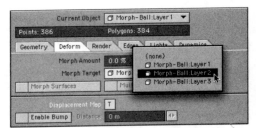

Figure 7.52 Select the object you want to morph to.

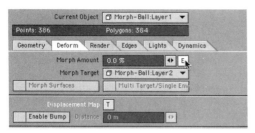

Figure 7.53 Click the E button next to an input field in Layout to open that channel in the Graph Editor.

Now you want the morph to occur over time, so you need to animate the Morph Amount value with an envelope.

To animate the Morph Amount:

1. From the Current Object pull-down menu, choose Morph-Ball:Layer1.

2. Select the Deform tab to display the morphing options.

3. From the Morph Target pull-down menu, choose Morph-Ball:Layer2 (**Figure 7.52**).

4. Click the E button next to the Morph Amount field (**Figure 7.53**) to open the Graph Editor (**Figure 7.54**).

5. Press Enter to open the Create Key dialog.

continues on next page

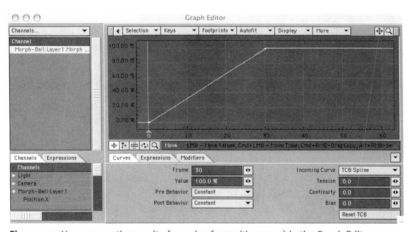

Figure 7.54 You can see the result of your keyframe (the curve) in the Graph Editor.

MORPHING OBJECTS

6. Type 30 in the Frame field to make the ball morph into the box over the course of 1 second and type 100 into the Value field (**Figure 7.55**) to make the ball completely morph into the box.

7. Click OK or press Enter to accept the input and close the Graph Editor. (For more about the Graph Editor, see Chapter 10, "Advanced Animation Tools").

8. Click the frame-slider play button. The sphere morphs into the box.

Where's the pyramid? Well, you need to add it to the morph target list. Now, you may have noticed that there's only one Morph Target pull-down menu for the sphere object. This is because each object can only have one morph target, so in order to continue the morph, you need to add a morph target for the box object. We can streamline the process a bit, however, by using the envelope for the sphere object to continue the morph, instead of creating a new morph envelope that morphs from the box to the pyramid.

You'll need to continue the morph "past" the box object. So if the sphere morphs to the box at 100 percent, what value could you use in order to morph to the pyramid? Think of it this way: To get from the sphere to the box is 100 percent, and to get from the box to the pyramid would be 100 percent. So we come up with a total of 200 percent to get to the pyramid from the sphere.

To continue the morph using the envelope:

1. In the Object Properties panel, click the Multi Target/Single Env check box to enable multiple-target morphing with a single envelope (**Figure 7.56**).

2. Click the E button next to the Morph Amount field to open the Graph Editor.

Figure 7.55 Create a keyframe for the morph effect at frame 30 and set the keyframe value to 100 so the ball morphs completely into the box.

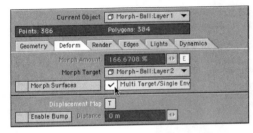

Figure 7.56 The Multi Target/Single Env option is a great timesaver when an object needs to make more than one transformation.

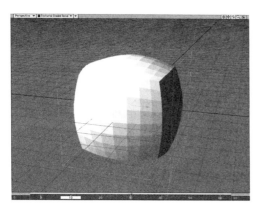

Figure 7.57 At frame 10 the sphere starts to transform into the cube.

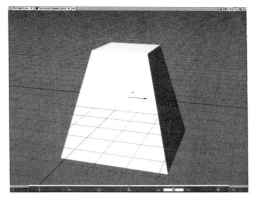

Figure 7.58 The transformation from cube to pyramid at frame 45.

3. Press [Enter] to open the Create Key dialog.

4. Type 60 in the Frame field to make the sphere morph into the pyramid after it has morphed into the box, and type 200 in the Value field to make the sphere morph completely into the pyramid at frame 60.

5. Press [Enter] to accept the values and close the Graph Editor.

6. From the Current Object pull-down menu, choose `Morph-Ball:Layer2`.

7. From the Morph Target pull-down menu, choose `Morph-Ball:Layer3`.

Steps 6 and 7 set the pyramid object as the morph target for the box object.

8. Click the frame-slider play button to preview your finished morph animation (**Figures 7.57** and **7.58**).

✔ Tips

- You can set up a separate Morph Amount envelope on the box object to continue the morph, but streamlining the process where possible saves a lot of time when setting up and troubleshooting your animations.

- If your objects have separate surface values you can enable the Morph Surfaces option to have the object's surface transform in addition to its geometry. This option will not work with Multiple Target/Single Env, though.

MORPHING OBJECTS

Using the Morph Mixer

The preferred method for morphing between geometry is the EndoMorph Mixer. It uses morph maps, which you may remember from Chapter 5, "Vertex Maps." The EndoMorph Mixer makes for more manageable morph sequences, because everything is consolidated in one interface and there's never more than one object to manage.

What we didn't mention in Chapter 5 is that when you create a morph map, the name you give it will become the name of a slider control in the Morph Mixer interface. The EndoMorph Mixer control panel is unique in that its controls and their location are defined by how you name your morph maps in Modeler as you create them.

Now, you can imagine that if you were animating a face, what with all the different possible facial expressions and eye and mouth positions, you could end up with a huge panel of morph sliders. You can prevent the EndoMorph Mixer's becoming unwieldy by using special notation to organize your slider groups into individual tabs as you name the morph maps in Modeler. The name to the left of the period determines what tab the slider belongs in while the name to the right determines the name of the slider control itself: <Tab Name.Slider Name>. For example, you might name all morph maps related to the mouth mouth.smile, mouth.frown, and so on. As you can see, the EndoMorph Mixer panel in **Figure 7.59** has controls for the mouth, eyes, brows, and so forth. There is no limit to how many tabs and sliders you can add to your morph object.

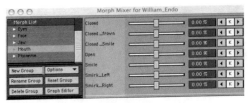

Figure 7.59 The EndoMorph Mixer is used to manipulate "endomorphs" (morph Vmaps).

Figure 7.60 Open the EndoMorph Mixer interface.

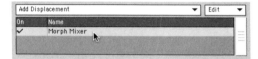

Figure 7.61 The EndoMorph Mixer is a powerful facial animation tool.

Figure 7.62 Keyframes are automatically created when you adjust a morph slider. Make sure you're on a frame where you want a key for this channel before you make any changes.

To use the EndoMorph Mixer:

1. Create an object that contains at least two morph maps and load it into Layout.

2. Click Item Properties or press $\boxed{p}$ to open the Object Properties panel, and select the Deform tab to display new options.

3. From the Add Displacement pull-down menu, choose Morph Mixer (**Figure 7.60**).

4. Double-click the Morph Mixer entry in the displacement list panel to open the mixing controls (**Figure 7.61**).

5. Go to frame 30 of the scene.

6. Drag one of your sliders to the right (**Figure 7.62**).

    The EndoMorph Mixer automatically creates a keyframe when you adjust the slider and a key icon appears on the button between the previous and next keyframe buttons at the end of the slider track. This indicates that there is a keyframe on this channel at this frame.

7. Create some more keyframes at different times for your various morph sliders.

8. Click the frame-slider play button to preview your EndoMorph Mixer animation.

✔ Tips

- If you want to manually modify a morph channel's envelope, click the Graph Editor button at the bottom of the EndoMorph Mixer panel to open the Graph Editor with all of the current object's morph channels selected.

- If you aren't sure that a morph slider has keyframes, you can use the next and previous keyframe buttons at the end of each track. Clicking one of these buttons jumps to the next (or previous) frame that contains a morph keyframe for the selected slider.

MORPHING OBJECTS

Working with Bones

Bones are unique to objects, because they're designed to flex and deform geometry. There are two ways to add bones. The first is to add an independent bone to the object. This is the default behavior for the first bone that you add to any object. An independent bone has no direct effect on any other bone in the object other than where their spheres of influence may overlap.

The second way is to add a "child bone" to an existing bone, which creates a bone that's connected to the first. (For more about parenting, see Chapter 10, "Advanced Animation Tools.") Add Child Bone, by default, adds an independent bone if there are not yet bones in the current object, as you'll see in the following exercise, which we've broken down into several parts to make it easier to follow.

To add bones to an object:

1. In Modeler, use the Disc tool to create a cylinder with the following attributes: axis Z, sides 24, segments 12, bottom 0m, top 4m, center X 0m, center Y 0m, center Z 2m, radius X 500mm, radius Y 500mm, radius Z 2m (**Figure 7.63**).

2. Press [s] to save the cylinder, name it Bone-Tube.lwo in the Save As dialog that appears, and send it to Layout.

3. From the View pull-down menu in the upper-left corner of the Viewport, choose Right (ZY) to switch views.

4. In Layout, choose Wireframe from the View Mode pull-down menu in the upper-left corner of the Viewport.

5. Press [=] to add a child bone.

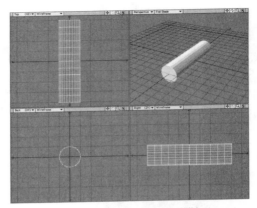

Figure 7.63 Create a cylinder that you will later deform with a pair of bones.

Figure 7.64 Click OK to accept the default name in the Bone Name dialog.

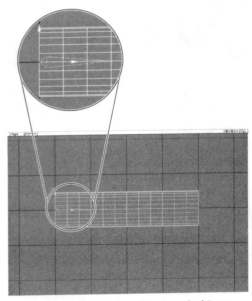

Figure 7.65 The default size of the bone (1m) is too small for this object. You want the bone to be at least half the length of the tube.

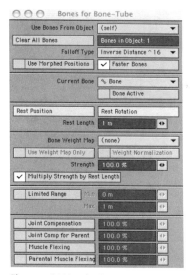

Figure 7.66 Use the Bones properties panel to adjust the bone's settings.

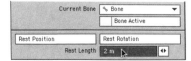

Figure 7.67 The Rest Length defines the bone's base area of influence.

6. When the Bone Name dialog appears, press Enter to accept the default name (**Figure 7.64**).

Notice that the bone is a little small for the object (**Figure 7.65**). In this example, we want the bone to affect half of Bone-Tube.lwo, which is 4 meters long, so we need to adjust the bone's length to two meters.

7. Click Item Properties or press p to open the Bones properties panel (**Figure 7.66**).

8. Type 2m in the Rest Length input field (**Figure 7.67**) to make the bone occupy half of Bone-Tube.lwo.

9. Repeat Steps 5-6 to add a child bone to the first one.

Bone (2) is already 2 meters long, fitting perfectly into the remaining half of Bone-Tube.lwo, because a child bone is automatically created with the attributes of the parent bone (**Figure 7.68**).

continues on next page

WORKING WITH BONES

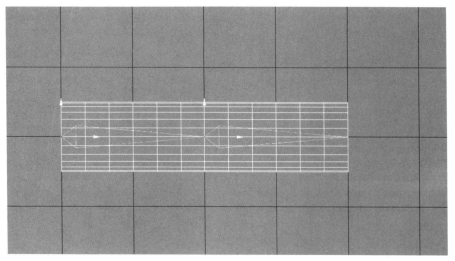

Figure 7.68 When you create a child bone, it automatically inherits the original bone's properties.

10. In the Bones properties panel, check the Bone Active check box to toggle on Bone (2) (**Figure 7.69**).

Notice that the bone outline changes from a dotted to a solid line so you know that the bone is affecting your geometry (**Figure 7.70**)

11. From the Current Bone pull-down menu, choose Bone (1).

12. Check the Bone Active check box to toggle on Bone (1).

13. Click Bone (2) in the Layout Viewport.

14. Select the Modify tab and choose Rotate from the Rotate tool group in the toolbar or press y and rotate Bone (2) to –90 degrees on the Pitch axis.

Now Bone-Tube.lwo bends with the bone (**Figure 7.71**).

✔ Tips

■ The child bone will not assume the new attributes of a parent bone that has been modified since the child bone was created.

■ Sometimes you'll want to move and rotate your bones into position before they affect the geometry. You can rotate Bone (2) -90 degrees on the Pitch axis, and you'll notice that as long as you haven't activated the bones yet, Bone-Tube doesn't bend with the bone (**Figure 7.72**).

■ When you add more than one of the same item and don't give them custom names, Layout will automatically "serialize" them. For instance, in the above exercise you added two bones to the scene without giving them unique names, so "Bone" became "Bone (1)" and the second bone became "Bone (2)."

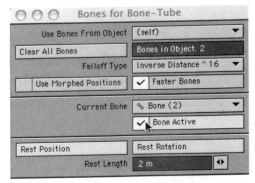

Figure 7.69 You don't want a bone to be active upon creation. This allows you to position the bone into its starting position without affecting the geometry.

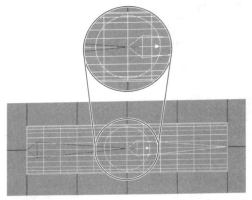

Figure 7.70 Bones that are active are drawn with solid lines, while those that are inactive are drawn with dotted lines.

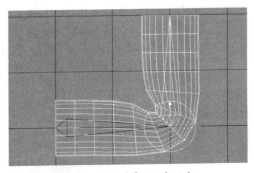

Figure 7.71 Now the bone deforms the tube.

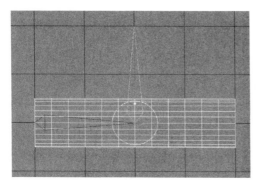

Figure 7.72 The tube didn't bend because you haven't yet activated the bone.

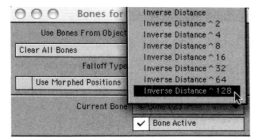

Figure 7.73 The falloff type determines how fast the bone's effect "wears off." The higher the number, the smaller the area of effect.

Adjusting bones

As you were rotating Bone (2), you probably noticed that it slightly affected the geometry around Bone (1) as it moved. This is because the bone's influence area doesn't fall off very quickly. Nothing to fret over: You can easily fix it by adjusting the bone's falloff value, which determines how fast the bone's influence over points falls off. The higher the number, the less it will affect geometry outside its immediate area.

To adjust bone falloff:

1. Follow the preceding procedure, "To add bones to an object."

2. In the Bones properties panel, choose Inverse Distance ^ 128 from the Falloff Type pull-down menu (**Figure 7.73**).

3. Click the green rotation handle on Bone (2) and rotate it up.

   This time the geometry around Bone (1) stays put.

✔ Tips

- Another way to resolve bone influence problems is with bone weight maps (covered in Chapter 5). You can set the active bone map for the current bone by selecting it from the Bone Weight Map pull-down menu in the Bones properties panel.

- You can adjust how much a bone deforms the geometry around it by changing the Strength setting in the Bones properties panel.

Now let's take a look at the geometry in the area where the two bones meet. As Bone (2) is rotated, the tube bends, but it "pinches" at the joint, much like a kinked garden hose (**Figure 7.74**). Sometimes this is the look you want, but if not you can use joint compensation to fix it.

To use joint compensation:

1. Follow the procedure in this section.

2. In the Bones properties panel, check the Joint Compensation check box at the bottom of the panel (**Figure 7.75**).

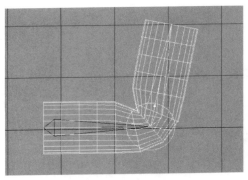

Figure 7.74 Your tube resembles a kinked garden hose.

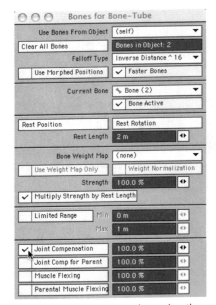

Figure 7.75 Joint Compensation makes the geometry around the joint maintain its size.

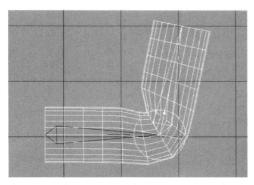

Figure 7.76 There are two sides to every joint and you've only compensated for one of them.

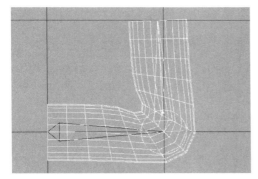

Figure 7.77 Using Joint Compensation For Parent will cause the geometry on the other side of the joint to act accordingly.

3. Select the Modify tab , then click Rotate or press $\boxed{y}$ and drag the bone around.

Notice that the geometry around the joint doesn't kink as much, but there is still a slight pinching on the Bone (1) side of the joint (**Figure 7.76**).

4. Check the Joint Comp for Parent check box.

Now the geometry around the joint pushes out to maintain its original shape (**Figure 7.77**).

✔ Tips

■ It's a good idea to check both Joint Compensation and Joint Comp for Parent when you want to fix kinking around bone joints.

■ You can adjust the amount of joint compensation by entering a percentage value in the input field or using the mini-slider arrows next to the corresponding control.

If you're working with characters, you may want to simulate a bicep flexing when an arm bends. You can achieve this quickly and easily using one of the muscle flexing options. But beware: Like Joint Compensation, the Muscle Flexing option applies to the currently selected bone. We wouldn't want to apply muscle flexing to Bone (1) however, because it wouldn't flex when we rotate Bone (2). Instead, we'll use the Parental Muscle Flexing option.

To use muscle flexing:

1. Follow the first procedure in this section.

2. Click Bone (2) in the Layout Viewport.

3. In the Bones properties panel, check the Muscle Flexing check box (**Figure 7.78**). Notice that the wrong part of the arm is flexing (**Figure 7.79**).

4. Uncheck Muscle Flexing box for Bone (2) and check Parental Muscle Flexing instead.

   Now the proper portion of the tube is flexing (**Figure 7.80**).

✔ Tip

■ You can use the numeric fields or mini-slider arrows next to each check box to adjust the muscle flexing percentage and modify how much the geometry bulges.

Figure 7.78 Muscle Flexing pushes the geometry around a bone out as it rotates, to create a flexing effect.

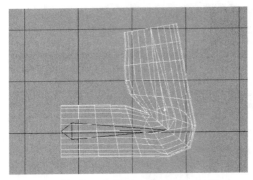

Figure 7.79 The Muscle Flexing option places the effect over the current bone. You want it to be over the previous bone to create a bicep.

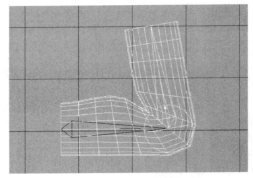

Figure 7.80 The geometry is now bulging in the appropriate place.

WORKING WITH BONES

Hood Armature by Christian Bloch (www.blochi.com)

A whole new kind of anti-hero by Emmy Award Nominee
Eddie Robison (www.pax-ill.com)

Mini Cooper by Fred Pienkos (www.edenfx.com)

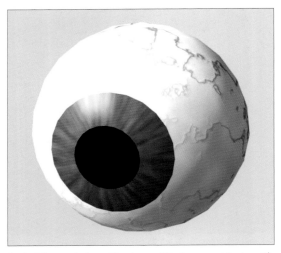

Eyeball (example from Chapter 12, "Surfaces and Textures")
by Brian E. Marshall (www.h2mw.com)

ELO by Christian Bloch (www.blochi.com)

©2003 kenneth woodruff

Palace 1 by Kenneth Woodruff (www.kennethwoodruff.com)

ELO Blue by Christian Bloch (www.blochi.com)

Stomping Mushrooms by John Savage and Matt Rasmussen (www.gigapixstudios.com)

Temple of E-sha by Christian Bloch (www.blochi.com). Concept art by Chris Thunig.

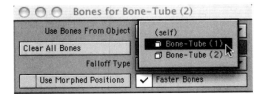

Figure 7.81 Use Bones From Object allows you to set up and animate a bone chain once and then apply its effect to multiple items.

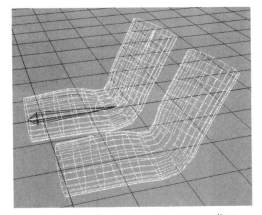

Figure 7.82 Both of the objects react as you adjust the bone in the original.

Using bones from other objects

Say you wanted to have multiple Bone-Tube objects flexing away in tandem in your scene. Instead of having to set up a complete bone chain with the desired options for each object, you can set them up once, and then have another object use them.

To use bones from another object:

1. Following the first procedure in this section, press + to load another copy of Bone-Tube.lwo.

   Layout will name it Bone-Tube (2) and rename the original we've been working with Bone-Tube (1).

2. From the View pull-down menu, change the Layout Viewport to Perspective view.

3. Click Bone-Tube (2) in the Layout Viewport.

4. Select the Modify tab to display new toolbar options, click Move from the translate tool group in the toolbar or press ⒨, and drag Bone-Tube (2) to 2m on the X axis.

5. Click the Bones button below the Current Item pull-down menu or press ⒮ʰⁱᶠᵗ+ⓑ to activate the bones edit mode.

6. Click Item Properties or press ⓟ to open the Bones properties panel, and choose Bone-Tube (1) from the Use Bones From Object pull-down menu (**Figure 7. 81**).

7. Click Rotate in the toolbar or press ⓨ, and rotate Bone (2) in Bone-Tube (1). Notice that both objects bend and flex (**Figure 7.82**).

Adding Skelegons

An important thing to understand is that bones are not saved with your object, they're part of your Layout scene. After you have an object set up with bones, saving the object and then loading it into another scene will not bring the skeleton with it.

One way around this is to use Layout's Load from Scene option in the File pull-down menu, which loads all of the components from the selected scene into the current scene.

The other method is to use Skelegons (covered in Chapter 3).

When loading objects that contain Skelegons, you can convert them to bones for use in your scene. Once converted, they'll have all of the same properties and options as bones created directly in Layout. The main benefit is that the Skelegon is embedded in the object itself and therefore transportable to any scene that you load it into.

To activate an object's Skelegons:

1. Load an object that contains Skelegons into Layout.

2. Select the Items tab and choose Bones > Convert Skelegons Into Bones from the Add pull-down menu in the toolbar (**Figure 7.83**).

   Your object now has bones (**Figure 7.84**).

✔ Tip

- It is important to understand that any changes made to the bones created from Skelegons are saved with the scene and not the object file, meaning that if you want to change the Skelegons themselves, you will need to reload the object into Modeler and manipulate them there.

Figure 7.83 Simply convert the Skelegons in your objects to create bones in their place.

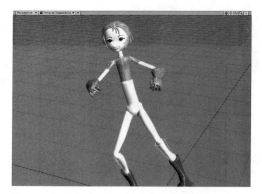

Figure 7.84 This character's skeleton was created with Skelegons in Modeler and then converted to bones in Layout. This is the most efficient way to transport a skeleton with an object from scene to scene.

ADDING SKELEGONS

LIGHTING

Figure 8.1 With a single light, this shot is flat.

Figure 8.2 Now that we've added a few more lights, it's more realistic.

Creating a beautifully rendered shot in LightWave often depends on properly lighting the scene. Hyper-accurate modeling or near-lifelike animation won't matter much if the final rendered image is flat and unrealistic. This kind of eyesore can totally ruin a well-designed shot.

For example, it looks strange when we use flat lighting on the interior of a medieval castle (**Figure 8.1**). But light the room with some candles and the shot looks more realistic and interesting (**Figure 8.2**).

A light not only illuminates space, it also adds shadows and more importantly, depth. While hard lights produce sharp, crisp shadows, soft lights produce much warmer, smoother shadows. Using a combination of these lights with the right placement and color can properly set the mood of the image, call attention to or away from something, show distance, and even illustrate the passing of time.

In this chapter, we'll discuss the different types of lights you can use and their effect on your scene. We'll also introduce special lighting effects and advanced lighting features such as Radiosity and Caustics. You can use any or all of these methods to achieve the exact effect you're looking for in your image.

Lights and Lighting Effects

Experienced users consistently refer to LightWave as a "virtual set." This is never truer than when we're discussing the complexities of lighting a scene. The designers of LightWave have tried to make each different light look and act just as it would in the real world. This attention to detail makes the lights very easy to use and understand.

LightWave has five different types of lights to choose from:

◆ **Distant:** A global light that emits at an angle, but affects all the objects in a scene, regardless of position. This light source acts much like sunlight.

◆ **Point:** Emits light in all directions (omnidirectional) from the designated point, much like an ordinary light bulb.

◆ **Spotlight:** A highly directional conical light source that can produce nice, smooth shadows at the edges. This works much like the stage light (of the same name) or a flashlight.

◆ **Linear:** A sizable line that emits light from everywhere but the ends, producing soft shadows, much like a fluorescent light.

◆ **Area:** A sizable card that emits light from both the front and back, but not from the edges. This works like a large, diffused fluorescent ceiling light.

By using a combination of these lights, you'll be able to re-create anything from a natural outdoor setting to an artificially lit room.

Special Effect Lights

LightWave also offers several high-end lighting special effects that add an extra level of realism to your scenes.

◆ Spotlights act as a movie projector when you use an image or movie as their light source.

◆ Lens Flares and Volumetrics allow a light's rays to be seen by the camera, simulating an extremely bright light or a dusty environment.

◆ Radiosity calculates the natural effect of light scattering and bouncing off surfaces.

◆ Caustics project focused light from reflective or transparent surfaces, producing incredibly realistic glass, water, or metallic shimmering effects.

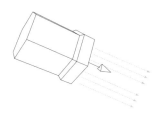

Figure 8.3 This is how a Distant light casts rays in Layout.

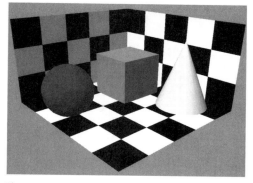

Figure 8.4 Here is an example of a simple lighting scene.

Adding Lights

Layout will automatically add a single light (a Distant light, by default) and a LightWave camera into any new scene you create. With this type of light, all the objects in the scene are lit with the same intensity, regardless of how close they are to the source (**Figure 8.3**). So it doesn't really matter where you place the light in the scene. However, by rotating it you'll change the angle of the rays cast and thus the shading and placement of shadows on the surfaces.

To add a Distant light:

1. Open or create a scene similar to **Figure 8.4** with a few basic shapes (primitives) and a floor or wall to cast shadows onto.

2. Select the Items tab to display new options in the toolbar (**Figure 8.5**).

3. Choose Distant Light from the Lights pull-down menu.(**Figure 8.6**).

continues on next page

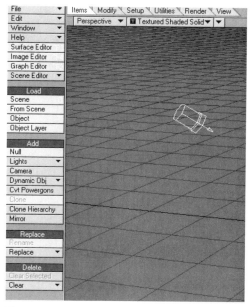

Figure 8.5 The Items tab gives you access to new toolbar options, including the Lights pull-down menu.

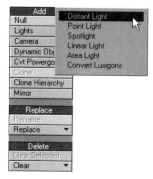

Figure 8.6 Create a Distant light by selecting Distant Light from the Lights menu.

ADDING LIGHTS

4. When the Light Name dialog appears, click OK to accept the default name (**Figure 8.7**).

5. Click the Modify tab to display new options in the toolbar.

6. Click Move in the toolbar or press ⌈t⌋ to activate the Move tool and drag the light to the upper-left quadrant of the screen.

Notice that the lighting effect on the objects in the scene doesn't change (**Figure 8.8**).

7. Click Rotate in the toolbar or press ⌈y⌋ to activate the Rotate tool and drag to adjust the light's casting angle.

Notice its effect on the surfaces in the scene (**Figure 8.9**).

8. Render the current frame ⌈F9⌋.

✔ Tip

■ You don't always need a Distant light in a scene, so naturally you can change the default Distant light to whatever light type you need. Distant was chosen as the default light type because it quickly and easily lights everything in the scene.

Figure 8.7 You can either accept the name Layout automatically generates or enter one of your own.

Figure 8.8 Move the Distant light from the origin to the upper-left-hand quadrant.

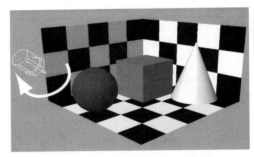

Figure 8.9 Rotate the light, and notice the affect on the object's shading.

ADDING LIGHTS

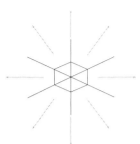

Figure 8.10 This is how a Point light casts rays in Layout.

Figure 8.11 If you move the Point Light to the upper quadrant, the shading will change.

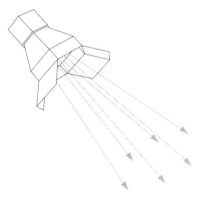

Figure 8.12 This is how Layout displays a Spotlight (we've illustrated the rays).

A Point light radiates light from all directions (**Figure 8.10**). However, because it's an omnidirectional light, rotating it will have no direct effect on either an object's shading or shadows.

To add a Point light:

1. Follow Steps 1 and 2 from the first procedure in this chapter, "To add a Distant light."

2. Select Point Light from the Lights pulldown menu.

3. When the Light Name dialog appears, click OK to accept the default name.

4. Select the Modify tab to display new options in the toolbar.

5. Click Move in the toolbar or press [t] and drag the light to the upper-left-hand portion of the screen.

   Notice how the movement affects the surface's shading (**Figure 8.11**).

6. Render the current frame [F9].

Where a Spotlight casts its light is determined by both its position and its direction. It emits rays in a conical pattern defined by the light's Cone Angle and the Soft Edge Angle (**Figure 8.12**).

To add a Spotlight:

1. Follow Steps 1 and 2 of the first procedure in this chapter.

2. Select Spotlight from the Lights pull-down menu.

3. When the Light Name dialog appears, click OK to accept the default name.

4. Select the Modify tab to display new options in the toolbar.

5. Click Move in the toolbar or press [t] and drag the light to the upper-left quadrant of the screen.

6. Click Rotate in the toolbar or press [y] and drag to adjust the light until it lights up some of the scene's objects (**Figure 8.13**).

7. Click the Properties button at the bottom of the screen or press [p] to open the Light Properties panel (**Figure 8.14**).

8. In the Spotlight Cone Angle and Spotlight Soft Edge Angle fields, use the numeric inputs or mini-sliders to narrow the light's cone angle to best fit the area.

9. Render the current frame [F9].
   Your scene should look like **Figure 8.15**.

Figure 8.13 Rotate the Spotlight to light up some of the objects.

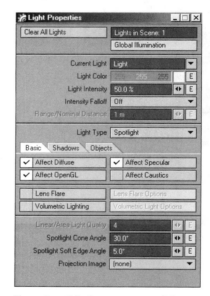

Figure 8.14 Edit the parameters of the scene's lights in this panel.

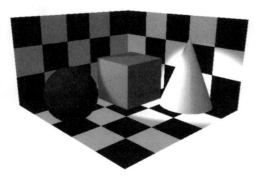

Figure 8.15 This is a rendering of the scene using a Spotlight.

Figure 8.16 This is how a Linear light casts rays in Layout.

Figure 8.17 This is a rendering of the scene using a Linear light.

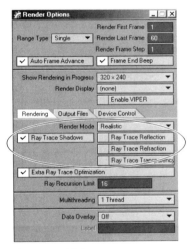

Figure 8.18 Click to turn on ray tracing in the Rendering menu.

Figure 8.19 This is a *better* rendering of the scene using a Linear light.

Linear Lights are represented in LightWave as a stretchable straight line. This works very much like a fluorescent bulb, emitting rays in all directions except the very ends (**Figure 8.16**). The shadows produced from ray-traced Linear lights are soft and gentle.

To add a Linear light:

1. Follow Steps 1 and 2 of the first procedure in this chapter.

2. Select Linear Light from the Lights pull-down menu.

3. When the Light Name dialog appears, click OK to accept the default name.

4. Select the Modify tab to display new options in the toolbar.

5. Click Move in the toolbar or press [t] and drag the light to the upper-left quadrant of the screen.

6. Render the frame [F9].
   Your scene should look like **Figure 8.17**, but you must enable ray tracing to make this light really show off what it can do.

7. Select the Render tab to display new options in the toolbar.

8. Click Render Options to display the Render Options window.

9. Toggle on Ray Trace Shadows (**Figure 8.18**). (For more about this option, see Chapter 13, "Rendering Your Scene.")

10. Re-render the frame [F9].
    Notice the soft shadows (**Figure 8.19**).

Area Lights act much like Linear Lights, producing soft shadows like a fluorescent bulb. However, instead of a line, they emit light from both sides of a resizable card (**Figure 8.20**).

To add an Area light:

1. Follow Steps 1 and 2 of the first procedure in this chapter.

2. Select Area Light from the Lights pull-down menu.

3. When the Light Name dialog appears, click OK to accept the default name.

4. Select the Modify tab to display new options in the toolbar.

5. Click Stretch in the toolbar or press (h) to activate the Stretch tool and drag the mouse to increase the length of the light.

6. Select the Render tab to display new options in the toolbar.

7. Click Render Options to display the Render Options window.

8. Toggle on Ray Trace Shadows.

9. Render the frame (F9) and it should look like **Figure 8.21**.

✔ Tips

■ Linear and Area lights require more time to render, but you can decrease it by adjusting the Linear/Area Light Quality parameter on the Light Properties panel (**Figure 8.22**). This setting ranges from 1 to 5, affecting the quality of shadows produced. A value of 1 produces the most artifacts in shadows, but is very fast. A value of 5 will look the best, but may take a long time to render.

■ A smaller-size light will also produce fewer artifacts.

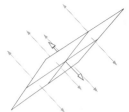

Figure 8.20 This is an Area light with its illustrated rays.

Figure 8.21 This is a rendering of the scene using an Area Light.

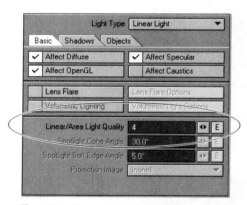

Figure 8.22 Decrease render times by adjusting Linear/Area Light Quality.

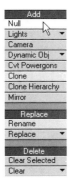

Figure 8.23 Select Null from the Items toolbar to create a Null object.

Figure 8.24 This is the Target_Null object's Motion Options panel.

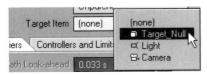

Figure 8.25 Select the Target_Null object as the Target Item, and the light will always be pointing towards the Null.

Aiming a light can be very difficult, especially if it needs to track a moving object. One useful feature that LightWave provides is the ability to have a light target an item. With this motion effect enabled, the light will always point itself to face whatever object you have set as its target.

To set a target object:

1. Follow Steps 1 and 2 of the first procedure in this chapter.

2. Select Null (**Figure 8.23**) from the toolbar.

3. When the Null Object Name dialog appears, name it Target_Null and click OK.

4. Click a directional light source in the scene, preferably a Spotlight.

5. Click Motion Options in the toolbar or press m to open the Motion Options panel (**Figure 8.24**).

6. From the Target Item pull-down menu, select the Target_Null object (**Figure 8.25**).

7. Select the Modify tab to display new options in the toolbar.

8. Click Move in the toolbar or press t and drag the light around in the Viewport. Notice how the light always points at the Target_Null object.

✔ Tip

■ Any LightWave item can target another item, not just lights and cameras. For geometry, LightWave will will use the object's positive Z axis to do the pointing.

Adjusting Light Parameters

Each of LightWave's lights has several properties you can adjust to fine-tune their effect on surfaces in a scene. Some of these values can be animated using Envelopes (see Chapter 10, "Advanced Animation Tools"), while others are simply static values.

The first, and probably the easiest attribute to change, is Color. Because not all lights are white (in fact very few real lights are), we can alter the individual color channels (red, green, or blue) of the rays coming from each light.

To set a light's color:

1. Create or open a scene with one or more simple shapes.

2. Click the Lights button at the bottom of the screen (**Figure 8.26**) or press [l] to switch Layout to Light selection mode.

3. Click any light in the scene to select it.

4. Click Properties or press [p] to open the Light Properties panel.

5. Click the Light Color swatch (**Figure 8.27**).

   Your system's installed color picker will appear.

6. Select a color for the light and click OK (**Figure 8.28**).

7. Render the frame [F9].

✔ Tip

- There's an alternate way to adjust a light's color. Click and drag the numbers in the Light Color field and you can manually scroll through the light's individual red, green, and blue channels. Right-clicking in this field lets you edit the channels using Hue, Saturation, and Value (HSV) settings.

Figure 8.26 Click the Lights button to switch Layout to Light selection mode.

Figure 8.27 You can change the light's color by clicking the color swatch on the Light panel.

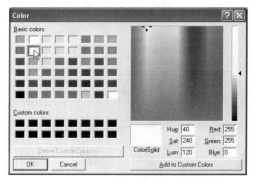

Figure 8.28 Using your system's color picker, select the color for the Light.

Figure 8.29 Select the light you want to edit from the Current Light pull-down menu.

Next you should decide how bright you want the light to be. This is controlled using the Light Intensity parameter, one of LightWave's more flexible settings. You can have both overdriven values (greater than 100 percent) and negative values that will absorb light from an area.

To set a light's Intensity:

1. Follow Steps 1 and 2 in the previous procedure.

2. Click Properties or press p to open the Light Properties panel.

3. From the Current Light pull-down menu, select the name of the light you want to edit (**Figure 8.29**).

4. In the Light Intensity field, use the numeric input or mini-slider to adjust the value.

   Observe your actions in the Viewport.

5. Render the frame F9.

ADJUSTING LIGHT PARAMETERS

LightWave gives you two options for customizing how lights influence a highlight created on a specular surface: Affect Diffuse and Affect Specular. When you create lights, both of these options are automatically enabled.

If you turn off the Affect Diffuse option, the selected light will no longer affect the color or brightness of the surfaces in the scene. It will only influence specular highlights. If you turn off the Affect Specular option, the light won't affect the specularity of any surfaces.

To turn off Affect Diffuse and Affect Specular:

1. Create or open a scene with a simple object (**Figure 8.30**).

2. Click the Lights button or press ⎯I⎯ to switch Layout to Light selection mode.

3. Click any light in the scene to select it.

4. Click Properties or press ⎯p⎯ to open the Light Properties panel.

5. Uncheck the Affect Diffuse check box or the Affect Specular check box (**Figure 8.31**).

6. Render the frame ⎯F9⎯.
Your scene should look like **Figure 8.32** or **Figure 8.33**.

✔ Tip

■ The Affect Caustics option works just like Affect Specular: You can enable or disable this light's effect.

Figure 8.30 This red sphere is highly specular. Notice the highlight.

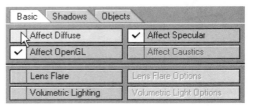

Figure 8.31 You can turn off the light's effect on the diffuse channel.

Figure 8.32 With Affect Diffuse off, the light only generates a specular highlight.

Figure 8.33 With Affect Specular off, even though the surface is very specular, the light isn't producing any highlights.

Figure 8.34 This toggle button lets you quickly turn on and off a light in the viewport.

Due to an Open Graphic Library (OGL) limitation, LightWave will allow a maximum of only eight lights to light or shade geometry in the Viewport. Naturally, there will be times when your scene has more than eight lights. Some may be less significant than others, so you can dismiss them from affecting the Viewport, allowing other, more important, lights to be used.

To turn off a light in the Viewport:

1. Follow Steps 1 through 4 in the previous procedure.

2. Toggle off Light Affects OpenGL (**Figure 8.34**).

   Notice that the Viewport gets dark.

✔ Tip

■ To avoid straining your computer's graphics card, Layout will use only one light (by default) to generate the OGL Viewport. Unless you have an antiquated machine, you can adjust this maximum number to 8 in the Display Options panel (press ☐ to open it). This setting only needs to be changed once.

Creating Shadows

Lights illuminate surfaces and create shadows. That's their job. The shadows created by LightWave's renderer can be hard, soft, colored, or monochromatic—it's your choice, really. Controlling the type of shadow created is simply a matter of setting some key attributes.

By default, the lights you've already created by selecting a light type from the Lights pull-down menu produced shading, not real shadows. With shading, rays of light will pass through any object they intersect, lighting the objects behind it as well. Though extremely quick to calculate, shading is not very realistic.

True shadows are created when a ray from a light source stops and can no longer illuminate any more surfaces. In LightWave, there are only two ways to stop a ray of light and create a shadow. The first, and fastest, way is to set the light's Intensity Falloff setting. This setting instructs the renderer to let rays travel only a certain distance from the light, and then stop. As this ray approaches its falloff distance, its intensity diminishes until it finally reaches zero.

To set a light's Intensity Falloff:

1. Follow Steps 1-3 in the "To add a Point light" procedure earlier in this chapter.

2. Click Properties or press [p] to open the Light Properties panel.

3. From the Intensity Falloff pull-down menu, select one of the following settings (**Figure 8.35**):

    ◆ Linear diminishes the light at a constant rate.

    ◆ Inverse Distance and Inverse Distance ^ 2 refer to the effect produced by the inverse square law (which governs real-world lighting falloff). These are the most realistic.

Figure 8.35 The Intensity Falloff settings let you mimic how light naturally diminishes over distance.

CREATING SHADOWS

Figure 8.36 The Range/Nominal Distance setting lets you enter a maximum distance the light will travel.

Figure 8.37 Set the Ambient Light Intensity to 0 percent.

Figure 8.38 This rendering shows a Point light with an Intensity Falloff set to Inverse Distance.

4. In the Range/Nominal Distance field, use the numeric input or mini-slider to set the falloff to determine how far the ray of light will travel (**Figure 8.36**).

A value of 2.5 works well here.

5. Click the Global Illumination button to display the Global Illumination window.

6. In the Ambient Light Intensity field, type 0% and click OK (**Figure 8.37**).

Only the light cast by the Point light will be seen.

8. Render the frame (F9) and your scene should look like **Figure 8.38**.

Notice that very little light is hitting any object farther away than the sphere.

✔ Tips

- Layout will illustrate the falloff as a circular dashed line around the light in any of the orthographic views. This represents the point where the light's rays are at 0 percent.

Ray-traced shadows

The second way to stop a ray of light is to ray trace the scene. In this method, when a ray of light intersects with a surface, it stops, essentially blocked by the surface. No light is cast on the surfaces behind it, producing a shadow. This is how real shadows work.

Due to the large number of calculations, ray tracing a scene can take a long time to render. Although the results are far better, ray tracing can come at an extremely heavy price when you start adding more and more lights. That's because when you enable ray tracing, you essentially turn on this feature for every light in the scene. Now every light will be producing shadows!

To create ray-traced shadows:

1. Create or open a scene with a simple object.

2. Select the Render tab to display new options in the toolbar.

3. Toggle on Ray Trace Shadows.

3. Render the frame $\boxed{\text{F9}}$ and your scene should look like **Figure 8.39**.

   Notice the shadows cast by and on the objects.

✔ Tip

■ There's actually a third way to create a shadow—a kind of hack. Negative lights absorb light from surfaces rather than illuminating them. Simply enter a negative value in the Light Intensity setting.

Figure 8.39 This rendering shows what ray tracing can do. Notice the shadows on the other objects and the background.

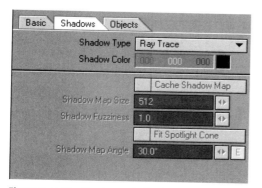

Figure 8.40 The Shadows tab displays the different shadow options for each light.

Figure 8.41 Select Shadow Map in the Shadow Type pull-down menu.

Figure 8.42 Adjust the quality of the shadow using the Shadow Map Size setting.

✔ Tips

- The smaller the size of the rendered shadow (not the shadow map), the better the quality of the shadows produced. If the shadow covers half the screen, it will look worse than if it just used a quarter.

- If there's no animation on the light, check the Cache Shadow Map check box on the Shadows panel and LightWave won't recompute the map for every frame.

Shadow maps

Spotlights can use the ray-tracing method to calculate shadows without having to ray trace the entire scene. This lets you save valuable rendering time by only ray tracing some of the lights and shading the rest. This is known as a generating a *shadow map*.

One advantage to the shadow map is that you can define exactly how much detail each shadow has by determining the resolution of the shadow map. This directly affects the quality of the visible shadow. And as long as the light isn't moving, rendering the shadows for the shadow map only has to be done once. This can save you a lot of time when you're rendering an entire scene.

Although they're a faster alternative to ray tracing, the trade-offs are that shadow maps are less accurate, take more memory, and are only available when using Spotlights.

To enable shadow maps:

1. Follow Steps 1-7 in the "To add a Spotlight" procedure earlier in this chapter.

2. Select the Shadows tab in the Light Properties panel to display new options (**Figure 8.40**).

3. From the Shadow Type pull-down menu, select Shadow Map (**Figure 8.41**) to display more options in the panel below.

4. In the Shadow Map Size field, use the numeric input or mini-slider to enter a value for the square resolution of the shadow map (**Figure 8.42**).

   The greater the size, the higher the resolution, and the better the shadow will be, so for this example we recommend 1024.

5. Render the frame F9 .

CREATING SHADOWS

By default, the color of a rendered shadow is a darker shade of the light affecting the object's surface color. You can change this so the ray-traced shadows are rendered in a totally different hue than the light casting the rays. Use this to create interesting environmental effects, such as moonlight shadows that are more blue than black.

To change the shadow's color:

1. Follow Steps 1 and 2 in the previous procedure.

2. Click the Shadow Color swatch and choose a new color (**Figure 8.43**).

3. Select the Render tab to display new options in the toolbar.

4. Toggle on Ray Trace Shadows.

5. Render the frame (F9).

In some very specific cases, you won't want an object to be affected by a light's rays at all. You can easily add any object in the scene to a list of objects that a light will ignore when rendering.

To exclude objects:

1. Follow any of the earlier procedures for adding lights and click the light you want to ignore objects when rendering.

2. Click Properties or press (p) to open the Light Properties panel.

3. Select the Objects tab in the middle of the panel to display new options.

4. Check the objects to be excluded from this light (**Figure 8.44**).

5. Render the frame (F9).
   The objects that you excluded are no longer lit by the light.

✔ Tip

■ Conversely, to remove a single object from multiple lights, use the light exclusion list in the Object Properties panel (see Chapter 13).

Figure 8.43 Change the color of the shadows created by this light with the Shadow Color setting.

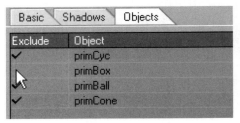

Figure 8.44 Exclude objects from this light's rays by checking off their names in the list.

Figure 8.45 This is a simple lens flare.

Figure 8.46 With Reflections turned on, you can simulate light being bounced around within a lens.

Lighting Special Effects

Lighting effects, when used correctly, can add another level of realism to your shot. However, when overused or used incorrectly, they can have the opposite effect: They can actually annoy the viewer.

Lens flares are one of the oldest lighting effects in computer graphics. Their popularity has grown over the years with their clever use in simulating rocket engines, stars, explosions, and light bulbs. They basically allow you to view the actual simulated light as a glowing object in space (**Figure 8.45**).

Consequently, a lens flare can also produce the artifacts you sometimes find when an extremely bright light bounces around in a camera lens (**Figure 8.46**). Granted, this effect is usually avoided by professional cameramen, but when used correctly, it can be extremely realistic, because it's what the viewer is expecting to see.

To make a Lens Flare:

1. Follow the steps to create a Distant, Point, or Spotlight light described earlier in this chapter.

2. Click Properties or press ⓟ to open the Light Properties panel.

3. Check the Lens Flare check box and click the Lens Flare Options button (**Figure 8.47**).

4. When the Lens Flare Options for Light panel appears, set the flare's strength, glow parameters, star filters, and ring effects (**Figure 8.48**). (Consult the software manual for detailed descriptions of these options.)

✔ Tip

■ LightWave's camera Viewport can approximate how a lens flare will be rendered. Turn on this option in the Display Options panel. The flare's quality and how well it displays in the Viewport depends on the power of your system's video card.

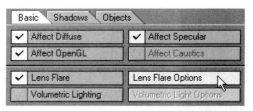

Figure 8.47 Turn on the light's lens flare using this check box and button to open the Options panel.

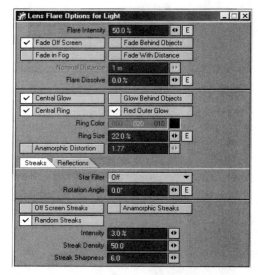

Figure 8.48 Adjust the light's lens flare setting using this Options panel.

LIGHTING SPECIAL EFFECTS

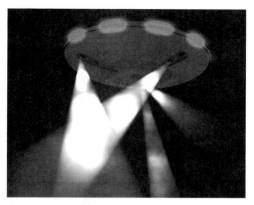

Figure 8.49 Volumetrics simulate visible light rays.

Figure 8.50 Turn on the light's volumetric effect using this check box and button to open the Options panel.

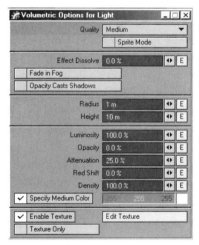

Figure 8.51 Adjust the light's volumetric effect in this Options panel.

When real light shines through dusty or murky space, its rays can make the particles in the air glow. This makes the light seem to be a solid shaft, or volume, of light, known as a *volumetric effect* (**Figure 8.49**).

Distant, Point, and Spotlight lights can all have visible rays of volumetric light.

To make volumetric lights:

1. Follow Steps 1 and 2 of the previous procedure.

2. Check the Volumetric Lighting check box and click the Volumetric Light Options button (**Figure 8.50**).

3. When the Volumetric Options for Light panel appears, modify the various settings, options, and values that define the volumetric effect (**Figure 8.51**). (Consult the software manual for detailed descriptions of these options.)

✔ Tips

- Layout will estimate the size of the light volume and display it in the Viewport as white lines (like a Spotlight). This happens automatically for any lights that have volumetric lighting enabled.

- Volumetrics can take a while to render. Be sure to read the sections in the manual on how to use LightWave's Viper and Presets to speed this process up.

- The various effects you can create with these settings could fill an entire book. Be sure to read the definitions and parameters in the manual supplied by NewTek and check out some online user tutorials (www.lightwave3d.com).

LIGHTING SPECIAL EFFECTS

227

Using Global Illumination

The Global Illumination panel does many things with lighting (**Figure 8.52**). You can adjust the intensity of all the lights and lens flares in the scene. This global adjustment can be handy when you have dozens of lights you want to change at once.

This panel lets you turn on lens flares, volumetrics, and shadow maps for all the lights in a scene. During the animation process, you may not want to wait for these effects to render every time. These options allow you to quickly turn on and off render-intensive effects, globally, until it's time to do the final render.

Area, Linear, and Radiosity lights can often create noisy shadows when they're rendered. Minimize these unwanted byproducts by checking the Shading Noise Reduction check box. If this process alters your image too much, or creates additional artifacts (which is possible), try using Enhanced Anti-Aliasing.

This panel also lets you control the amount and color of the ambient light that gets added to every object on every frame. It has no angle or position, it just exists.

Radiosity

In nature, when light rays encounter a bright surface, they will often absorb the properties of the surface, bounce off, and continue to light the scene for a short distance. This is known as the Radiosity effect.

The object in **Figure 8.53** is very bright red. The little speckles you see on the background and surrounding objects are actually red light rays that have bounced off and are being cast onto these other surfaces. In effect, this red surface has become a very dim light source itself, producing what's known as *radiant light*.

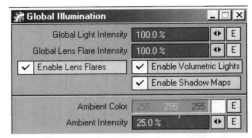

Figure 8.52 The top portion of the Global Illumination panel lets you adjust several lights at once.

Figure 8.53 Radiosity bounces light from one surface to another. The speckles in this image are red rays bounced off the red box.

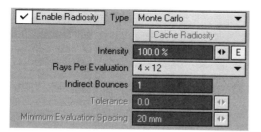

Figure 8.54 These settings control the Radiosity effect.

LightWave lets you simulate this effect by checking Enable Radiosity on the Global Illumination panel (**Figure 8.54**). Naturally, because it has to calculate each ray from each light (and luminous surface) bouncing all over the place, this effect can take a very long time to render. Its quality and render speed can be controlled mostly by changing the Rays per Evaluation and Indirect Bounces values. The higher you set these values, the better quality the render will be, and the longer it will take.

✔ Tip

- Because of the incredibly long render times associated with Radiosity, users have been developing hacks and tricks to fake this effect for years. Doing a little online research may result in a method that is not only faster, but will also produce acceptable renders.

Caustics

Curved reflective or transparent surfaces such as metal, glass, and water tend to bend and refocus light rays into bright single spots (**Figure 8.55**). LightWave can calculate this effect if you check the Enable Caustics box on the Global Illumination panel (**Figure 8.56**). Just like with Radiosity, this effect computes the rays bouncing off surfaces, so using this effect can drastically increase a scene's render time.

These are the parameters of the Caustics effect:

◆ **Intensity** controls the strength of the caustics effect. If the caustics aren't bright enough, turn up this setting.

◆ **Accuracy** determines how much time the renderer will spend calculating this effect. Lowering this setting can not only reduce render times, but it will also reduce the quality of the effect.

◆ **Softness** controls how sharp or soft the rendered effect is. For smooth caustics, use a high setting. For a sharp effect, use a low value.

✔ Tip

■ Because of it's rendering complexity, it is very difficult to animate using Caustics. The rendered result is often hard to control or predict. Typically, it's used for still work, and extremely limited effects work.

Figure 8.55 Caustics refocus light rays from shiny objects and redirect them. Notice the shimmering light underneath the sphere.

Figure 8.56 These settings control the Caustics lighting effect.

CAMERAS

LightWave cameras are used to record the elements and actions in your scene, whether it's a simple preview or a complex animation. They're designed not only to match their real-world counterparts, but to mimic real-world effects as well. Cameras are the final element in our virtual set analogy.

There are several books out there that teach cinematography, including how to use camera angles, zooms, and focusing tricks effectively. These traditional methods, like dolly, track, pan, zoom, and focus, are all easy to mimic in Layout, and they can dramatically increase the quality of your animations.

In this chapter, we'll show you how to set up the virtual camera's resolution and digital lens. We'll also cover several in-camera special effects, such as Motion Blur and Depth of Field, which can make your shot look more realistic.

Camera Management

In LightWave, a camera is represented in the Viewport as a wireframe outline of a typical film camera (**Figure 9.1**). It can be moved, rotated, and animated just like any of the other items found in LightWave.

When selected, the camera's viewing angle is displayed in the Viewport as a four-sided pyramid emanating from its lens (**Figure 9.2**). This helps the animator visualize, from any of the views, where the camera is pointing and what it's seeing.

When you create a new scene, LightWave automatically adds both a camera and a light to the scene. Although this camera is set up as a default camera, with default settings, it's perfectly fine to use in your scene. Simply adjust its settings to fit your needs.

You can have as many cameras in your scene as you need, and adding another camera is as easy as adding any other item in Layout. Using multiple cameras can give you greater flexibility in creating your scene. For example, you can render the different angles of an animated scene, or switch back and forth between cameras with extremely different parameters. This can save you a lot of time when you want to test possible camera angles and positions. However, one thing you should keep in mind is that you can only generate images or previews from one camera at a time.

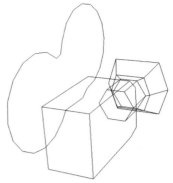

Figure 9.1 This is the wireframe representation of the camera in Layout.

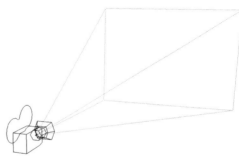

Figure 9.2 Layout illustrates the camera's viewing angle to help you create your shots.

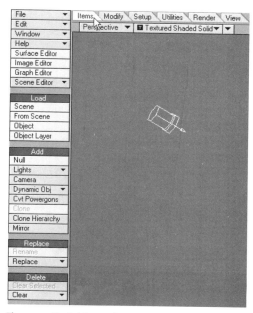

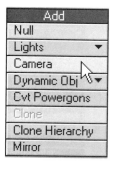

Figure 9.3 Switching to the Items tab will display the new options in the toolbar.

Figure 9.4 Create a new camera by clicking the Camera option in the toolbar.

Camera Name

Camera

OK

Cancel

Figure 9.5 Either accept the default camera name or type your own.

To add a camera to a scene:

1. Create or open a scene.

2. Select the Items tab to display new options in the toolbar (**Figure 9.3**).

3. From the Add section of the toolbar, select Camera (**Figure 9.4**).

4. When the Camera Name dialog appears, click OK to accept the default name for the new camera or make up your own (**Figure 9.5**).

✔ Tips

- It's important to remember that no matter how many cameras are in the scene, only one can actually render at a time. An image or animation will be rendered from the last camera selected.

- Use LightWave's Item Picker Master plug-in or the Schematic View to easily toggle between several cameras in your scene.

- Like a light in Layout, cameras are invisible to the renderer. This way, other cameras can't accidentally render it.

- Because it doesn't make much sense to animate the size or shape of a camera, Layout's Size and Stretch tools are disabled whenever a camera is selected.

CAMERA MANAGEMENT

Having a lot of unused cameras in your scene can get confusing (**Figure 9.6**). Although it's not necessary, you can opt to remove any unwanted cameras from your scene as easily as you added it. Be careful not to accidentally remove the camera you intend to render from. After a camera is removed, all its settings, effects, and animation are removed as well, and unfortunately, this action cannot be undone.

To remove a camera from a scene:

1. Click the Camera button at the bottom of the screen or press c to switch Layout into Camera selection mode.

2. Click the camera(s) you want to remove.

3. Click the Items tab to display new options in the toolbar.

4. From the Delete section of the toolbar, choose Clear Selected (**Figure 9.7**) or press −.

5. When the Clear Camera dialog appears, check that this is the right camera and click Yes (**Figure 9.8**).

LightWave will always need at least one camera in the scene, so Layout won't let you remove all of them.

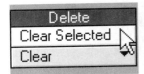

Figure 9.7 Select Clear Selected to remove the selected camera.

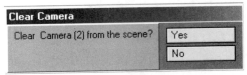

Figure 9.8 Verify that you want to clear the item.

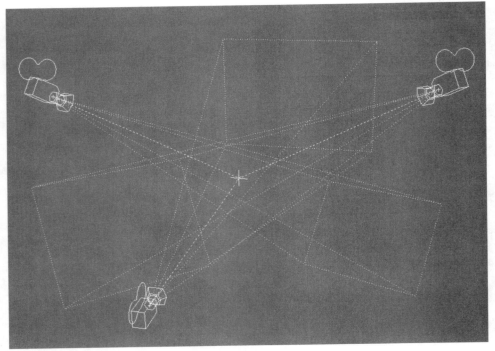

Figure 9.6 Multiple cameras can create a lot of confusion.

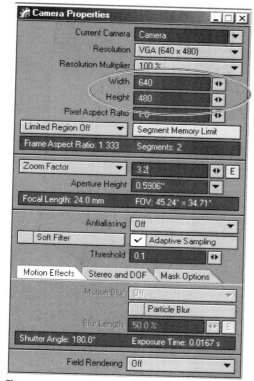

Figure 9.9 Use the Camera Properties panel to set the resolution of a camera, including the width or height of the images or animation to be rendered.

Image resolution

In LightWave, an image's resolution is measured in colored dots, or *pixels*, by counting the number of pixels both across the image (width) and down (height). These numbers have a bearing not only on the image's dimensions, but also on its file size, memory used, and render times. Determining the resolution of the render is incredibly important. Knowing the medium you plan to end in is a good place to start.

For example, the D1 video format (NTSC) has 720 pixels across and 486 pixels down. The resolution of an image rendered at this size would be 720 by 486 or 720 × 486. For film or print, where the resolution is much higher, you might have to render up to four or five times that size!

To set the resolution of a camera:

1. Click the Camera button or press [c] or to switch Layout into Camera selection mode.

2. If there's only one camera in the scene, it will automatically become selected. If not, simply click the camera you want to use in the Viewport.

3. Click the Properties button at the bottom of the screen, or press [p] to open the Camera Properties panel (**Figure 9.9**).

4. In the Width field, use the numeric input or mini-slider to set the number of pixels across.

   The default setting is 640.

5. Press [Tab] to jump to the next field.

6. In the Height field, use the numeric input or mini-slider to set the number of pixels vertically, and press [Enter].
   The default setting is 480.

✔ Tip

■ A good indication that your resolution is off is if your images or animations have black borders or the image looks stretched when viewed on your target medium.

Pixel aspect ratio

The Pixel Aspect Ratio setting lets you alter the shape of rendered pixels from square to rectangle. Why would you ever want to change the shape of a pixel? This might seem like a strange thing to do, but it's actually incredibly important.

Pixels displayed on computer monitors are square, with a pixel aspect ratio of 1. These pixels work well for Web, print, and video-game work. However, television pixels are rectangular in shape—longer than they are high. **Figure 9.10** illustrates what a simple box produced for the computer screen looks like when displayed on a television monitor. Although it's subtle, when this effect is multiplied by the thousands of pixels that make up an image, it can make your image look squashed or stretched.

You can have LightWave compensate for rectangular pixels by changing the Pixel Aspect Ratio setting to .86 or .9. This slight change keeps your render from looking stretched when you display it on a television.

To change the pixel aspect ratio:

1. Follow Steps 1–3 in the previous procedure, "To set the resolution of a camera."

2. Enter your medium's correct aspect ratio in the Pixel Aspect Ratio field (see the "Pixel Math" sidebar) (**Figure 9.11**).

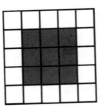

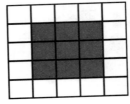

Figure 9.10
The top image is rendered with square pixels, whereas the bottom has rectangular pixels.

Figure 9.11 Use the Pixel Aspect Ratio setting to adjust the shape of the pixels.

Pixel Math

To determine the correct pixel aspect ratio, simply divide the width of your medium's pixel by its height. This ratio can usually be found online.

Pixel Aspect Ratio = pixel width ÷ pixel height

Calculate the frame aspect ratio by dividing the width (in pixels) of the image by its height, and then multiplying the result by the pixel aspect ratio.

Frame Aspect Ratio = (image width ÷ image height) × Pixel Aspect Ratio

CAMERA MANAGEMENT

Figure 9.12 The starting resolution is 640 × 480.

Figure 9.13 Switch the Resolution Multiplier to 50%.

Reducing rendering times

It's said that 3D artists can spend up to one quarter of their professional lives waiting for their images to render. This wasted time (often spent sleeping) decreases as both our talents and our machines improve. That said, render time is something you should always try to minimize. This is especially true when you're making test renders and previews.

One way to cut back on this time is to reduce the amount of the screen you render. Your first option is to change the Resolution Multiplier from 100 percent to 50 or even 25 percent. This option reduces the output resolution to a smaller, more manageable size.

To change the Resolution Multiplier:

1. Follow Steps 1–3 in the procedure titled, "To set the resolution of a camera."

   Note the camera's current resolution: 640 × 480 (**Figure 9.12**).

2. From the Resolution Multiplier pull-down menu, choose 50%.

   Notice the camera's new resolution (**Figure 9.13**).

3. Switch the Resolution Multiplier back to 100%, and the resolution should go back to normal.

✔ Tip

- Although LightWave gives you the option of customizing practically every aspect of your camera, it also makes your job a lot simpler by providing some camera presets. Each preset not only sets the correct size (width and height) for the medium, but it also corrects the pixel aspect ratio to match. You just select your format, and LightWave will do the rest.

Selecting Film

OK. We don't really use film in our LightWave cameras. It's more like digital film of sorts. In the real world, where the end result of a film shoot is a piece of celluloid, your shot becomes a rendered image (or animation). In LightWave, you can choose to make that image into a picture for a wall, a shot in a movie, or a graphic for a Web site. The rendering is done; what you do with it is up to you.

However, selecting the right film for a camera is just as important in the digital realm as it is to cinematographers. LightWave cameras have to be set up specifically to match the image's final medium. Settings vary—drastically sometimes—among film, television, Web, and print. Setting the wrong camera parameters can result in a useless shot, a lot of clean-up work, or some extremely long render times. So before you set your scene up to render those 1,000 frames, be sure to double-check your camera settings!

Your second option is to render using Limited Region. This setting confines the renderer to a predefined, rectangular portion of the screen, rather than the whole thing. You can edit this region so that only what you're currently working on renders, ignoring time-intensive effects and drastically reducing rendering times.

To use Limited Region:

1. Follow Steps 1–3 in the procedure titled, "To set the resolution of a camera."
2. From the Limited Region pull-down menu, select Limited Region Borders (**Figure 9.14**).
3. From the Viewport's current view pull-down menu, choose Camera View (**Figure 9.15**) or press 6.
4. Press I to activate the Limited Region tool and adjust the region. You'll see a dashed yellow rectangle around the screen.
5. Drag the edges of the rectangle to define the area you want to render (**Figure 9.16**).
6. Render the frame by pressing F9, and your scene should look like **Figure 9.17**.

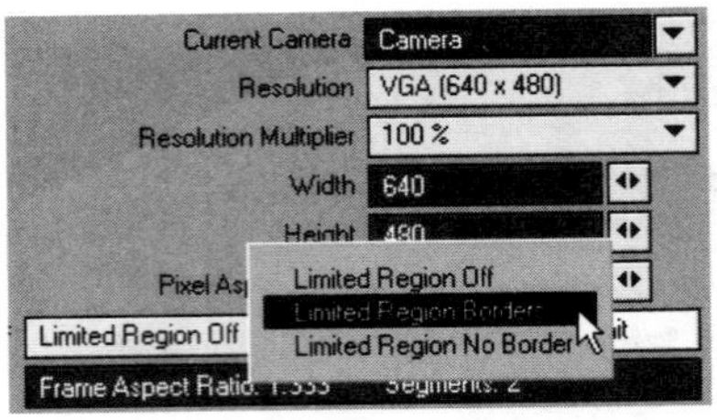

Figure 9.14 Turn on Limited Region by selecting either Limited Region Borders or Limited Region No Borders from this pull-down menu.

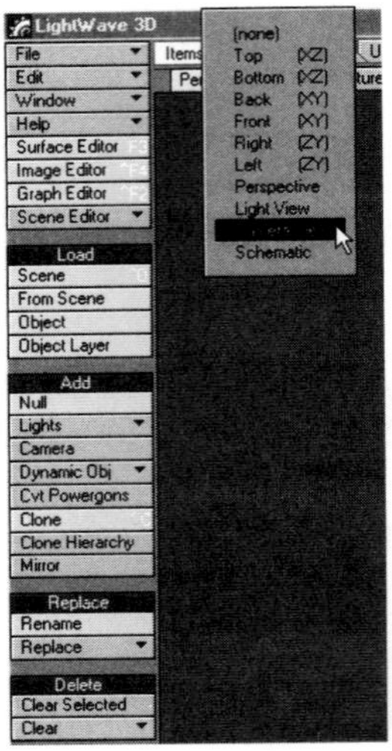

Figure 9.15 Switch the Viewport to Camera View.

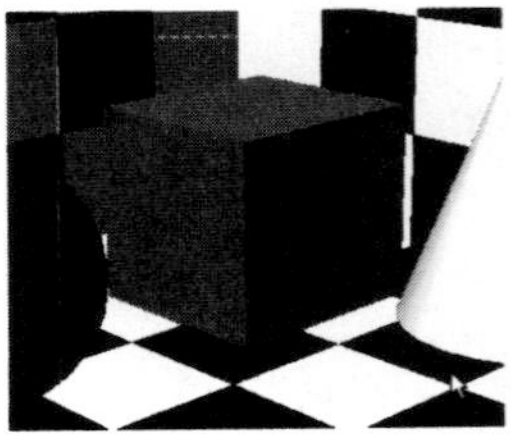

Figure 9.16 Adjust the yellow box to render only what you want to see.

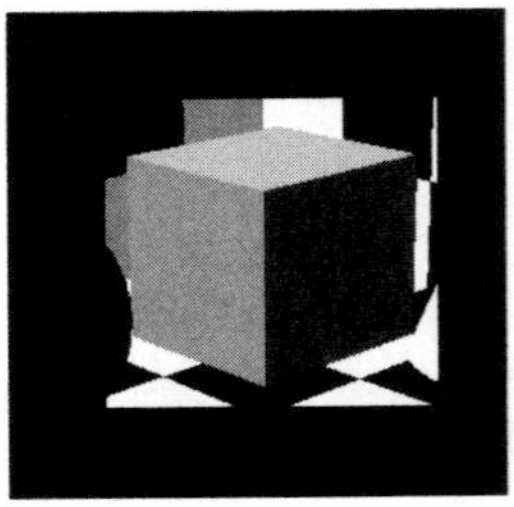

Figure 9.17 Only the area inside the box is rendered.

Customizing the Lens

Just as LightWave lets you modify the type of film that the camera uses, several of the lens parameters are also adjustable. You'll usually adjust these settings when trying to match footage previously shot on location.

For the effect to appear seamless, both the fields of view and the aperture settings of your lens have to match those of the existing footage. It's the job of the on-location visual effects supervisor to take notes on the lighting, reference points, film stock, and lenses used. All this information helps you insert digital elements seamlessly into a shot later.

Lens manipulation isn't only used for matching footage. These settings can be animated or combined with various other methods to create highly stylized effects, such as zooms, pulls, pushes, and rack focuses.

✔ Tip

- It's a good idea to modify a camera's lens before any animation is laid out. If the field of view changes later, existing camera angles might be off their marks or no longer acceptable.

Adjusting Segment Memory

As your scenes get larger, they'll start to require more and more memory. At some point, you might find that simply rendering a frame can suddenly cause you to run out! What's happening is that LightWave needs memory to set up buffers, compute shadows, do anti-aliasing, and so forth, and you just happened not to have enough. Luckily, you can adjust exactly how much memory the renderer can use by entering a value (in MB) in the Segment Memory setting in the Camera Properties panel.

With this value set, LightWave calculates how many segments it needs to stay within this maximum memory allotment. A low Segment Memory limit produces a large number of segments, whereas a high number keeps the segment count low. The more render segments you use, the longer it takes to calculate anti-aliasing, motion blur, and depth of field.

Wide or telephoto?

Because of its large field of view, a wide-angle lens can display a huge portion of your scene (**Figure 9.18**). This can come in handy when you're rendering large panoramic or environmental shots, but it can also create what's known as the "wall-eyed effect." That's when objects' proportions become exaggerated, with geometry closer to the camera appearing larger than geometry farther away, sort of like the typical front-door peephole (**Figure 9.19**).

A telephoto lens has exactly the opposite effect. Its narrow field of view compresses distance, reducing perspective and resulting in a much more straight-on image (**Figure 9.20**). This can be helpful when you're producing template images or interface graphics, where perspective isn't always wanted.

There are four settings that determine whether the camera lens is wide or telephoto:

◆ Zoom Factor

◆ Lens Focal Length

◆ Horizontal FOV

◆ Vertical FOV

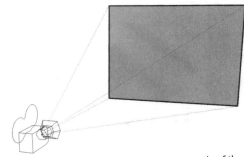

Figure 9.18 Layout displays the viewing angle of the camera lens.

Figure 9.19 A wide-angle lens produces the wall-eyed effect.

Figure 9.20 A narrow lens compresses distance and creates a flat image.

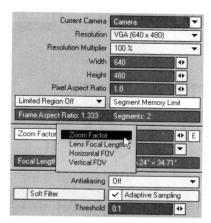

Figure 9.21 Select the setting you want to change from this pull-down menu.

All these settings are located in the Zoom Factor pull-down menu in the Camera Properties panel (**Figure 9.21**). You'll notice that if you adjust the Zoom Factor setting, the others will update as well. That's because all four of these settings are basically adjusting the same thing. LightWave gives you the different options because various animators have different backgrounds and can understand certain settings better than others.

✔ Tips

- If you're just starting out and none of these settings are familiar to you yet, use Zoom Factor. It's been with LightWave the longest and has the most documentation.

- For people familiar with the affect of lenses on certain film stocks, LightWave offers various presets that range from 8 mm to 65 mm stock, and one-third-, two-third-, and one-half-inch chip video cameras. This affects the Lens Focal Length setting and can strengthen the depth of field effect.

Using Anti-Aliasing

Images that have round or diagonal elements create the 2D effect called *aliasing*. Aliased pixels have a sort of stair-stepped edge that can give your images a jagged or rough look (**Figure 9.22**). This is usually unwanted and can be corrected using LightWave's anti-aliasing feature.

Anti-aliasing is the process of smoothing or blending these jagged lines out of the image. LightWave achieves this by sampling the surrounding pixels and overlaying a blended pixel in between them (**Figure 9.23**). To the human eye, this smoothes out the stair-steps.

Each anti-aliasing pass that LightWave's renderer makes decreases the aliased look a little more. Although the results are nicer, smoother edges, it can cost you some serious rendering time, depending on the quality of anti-aliasing you set up.

There are several levels of anti-aliasing available, ranging from low to high. Each increased level adds additional passes to the rendering process, thus increasing rendering time but producing a much better-looking image.

Video production work requires at least low anti-aliasing to look good on a television (medium is usually preferred). However, you might find that images with larger resolutions require less anti-aliasing when they're resized because of their added detail. Before setting up an animation to render, do some render tests and compare their times and quality.

Figure 9.22 This line is extremely aliased.

Figure 9.23 Anti-aliasing samples surrounding pixels to smooth out this line.

✔ Tips

■ The Enhanced Low to Enhanced High anti-aliasing settings offer more passes and an alternative algorithm for smoothing out aliased lines. This is especially useful for Radiosity and Area Light work.

■ Instead of anti-aliasing, some animators actually render at higher resolutions, and then shrink the image to the correct size in a paint program.

Figure 9.24 The white parts of this image have been selected for smoothing out with Adaptive Sampling.

Determining edges

You can instruct LightWave's renderer to anti-alias only certain edges, rather than the entire image, by using the camera's Adaptive Sampling feature (**Figure 9.24**). Only edges that fall within the Threshold parameter that you set are actually processed in each of the anti-aliasing passes. A good Threshold value can drastically reduce the time LightWave spends anti-aliasing your image.

To adjust the Threshold setting:

1. Create or open a scene.

2. Select the Render tab to display new options in the toolbar.

3. Click Render Options in the toolbar to display the Render Options panel.

4. Choose a resolution setting from the Show Rendering in Progress pull-down menu (**Figure 9.25**).

    This will let you view the render as it happens.

5. Click the Camera button or press c to switch Layout into Camera selection mode.

continues on next page

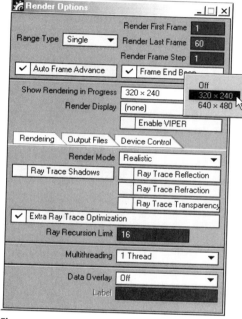

Figure 9.25 In the Render Options panel, set the resolution to adjust the Threshold value.

USING ANTI-ALIASING

243

6. Click the Properties button or press $\boxed{p}$ to open the Camera Properties panel.

7. From the Anti-aliasing pull-down menu, select a level of anti-aliasing (**Figure 9.26**).

8. Check the Adaptive Sampling check box.

9. In the Threshold field, use the numeric input or mini-slider to adjust the value. Start with a value less than .1 (the default value).

10. Render the frame by pressing $\boxed{F9}$.

When an anti-aliasing pass begins, a white line surrounds the areas of the image that are being blurred.

11. Repeat Steps 8 and 9, decreasing the Threshold value until the anti-aliasing pass affects only the edges you want smoothed out.

✔ Tip

■ The Soft Filter option renders the scene's objects smoothly, mimicking the film look. It's important to note that this effect does not process backgrounds.

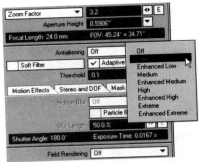

Figure 9.26 Select a level of anti-aliasing.

Figure 9.27 The Depth of Field feature lets you control what's in and out of focus.

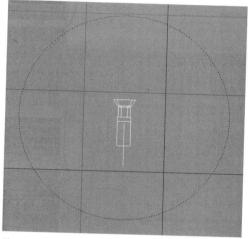

Figure 9.28 This circular dashed line around the camera represents the focal distance.

Depth of Field

LightWave can render surfaces in and out of focus by calculating the camera's depth of field, or DOF (**Figure 9.27**). Adjusting the camera's Focal Distance and Lens F-Stop values controls the look of this effect.

Focal distance

First, you need to determine the distance from the camera that will be in focus. This is known as the camera's *focal distance*. To see where this focus point is, view the camera in one of the Viewport's orthographic (top, side, front, and so on) views. When DOF is enabled, a dotted circle indicates the point that will be in focus (**Figure 9.28**).

Pixels that fall right on this circle will be rendered in focus. Surfaces situated both in front of and behind this line will be, to some degree, out of focus.

Lens F-Stop

Next, we need to adjust the strength of focus, so to speak—an area around the focal distance that's still in focus. Adjusting the Lens F-Stop value controls this.

As the Lens F-Stop gets smaller, the in-focus area around the focal distance also gets smaller. As this value increases, more and more pixels around the focal distance are in focus. This is how you control which surfaces are displayed in and out of focus.

To use Depth of Field:

1. Follow Steps 1–3 of the "To set the resolution of a camera" procedure earlier in this chapter (Figure 9.9).

2. From the Anti-aliasing pull-down menu, choose Medium (**Figure 9.29**).

3. Select the Stereo and DOF tab in the Camera Properties panel to display new options, and check the Depth of Field check box (**Figure 9.30**).

4. Use the Move [t] and Rotate [y] tools to drag and rotate the camera into the desired position.

5. In the Focal Distance and Lens F-Stop fields, use the numeric inputs or mini-sliders to adjust the values.

6. Render the frame [F9].

7. Repeat Steps 5 and 6 until you achieve the desired focal settings in your image.

✔ Tips

- The Depth of Field effect requires at least medium anti-aliasing. The higher the anti-aliasing level, the better the effect will look.

- Press [Ctrl]+[F9] to have LightWave render a preview of the Depth of Field effect in the OpenGL Viewport.

Figure 9.29 Depth of Field requires some anti-aliasing.

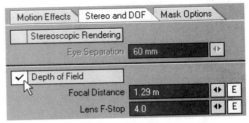

Figure 9.30 Enable the Depth of Field feature.

DEPTH OF FIELD

Figure 9.31 Notice the blurring that occurs as this ball travels through the frames.

Figure 9.32 Fast motion produces an effect known as *motion blur*.

Figure 9.33 Adjust the type of blur and the length of the effect.

Rendering Motion

Through the persistence of vision, our eyes and brain interpret movement when they see 24–30 sequential static images per second. This is the basis of all motion pictures, television, and animation.

In the real world, motion is blurred as objects travel between two points (**Figure 9.31**). This same blurring effect is captured successfully in film and television, but must be simulated in animation for motion to look realistic.

The best example of what happens when this isn't done correctly is early stop-motion animation. Jerky and strobe-like artifacts made these animations revolutionary, but not very life-like. As the process was perfected, the blurring effect was incorporated into the images, producing much more realistic animations.

Motion blur

To create the illusion of fast movement, LightWave can blur moving objects. Given an item's motion and a blur percentage, LightWave layers several semitransparent images on top of each other, streaking them along their path. This produces a blurring effect (**Figure 9.32**).

Like DOF, motion blur requires some kind of anti-aliasing. The more anti-aliasing passes that are rendered, the more layers are added to produce the motion blur effect.

You can adjust the amount of blur by setting the feature's Blur Length parameter, which can be found on the Motion Effects tab of the Camera Properties panel, as long as you have a camera selected. The quality can be further adjusted by selecting Normal or Dithered from the Motion Blur pull-down menu (**Figure 9.33**).

Field Rendering

An animation created for video or television plays at 30 frames per second (FPS). Each frame is actually made up of two interlaced fields. If you turn on Field Rendering in the Camera Properties panel (**Figure 9.34**), LightWave will split the motion information between the frame's two fields, saving one-half of the motion in one field and the other half in the other.

When the animation is played at 60 fields per second, the motion will look much smoother. This is because the same distance is now covered in 60 pieces instead of the normal 30. Field Rendering comes in handy when you're animating small objects moving quickly across the screen, especially text.

When you turn on Field Rendering, you're given the choice of rendering the even or odd scan lines in the first field. This is dictated by your hardware. If your field-rendered motion flashes during playback, producing a strobe-like effect, simply switch the even and odd field selection.

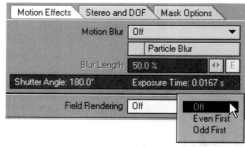

Figure 9.34 Turn on Field Rendering to split the motion information between two fields.

✔ Tip

■ Because of the technical trickery that Field Rendering performs, only use this effect if you're outputting to television or video. All other areas of displaying animation don't use fields and won't work correctly.

ADVANCED ANIMATION TOOLS

There is much more to animating items in Layout than just selecting and moving them. LightWave offers many tools that make complex animation, such as creating characters, much easier. You'll also find several tools you can use to refine your animation, adding that little touch that makes your scene come to life.

For instance, you can do keyframe management with the Graph Editor, parent items to one another, and use inverse kinematics to animate item chains. There are also a number of modifiers that you can apply to your item motions in order to automate certain tasks, making your job as an animator easier.

In this chapter, you explore some of the advanced animation capabilities of Layout and learn when to apply them.

Keyframe Automation

One of the advanced features of Layout is actually more of a convenience. It allows Layout to create new keyframes whenever you manipulate an item in a frame that doesn't have one and to modify keyframes when you manipulate an item in a frame that does. There are both pros and cons to this approach and in the end, it will come down to your personal preference.

One pro of the Auto Key Create option is that it allows you to quickly and easily rough out a motion path for an item. Simply advance to the frames where you want keyframes created and then move the item for which you want to create the keyframes.

The Auto Key option (located on the main Layout Viewport below the frame slider) on its own allows you to modify the values of an existing keyframe when you change items. But it's important to understand that just because Auto Key is active, that doesn't mean that Auto Key Create is active. So you may be modifying existing keyframes when you meant to create new ones.

Auto Key also serves as a master switch for both options. If it isn't active, then both Auto Key Modify and Auto Key Create are disabled. Auto Key Create is dependent on Auto Key being active, but Auto Key can be active while Auto Key Create is disabled. This allows you to modify existing keyframes without accidentally creating new ones. It's a little confusing at first, but as we progress through this chapter it will become clear.

Figure 10.1 Auto Key is the master switch for the whole Auto Key system.

Auto Key and Auto Key Create are both on by default in the standard LightWave installation. The remainder of this chapter assumes that both Auto Key and Auto Key Create are active, so you can explore how they'll fit into your workflow. We had you turn them off in Chapter 6, "Beginning Animation," so they may still be disabled. But never fear: We'll walk you through turning them back on.

To turn on Auto Key features:

1. Click the Auto Key button just below the frame slider track to activate it (**Figure 10.1**).

2. Select General Options from the Edit pull-down menu in the toolbar or press o.

   The Preferences panel opens with the General Options tab showing (**Figure 10.2**).

3. From the Auto Key Create pull-down menu, choose All Motion Channels (**Figure 10.3**).

4. Close the Preferences window.

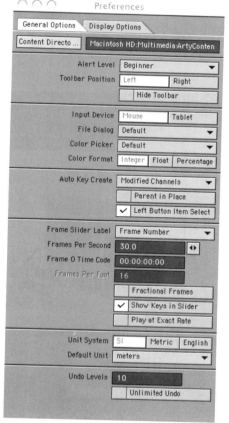

Figure 10.2 Use the General Options tab of the Preferences panel to turn on Auto Key features.

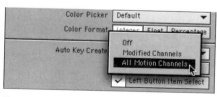

Figure 10.3 The Auto Key Create feature has two options. Modified Channels will create keys for only channels you manipulate, and All Motion Channels will create keys for every channel in the item.

To create and modify keyframes automatically:

1. Create or load an object into Layout.

2. Select the Modify tab, and then click Move in the Translate tool group of the toolbar or press ⊤ to activate the Move tool and drag the object to –2m on the Z axis (**Figure 10.4**).

3. Go to frame 30 of the scene.

4. Drag the object to 0m on the Z axis and 2m on the X axis.

   Notice that you didn't have to bring up the Create Motion Key dialog and accept the values before Layout drew the motion path for your object. Layout automatically created a keyframe for your object at frame 30 as soon as you moved it (**Figure 10.5**).

5. Go to frame 60 of the scene.

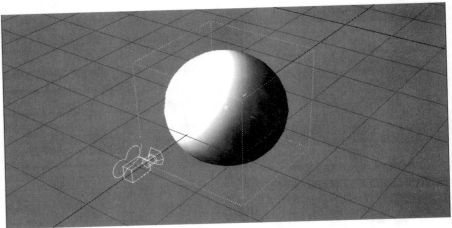

Figure 10.4 Use the Move tool to move your object to –2m on the Z axis.

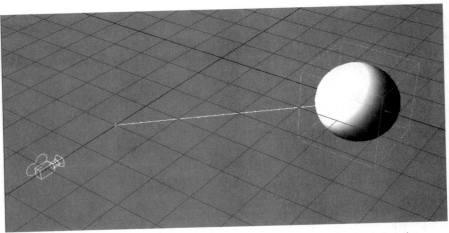

Figure 10.5 You don't need to use the Create Motion Key dialog when Auto Key Create is active.

6. Drag the object to 2m on the Z axis and 0m on the X axis.

Once again Layout automatically creates a keyframe and draws the motion path (**Figure 10.6**).

7. Go back to frame 30 of the scene.

8. Drag the object to 1m on the X axis.

Layout updates the motion path as you move the object because frame 30 contains a keyframe for your object (**Figure 10.7**). So as you adjust its position, Layout automatically updates the keyframe values.

✔ Tip

■ Auto keyframing can be very useful, but can also inadvertently modify your animation, so use these options carefully. Also understand that Layout's Undo feature will not undo inadvertent keyframe creation or changes made with the Auto Key features.

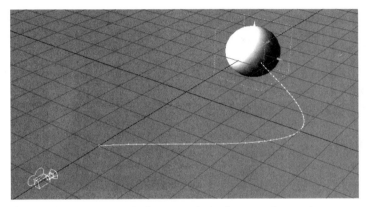

Figure 10.6 Layout automatically creates the keyframes and connects the dots.

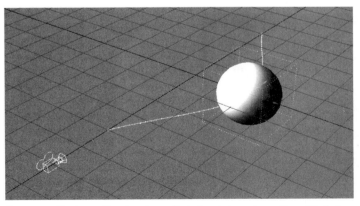

Figure 10.7 Moving an item in a frame that already has a key will modify that keyframe's values.

Managing Keyframes

While animating your scenes, you're going to notice an abundance of keyframes. In fact, you'll probably end up with multiple keyframes for several of the items in your scene. Though the Layout Viewport and frame slider track are good visual aids for identifying keyframes, they aren't well suited to managing them.

The Graph Editor is the best place to view and manipulate keyframes (**Figure 10.8**). You'll be spending a lot of time working in the Graph Editor, so it's very important to become familiar with it. Many functions of the Graph Editor are beyond the scope of this book, so we just focus on the basic functions you use every day.

The Graph Editor interface

First, let's examine the major components of the Graph Editor interface (**Figure 10.9**).

◆ **Channel bin:** This list displays the channels currently available for editing.

◆ **Channel list:** This hierarchical list allows you to select channels from the current scene and add them to the channel bin.

◆ **Motion graph:** This area displays the motion curves for the channels currently in the channel bin. This is where you manipulate your keyframes. The values along the left edge represent the keyframes' current values, and the numbers along the bottom edge represent time.

◆ **Curves:** This area displays information for the currently selected keyframe(s).

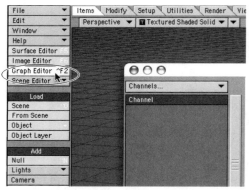

Figure 10.8 To open the Graph Editor, click the button in the upper-left corner of the toolbar (visible no matter what panel you're working in) or press [Ctrl]+[F2].

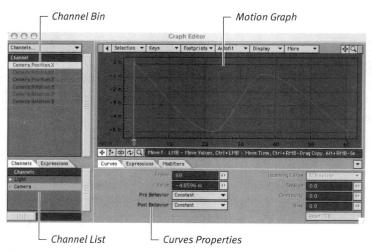

┌ *Channel Bin*   ┌ *Motion Graph*

└ *Channel List*   └ *Curves Properties*

Figure 10.9 The Graph Editor is an essential tool for managing your keyframes.

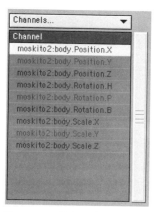

Figure 10.10 Select channels for editing in the channel bin.

To select channels for editing:

1. Create or load a scene with animation.

2. Select an item in the scene that has keyframes by clicking it.

3. Click Graph Editor in the toolbar or press `Ctrl`+`F2` to open the Graph Editor.

   The channel bin will contain the motion channels for the item you selected (**Figure 10.10**).

4. Click the Position.Z channel in the channel bin.

   Notice that the blue motion curve in the motion graph becomes highlighted, meaning that the curve is active for editing (**Figure 10.11**).

continues on next page

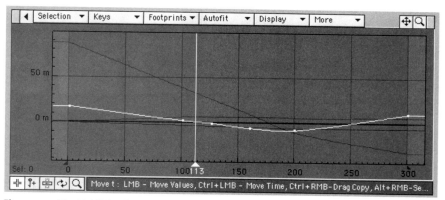

Figure 10.11 The highlighted curves in the motion graph are active for editing.

MANAGING KEYFRAMES

5. (Ctrl)-click the Position.X channel in the channel bin.

The Graph Editor adds this to your selection and now both the red and blue motion curves are highlighted (**Figure 10.12**).

6. (Shift)-click the Scale.Z channel.

Now all of the motion curves in the bin are active for editing in the motion graph (**Figure 10.13**).

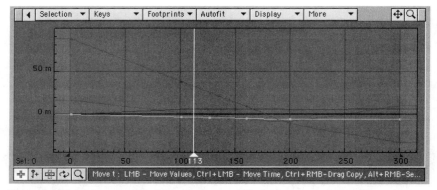

Figure 10.12 Hold down Control while selecting to add individual channels for editing.

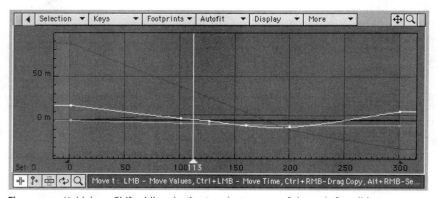

Figure 10.13 Hold down Shift while selecting to select a range of channels for editing.

Figure 10.14 Double-click an item in the channel list to move its channels to the channel bin, replacing the channels that were previously there.

Figure 10.15 Hold down Shift while double-clicking an item to add its channels to the channel bin.

To add channels for a new item to the channel bin without selecting the item in the Layout Viewport, use the channel list, located directly below the channel bin.

To add channels to the channel bin:

1. Create or load a scene with multiple animated items.

2. Click Graph Editor in the toolbar or press Ctrl+F2 to open the Graph Editor.

3. Double-click one of the items in the channel list.

   The channels for the item you selected in the hierarchical list replace the channels that were in the channel bin (**Figure 10.14**).

4. Shift-double-click another item in the channel list.

   The channels for the new item you selected are added to the channel bin (**Figure 10.15**).

continues on next page

MANAGING KEYFRAMES

257

5. Click the arrow next to one of the items in the channel list to expand it and see all the channels it contains (**Figure 10.16**).

6. Double-click one of the channels you just expanded.

It replaces the channels that were in the channel bin (**Figure 10.17**).

7. [Shift]-double-click another channel. This new channel is added to the channel bin.

✔ Tip

■ The Graph Editor will not automatically give you the channels for items as you select them in the Layout Viewport. If this is the desired mode of operation, check the Track Item Selections check box in the Graph Editor options panel.

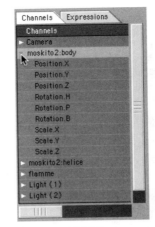

Figure 10.16 Click the arrow next to an item name to expand it so you can see its channels.

Figure 10.17 Add individual channels to the channel bin by holding Shift while selecting them.

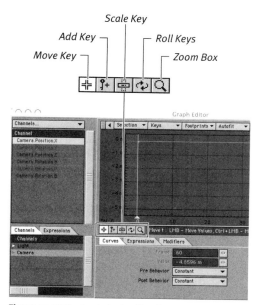

Scale Key

Add Key

Move Key

Roll Keys

Zoom Box

Figure 10.18 The basic tools of keyframe management.

Editing motions with the Graph Editor

Now that you know how to select and add channels to the channel bin, it's time to learn how to edit the motion curves. The Graph Editor has several tools with which to modify your keyframes (**Figure 10.18**).

Move Key: This tool allows you to move keyframes around in the motion graph portion of the Graph Editor. Just dragging will modify the keyframe values, and holding Ctrl while dragging will move them in time.

Add Key: This tool allows you to add or remove keyframes from the selected motion curve. Clicking a curve adds a keyframe at that point, and holding Ctrl while clicking a keyframe removes it.

Scale Key: This tool scales the values of a selected range of keys or a whole motion curve when you click and drag in the Motion Graph. Holding Ctrl while dragging scales the timing of the keys or motion.

Roll Keys: This tool effectively inverts the values of the keyframes in the selected range. For example, if you had an animated walk cycle for the right leg of a character and copied the motions to the left side, you could use this to invert them so the rotations are correct.

Zoom Box: This tool zooms in on the selected area.

To add and remove keyframes:

1. Create or load a scene with some animation.

2. Click an item in the scene that has keyframes.

3. Click Graph Editor in the toolbar or press Ctrl+F2 to open the Graph Editor.

   The motion curves for your selected item should be in the motion graph (**Figure 10.19**).

4. Click one of the keyframe dots to select it (**Figure 10.20**).

   Notice that it becomes highlighted in yellow and two handles appear, one on either side.

5. Press Del to remove the keyframe from the motion curve (**Figure 10.21**).

6. Click the Add Key tool in the Graph Editor or press +.

7. Click anywhere in the motion graph area to add a keyframe to the current motion curve (**Figure 10.22**).

✔ Tip

- Dragging with the right mouse button in the motion graph area performs a bounding box selection. This is very useful for selecting multiple keyframes at once.

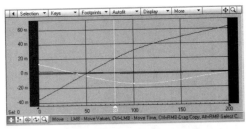

Figure 10.19 The Graph Editor automatically tracks your current selection in Layout and loads the appropriate motion channels.

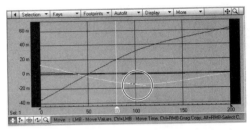

Figure 10.20 Click directly on a keyframe to select it.

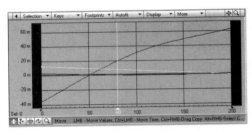

Figure 10.21 Press Delete to remove any selected keyframe(s) from the current motion curve.

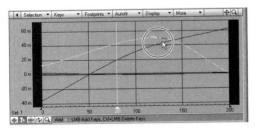

Figure 10.22 Click on the motion curve at the point where you would like the keyframe.

MANAGING KEYFRAMES

Figure 10.23 Select a channel in the bin for editing.

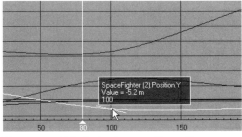

Figure 10.24 Select a keyframe on the motion curve.

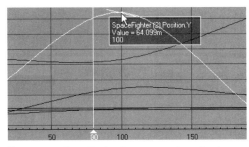

Figure 10.25 Drag the keyframe up or down to change its position.

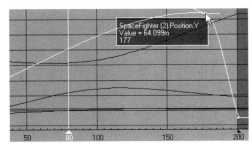

Figure 10.26 Hold Control while dragging left or right to adjust the keyframe's position in time.

To modify an existing keyframe:

1. Create or load a scene with some animation.

2. Click an animated item.

3. Click Graph Editor in the toolbar or press Ctrl+F2 to open the Graph Editor.

4. In the channel bin, click a channel with a motion curve (**Figure 10.23**).

5. Click the Move Key tool in the Graph Editor or press t.

6. Click one of the keyframes on the curve (**Figure 10.24**).

7. Drag the keyframe.

   As you drag left to right, nothing happens, but as you drag up and down, the value changes (**Figure 10.25**).

8. Hold Ctrl while dragging the keyframe.

   As you drag up and down nothing happens, but as you drag left to right, the timing changes (**Figure 10.26**).

✔ Tip

- Move the mouse over a keyframe in the motion graph to display the keyframe's current values.

- You can also change the timing of your keyframes by selecting and dragging them in the Dope Track. Managing the timing of multiple keyframes can be accomplished in the Dope Sheet View of the Scene Editor.

Whether you're scaling a motion over time or changing the values of multiple keyframes simultaneously, you will eventually need to modify multiple keyframes on a single curve, or even multiple curves. In this next example, you scale the timing of a motion curve.

To modify multiple keyframes:

1. Create or load a scene with some animation.

2. Click Graph Editor in the toolbar or press [Ctrl]+[F2] to open the Graph Editor.

3. In the channel bin, click a channel with multiple keyframes (**Figure 10.27**).

4. Click the Scale Key tool in the Graph Editor or press [h].

5. Right-click and drag a box around a couple of the keyframes to select them (**Figure 10.28**).

6. Using the left mouse button, [Ctrl]-drag in the motion graph area to scale the time that falls in between the keyframes.

    As you drag to the right, the keyframes become more spread out, lengthening the time between them (**Figure 10.29**). As you drag to the left, they come closer together, shortening the time between them (**Figure 10.30**). The time scaling operation uses the current mouse position as the center of the scaling effect.

Figure 10.27 Select a channel in the bin that has more than one keyframe.

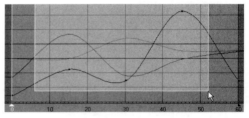

Figure 10.28 Right-click and drag to select a range of keyframes.

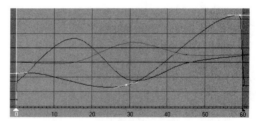

Figure 10.29 Drag right to expand the motion curve's time.

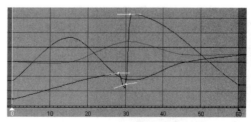

Figure 10.30 Drag left to contract the motion curve's time.

MANAGING KEYFRAMES

Figure 10.31 Move the camera's channels to the channel bin.

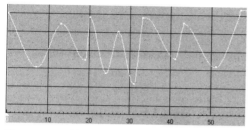

Figure 10.32 Add several keyframes relatively close together.

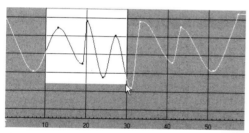

Figure 10.33 Select a portion of your motion curve to examine.

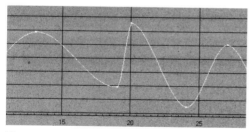

Figure 10.34 Zoom in on your keyframes.

If you have multiple keyframes on a single motion curve, it can sometimes be difficult to get in between them to refine your motion. Use the Zoom Box tool to expand your view of these areas and it'll be much easier.

To zoom in on a range of keyframes:

1. Click Graph Editor in the toolbar or press Ctrl+F2 to open the Graph Editor.

2. Double-click the camera entry in the channel list tree pane (**Figure 10.31**).

3. Click the Add Key tool in the Graph Editor or press +.

4. Add 10 to 15 keyframes to the Camera.Position.X channel (**Figure 10.32**).

5. Click the Zoom Box tool in the Graph Editor or press m.

6. Drag a box around a range of keyframes on the curve (**Figure 10.33**).

   The motion graph zooms in on the selection you just made (**Figure 10.34**).

7. Right-click anywhere in the motion graph area to zoom back out.

MANAGING KEYFRAMES

Adjusting the Curve Properties

As you may have noticed, when you select a keyframe, the controls in the Curves panel at the bottom of the Graph Editor change to display the keyframe's properties. You can use these controls to manually adjust your keyframes when you can't get the precision you need with the mouse (**Figure 10.35**).

Frame: This field displays the frame number at which this keyframe resides. Just like in the main Layout interface, typing a new frame number into the Frame field moves the keyframe to that frame in the animation.

Value: This field displays the current value of the selected keyframe. Just like in the main Layout interface, typing a new value into the Value field changes the position of the keyframe on the selected curve.

Pre Behavior: This control lets you set how your incoming curve behaves.

Post Behavior: This control lets you set how your outgoing curve behaves.

Incoming Curve: This control defines the type of curve preceding the keyframe.

Tension: You can think of this as "ease in" and "ease out" for the keyframe. A negative value slows the item as it approaches and passes through the keyframe, and a positive value speeds an item up as it approaches and passes through the keyframe. This control accepts values between –1.0 and 1.0.

Continuity: Continuity can be thought of as the transition of the motion at the keyframe. A negative value results in a sharp transition in the motion between the current keyframe and the next while a positive value results in a smooth transition. As with Tension this control accepts values between –1.0 and 1.0.

Bias: Bias determines whether the item will "undershoot" or "overshoot" the current keyframe. A negative value leaves slack in the curve before the keyframe causing the item to undershoot, and a positive value causes the item to overshoot the keyframe. As with tension and continuity, this control takes value between –1.0 and 1.0. The Pre and Post Behavior menus allow you to change the behavior of a motion. For instance, setting Post Behavior to Repeat will repeat the motion infinitely.

For a more in-depth overview of Tension, Continuity, and Bias as well as the different Incoming Curve types, please refer to the LightWave 3D User's Manual.

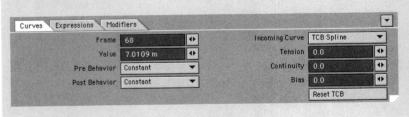

Figure 10.35 You can change the selected keyframe's properties in the Curves panel.

For this next example, you'll create a simple animation: a bouncing ball. Let's say you want the ball to bounce three times in the course of six seconds. You have two options—manually add keyframes or set Post Behavior for the Y channel to Repeat.

To set Post Behavior for a motion:

1. Create a 1-meter-by-1-meter sphere in Modeler and load it into Layout.

2. Go to frame 30 of the scene.

3. Click the sphere in the Layout Viewport.

4. Click the Modify tab to display new options in the toolbar.

5. Click Move in the Translate tool group of the toolbar or press [t] and drag the sphere to 2 meters on the Y axis (**Figure 10.36**).

continues on next page

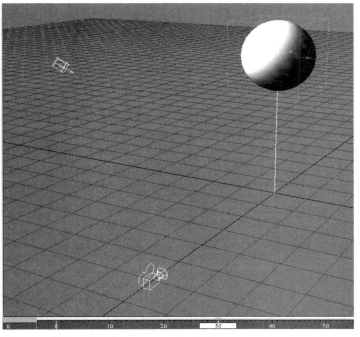

Figure 10.36 Place the sphere at 2m on the Y axis.

6. Go to frame 60 of the scene.

7. Click Reset in the General tool group of the toolbar to move the sphere back to its original position (**Figure 10.37**).

8. Click the forward play button under the frame slider to preview your motion.

The sphere moves up and down once.

9. Double-click in the frame slider end-frame input field and type 180 (30 fps × seconds = 180 frames).

Now the ball bounces once and then sits motionless for the remainder of the animation.

10. Click the pause button below the frame slider to stop the animation.

11. Click Graph Editor in the toolbar or press Ctrl+F2 to open the Graph Editor.

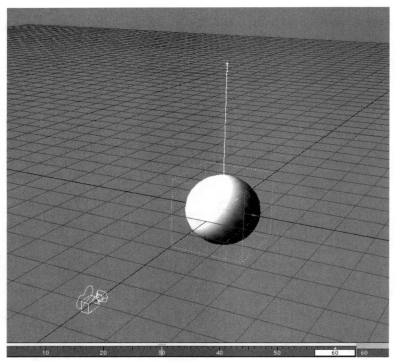

Figure 10.37 Reset the sphere's position.

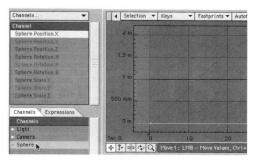

Figure 10.38 Move the sphere's motion curves to the channel bin.

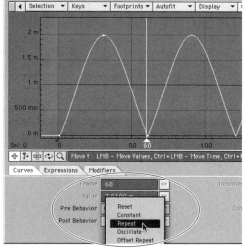

Figure 10.39 Setting the Post Behavior to Repeat is an excellent way to create looping motions.

12. Double-click the sphere in the channel list to move its channels into the channel bin (**Figure 10.38**).

13. Select the Sphere.Position.Y channel in the channel bin.

14. In the Post Behavior pull-down menu, choose Repeat.

Notice how the motion curve updates to repeat itself after frame 60 in the motion graph (**Figure 10.39**).

15. Click play again and your sphere now repeats its motion, bouncing up and down for the full 180 frames.

Using Channel Modifiers

LightWave 3D includes a number of useful channel modifiers for automating some effects in your motion channels. We'll take a quick look at the Oscillator here, but for a complete list and description of all of them, please refer to the LightWave 3D User's Manual.

Let's use the scene from the previous exercise as an example. The sphere was moving up and down to simulate a bouncing ball. Though the animation certainly accomplished this, it wasn't very realistic. In the real world, the loss of momentum would make each bounce lower than the previous one, until the sphere finally came to rest.

Rather than manually creating keyframes to simulate this motion, you can use what's referred to as a *channel modifier* to do the work for you. By using a modifier on the sphere's Y channel, you also avoid having to figure out the physics of the bouncing ball. Channel modifiers are an important part of the animation process, helping you save time so that you can focus on the more complex portions of animation.

To apply a channel modifier to a motion curve:

1. Load the sphere object you used in the previous task.

2. Type 180 into the frame slider end-frame input field.

3. Click Graph Editor in the toolbar or press Ctrl+F2 to open the Graph Editor.

4. Double-click the sphere in the channel list to add its motion channels to the channel bin.

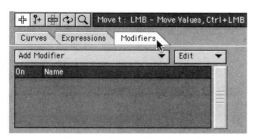

Figure 10.40 Click the channel Modifiers tab.

5. Click the Sphere.Position.Y channel in the channel bin.

6. Select the Modifiers tab in the Graph Editor to display new options (**Figure 10.40**).

7. From the Add Modifier pull-down menu, choose Oscillator (**Figure 10.41**).

Oscillator now appears in the list below the Add Modifier menu (**Figure 10.42**).

continues on next page

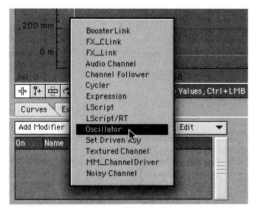

Figure 10.41 Apply the Oscillator channel modifier.

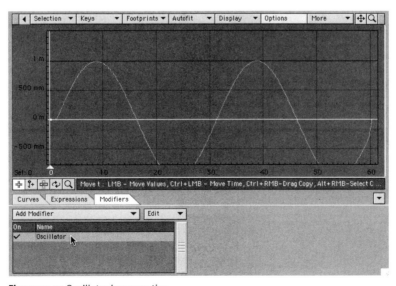

Figure 10.42 Oscillator is now active.

USING CHANNEL MODIFIERS

8. Double-click Oscillator in the list to open the Oscillator properties panel (**Figure 10.43**).

9. Type 180 in the frame slider end-frame input field.

10. Type 2m in the Wave Size input field.

11. In the Damping field, use the numeric input or mini-slider arrows to change the value to 75.

12. Click Continue to close the Oscillator properties panel.

The motion graph has drawn a dotted line to display the curve created by the channel modifier (**Figure 10.44**).

13. Click the play button below the frame slider to preview the animation.

As the sphere bounces up and down, the motion dissipates over time, providing for a more realistic effect.

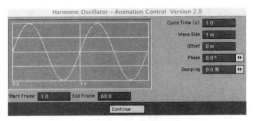

Figure 10.43 Open the Oscillator interface.

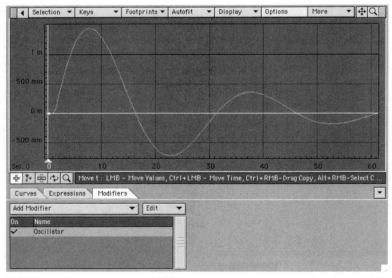

Figure 10.44 The Graph Editor will always present you with a visual representation of how a modifier is affecting the channel.

USING CHANNEL MODIFIERS

Targeting Items in Layout

In Chapter 8, "Lighting," we covered using target objects to aim a light. Targeting may be used for any of the Layout item types. As a quick refresher, now you will target the camera to a Null.

To target items:

1. Select the Items tab to display new options in the toolbar.

2. Click Null in the Add tool group of the toolbar.

3. Type Camera-Target in the Null Object Name dialog and then press Enter to accept it.

4. Select the Modify tab, and then click Move in the Translate tool group of the toolbar or press t and drag Camera-Target to 2m on the Y Axis.

5. Click the camera in the Layout Viewport.

6. Select the Setup tab to change the toolbar options.

7. Click Motion Options in the Motions tool group of the toolbar or press m to open the Motion Options panel.

8. From the Target Item pull-down menu, choose Camera-Target (**Figure 10.45**).

   The camera rotates to face the Camera-Target object and Layout displays a dotted red line to indicate which item the camera is targeting.

9. Drag the Camera-Target object to −4m on the X axis (**Figure 10.46**).

10. Go to frame 60 of the scene.

11. Drag the Camera-Target object to 4m on the X axis (**Figure 10.47**).

12. Click the play button under the frame slider.

    As the Camera-Target object moves from −4m to 4m on the X axis, the Camera pans to follow it.

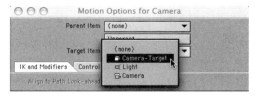

Figure 10.45 Targeting is very useful for having items track one another.

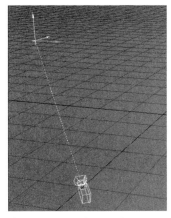

Figure 10.46 Set the initial position of Camera-Target.

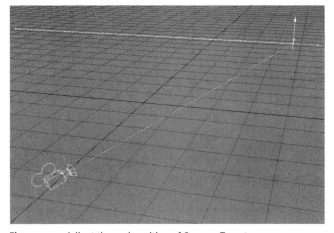

Figure 10.47 Adjust the end position of Camera-Target.

Parenting Items in Layout

Parenting is a simple yet powerful feature that lets you define the position, rotation, and size values of one item based on the values of another item. When you create a parent/child relationship, whatever the parent does, the child does. The simplest use is when you need two items to move together as one during the course of your animation.

Parenting is not limited to two items, however. Any number of items may be parented together. This can be multiple items attached to a single master item or a series of objects parented in succession, creating what is referred to as an "item hierarchy."

To parent items to one another:

1. Create or load an object into Layout. For this example, we used a sphere.

2. Select the Items tab to display new options in the toolbar.

3. Click Null in the Add tool group of the toolbar.

4. In the Null Object dialog that appears, name the new object Object-Parent and press (Enter).

5. Select the Modify tab then click Move in the Translate tool group of the toolbar or press (t) and drag Object-Parent to 2m on the Y axis (**Figure 10.48**).

6. Click your object (the sphere in our example) in the Layout Viewport.

7. Select the Setup tab, and then click Motion Options in the Motion tool group of the toolbar or press (m) to open the Motion Options panel.

8. From the Parent Item pull-down menu, choose Object-Parent (**Figure 10.49**).

Figure 10.48 Set the initial position of the parent item.

Figure 10.49 Parenting is a powerful feature that you'll use often.

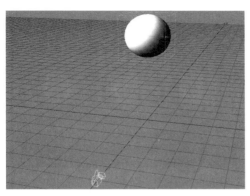

Figure 10.50 The sphere is now bound to Object-Parent.

Figure 10.51 Wherever the parent goes, the child must follow.

Figure 10.52 Reset the parent's position at frame 60.

You have just created a parent/child relationship, and the sphere (the child object) will jump to the position of Object-Parent (**Figure 10.50**).

9. Go to frame 30 of the scene.

10. Drag Object-Parent to 2m on the X axis. Notice that the object follows along (**Figure 10.51**).

11. Go to frame 60 of the scene.

12. Select the Modify tab, and then click Reset in the General tool group of the toolbar to return Object-Parent to its original position.

The sphere moves along with it (**Figure 10.52**).

13. Click the play button below the frame slider to preview the animation.

As Object-Parent moves along, the sphere follows.

In the previous example, you saw that the child object snapped to the position of Object-Parent after you had selected it as the parent. This is because when you parent one item to another, the child will move its center, or pivot point, to the position of the parent's center. This is OK for many applications, but sometimes you want an item to attach to another while retaining its initial position.

Take for example, the wheels on a car. Obviously, you want the wheels themselves to be separate from the car so you can animate their rotation, but when you parent the wheels to the chassis you don't want them to snap to its original position. Instead, you want to place the four wheels in the appropriate positions and then parent them to the chassis where they sit. To accomplish this, turn on the Parent in Place option.

To parent an item in place:

1. Create or load an object into Layout. For this example, we use a sphere.

2. Select the Items tab to display new options in the toolbar.

3. Click Null in the Add tool group of the toolbar and name the new object Object-Parent.

4. Select the Modify tab, and then click Move in the Translate tool group of the toolbar or press (t) and drag Object-Parent to 2m on the Y axis.

5. Press (o) to open the General Options panel of Preferences.

6. Check the Parent in Place check box (**Figure 10.53**).

7. Click your object in the Layout Viewport (the sphere, in our example).

8. Select the Setup tab, and then click Motion Options in the Motions tool group of the toolbar or press (m) to open the Motion Options panel.

9. From the Parent pull-down menu, choose Object-Parent.

   Notice that the sphere doesn't jump to the position of Object-Parent.

10. To check whether the item is parented, click Object-Parent to select it.

11. Drag Object-Parent to –2m on the Z axis.

    Notice that the sphere moves along the Z axis with Object-Parent, while retaining its own original position on the Y axis (**Figure 10.54**).

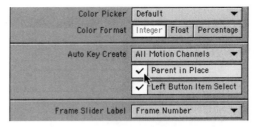

Figure 10.53 Use the Parent in Place option to parent items after they've already been positioned.

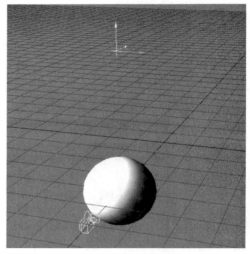

Figure 10.54 Even though the object follows Object-Parent, it retains its initial relative distance from it as it moves.

12. Go to frame 60 of the scene.

13. Drag Object-Parent to 2m on the Z axis (**Figure 10.55**).

14. Click the play button below the frame slider to preview the animation.

✔ Tip

- It is generally most desirable to enable Parent in Place on any items at frame 0. Although the Parent in Place operation itself is not keyframeable, enabling this feature later in your animation may create unwanted keyframes.

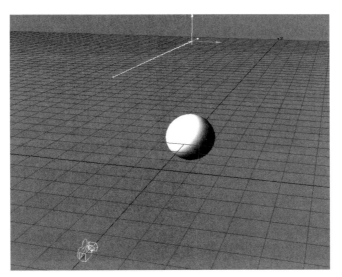

Figure 10.55 Move the parent to 2m on the Z axis to create a simple animation.

Working with Inverse Kinematics

In order to fully understand Inverse Kinematics, or IK, you first need to understand Forward Kinematics. All your animation up to this point has been accomplished by directly manipulating each item and creating keyframes. This is often referred to as Forward Kinematics, or FK.

IK is basically an advanced form of targeting. When you animate a target item so that the end of a chain of parented items is always pointing at it, that's IK. Remember the camera you had targeting the Null object earlier in this chapter? As the object moved along its motion path, the camera would rotate to continue pointing at it. IK works in a similar manner, but instead of a single item pointing at the target, the end of a "chain" of parented items points at the target. The actual IK comes into play if the item at the end of the parented chain can't point at the target; then the items further back in the chain will rotate so that it can.

The best way to illustrate is with your arm. Pick up a pencil and hold it in front of your face. Now think of the pencil you picked up as your arm's IK goal. As you lifted it toward your face, your hand and arm followed, and in order for you to examine it closely and in the proper orientation, you had to bend your elbow and wrist. Your hand and the bones of your forearm and upper arm are like the parented items that make up an IK chain.

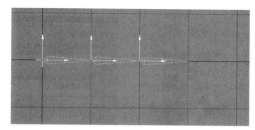

Figure 10.56 This is a simple chain of parented items.

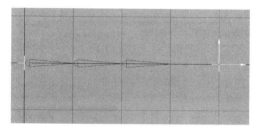

Figure 10.57 Create the goal object and position it in relation to the end of the chain.

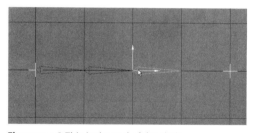

Figure 10.58 This is the end of the chain.

To create an IK chain:

1. From the View pull-down menu in the upper left corner of the Layout Viewport, choose the Right (ZY) view.

2. Select the Items tab to display new options in the toolbar.

3. Click Null in the Add tool group of the toolbar and name the new object IK-Chain.

4. Select the Setup tab to change the toolbar options.

5. Click Bone in the Add tool group of the toolbar or press $=$ to add a bone to IK-Chain.

6. When the Bone Name dialog appears, name the bone Upper-Arm and press (Enter) to accept it.

7. Press $=$ to add a child bone to Upper-Arm and name it Lower-Arm.

8. Press $=$ again to add a child bone to Lower-Arm and name it Hand.

   You should end up with a chain of bones like the one in **Figure 10.56**.

9. Repeat Step 3 and name the new Null object Arm-Goal.

10. Select the Modify tab, and then click Move in the Translate tool group of the toolbar or press (t) and drag Arm-Goal to 4m on the Z axis, which will position it at the end of the bone chain (**Figure 10.57**).

11. Click the Hand bone to select it in the Layout Viewport (**Figure 10.58**).

continues on next page

WORKING WITH INVERSE KINEMATICS

12. Select the Setup tab, and then click Motion Options in the Motions tool group of the toolbar or press m to open the Motion Options panel.

13. From the Goal Object pull-down menu, choose Arm-Goal (**Figure 10.59**).

All of the IK motion options become active and Layout draws a dashed blue line between Arm-Goal and the pivot point of Hand as well as a solid blue line from Arm-Goal to IK-Chain (**Figure 10.60**). The solid blue line indicates which chain of objects the goal belongs to, and the dashed blue line indicates the direction of the goal from the end of the chain.

14. In the Motion Options panel, check the Full-time IK check box (**Figure 10.61**).

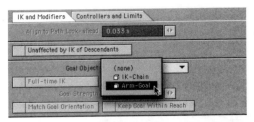

Figure 10.59 Select Arm-Goal as the goal item for the end of the chain.

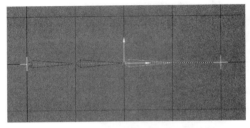

Figure 10.60 Layout draws visual indicators so you won't lose track of which goal item belongs to which IK chain.

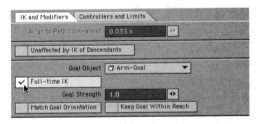

Figure 10.61 Full-Time IK makes Layout constantly calculate and update your IK chains.

WORKING WITH INVERSE KINEMATICS

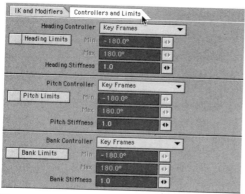

Figure 10.62 Click the Controllers and Limits tab to find the rotational controllers and limits.

Figure 10.63 You want Inverse Kinematics to control the pitch of this item.

15. Select the Controllers and Limits tab in the middle of the panel to display new options (**Figure 10.62**).

16. From the Pitch Controller pull-down menu, choose Inverse Kinematics (**Figure 10.63**).

17. Click Lower-Arm in the Layout Viewport. The Motion Options panel automatically updates to display the options for the new item (**Figure 10.64**).

18. Repeat Step 15 for Lower-Arm.

19. Click Upper-Arm in the Layout Viewport.

20. Repeat Step 15 for Upper-Arm, and then close the Motion Options panel.

21. Click the Arm-Goal Null object in the Layout Viewport.

continues on next page

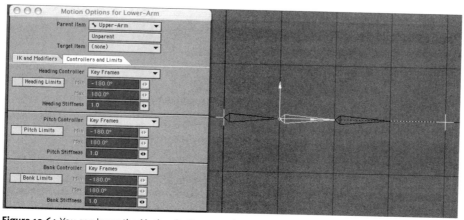

Figure 10.64 You can leave the Motion Options panel open and select the next item whose options you want to adjust.

WORKING WITH INVERSE KINEMATICS

22. Click the green tool handle and drag the `Arm-Goal` object up and down on the Y axis.

The base of the bone chain bends so that Hand always points at Arm-Goal (**Figure 10.65**).

23. Drag the `Arm-Goal` object to 500mm on the Y axis.

24. Click the blue tool handle and drag the `Arm-Goal` object to 600mm on the Z axis.

The closer `Arm-Goal` gets to `IK-Chain`, the more `Upper-Arm` and `Lower-Arm` have to rotate in order for Hand to continue pointing at it (**10.66**).

25. From the File pull-down menu, choose Save > Save Scene or press ⒮ to open the Save Scene dialog.

26. Name the scene `IK-Rig.lws` and click OK or press ⏎ Enter to save it.

We'll use this setup for the next few exercises.

✔ Tip

■ The more IK chains you have in a scene, the more computation required. With Full-Time IK active, Layout will constantly calculate and update all IK chains in the scene even if you aren't working with them. If Layout starts to slow down you can turn off the Full-Time IK option so that Layout will only calculate the IK for the chain you are directly working with. However, there will be situations where disabling this option will create erratic results with your IK setup and you will want to reenable this feature.

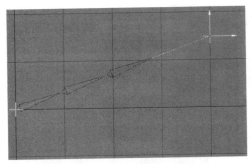

Figure 10.65 As you drag the goal item, the IK chain always points at it.

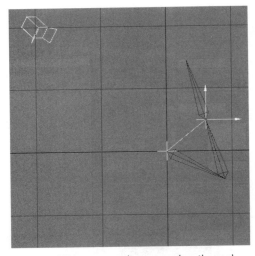

Figure 10.66 You can see that as you drag the goal beyond the normal reach of the end of the chain, the other items in the chain change pitch so the end can still point at the goal.

Figure 10.67 This option will turn your IK goal into an animation handle of sorts.

Keeping the goal within reach

Now that you have a basic understanding of how IK works, let's take a look at some of the different IK-related options. We focus only on the major IK options, as a more in-depth look at IK and its applications in character animation is beyond the scope of this book.

When you're working with multiple IK chains in a scene, having all of those goal objects floating around can become a bit confusing. The dashed blue line is a good indicator of which goal belongs to which IK chain, but even that can get a little overwhelming when you have multiple chains and goals.

In order to alleviate some of the clutter, you can turn on Keep Goal Within Reach in the Motion Options panel for the item at the end of the chain. This will snap the goal to the pivot point of the end item and keep it there. Some animators prefer to work this way because it turns the goal into a sort of animation handle.

To use Keep Goal Within Reach:

1. Load the IK-Rig.lws scene from the previous set of steps into Layout.

2. Select the Hand bone in the Layout Viewport.

3. Select the Setup tab, and then click Motion Options or press (m) to open the Motion Options panel.

4. Check the Keep Goal Within Reach check box and close the Motion Options panel.
   Arm-Goal snaps to the pivot point of Hand (**Figure 10.67**).

5. Click the Arm-Goal object in the Layout Viewport.

continues on next page

6. Click and drag anywhere in the Layout Viewport.

No matter where you move the mouse, the Arm-Goal object will not move from the pivot point of Hand (**Figure 10.68**). Working this way is much more like using a handle for animating IK-Chain.

Matching goal orientation

Remember when you picked up that pencil and examined it as a demonstration of IK? We mentioned that you had to bend your wrist to orient the pencil properly for examination. In Layout, you can have the end item in the chain match the orientation of the goal item. This is extremely useful for easily animating a wrist bending to match the orientation of an item the character picked up, for example, or the head of a snake that stays at one angle while tracking its prey. There are many applications for this option, and you'll find it's a great timesaver for performing seemingly simple animation operations that are actually complex.

To use Match Goal Orientation:

1. Load the IK-Rig.lws scene into Layout.

2. Click the Hand bone in the Layout Viewport.

3. Select the Setup tab, and then click Motion Options or press m to open the Motion Options panel.

4. Check the Match Goal Orientation check box (**Figure 10.69**).

5. Click Arm-Goal in the Layout Viewport.

6. Click the green tool handle and move Arm-Goal up and down on the Y axis.
Notice how Hand stays level as it follows Arm-Goal (**Figure 10.70**).

7. Click Rotate in the toolbar or press y.

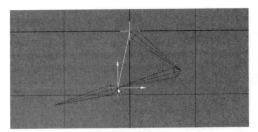

Figure 10.68 The goal is stuck to the pivot point of the Hand bone.

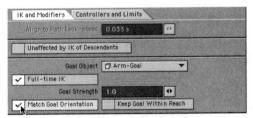

Figure 10.69 Match Goal Orientation keeps the rotation of the chain's end the same as that of the goal object.

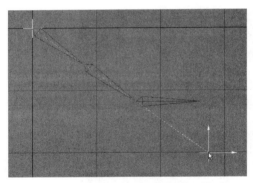

Figure 10.70 As you move the goal, the Hand bone stays level instead of rotating to point at the goal.

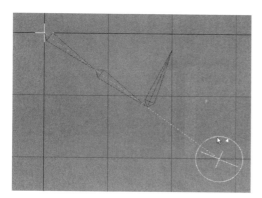

Figure 10.71 If you rotate the goal, you'll see that Hand rotates with it.

Figure 10.72 Activate Pitch Limits for the item.

8. Click the green tool handle and rotate Arm-Goal on the Pitch axis.

As Arm-Goal rotates, Hand rotates on the Pitch axis as well to orient itself to its goal (**Figure 10.71**).

✔ Tip

■ If the end of your IK chain is not behaving as expected with Match Goal Orientation, a quick fix is to parent the goal to the end item in the IK chain, enable Parent in Place and then unparent the goal item. This effectively aligns the two items together which should resolve the problem.

Setting rotational constraints

You probably noticed as you were dragging the goal around that if you moved it far enough down on the Y axis, the lower arm bone would hyperextend to follow it. That isn't a very realistic motion for an arm. Each joint on your arm has a specific range of motion, a certain angle beyond which it cannot bend without breaking. You can also define these ranges of rotation in LightWave.

To set rotational constraints:

1. Load the IK-Rig.lws scene into Layout.

2. Click the Lower-Arm bone in the Layout Viewport.

3. Select the Modify tab, and then click Rotate in the Rotate tool group of the toolbar or press ⓨ.

4. Select the Setup tab, and then click Motion Options in the Motions tool group of the toolbar or press ⓜ to open the Motion Options panel.

5. Click the Controllers and Limits tab and check the Pitch Limits check box to activate rotational limits on the Pitch axis (**Figure 10.72**).

continues on next page

6. Type **–150** in the Min input field and **4** in the Max input field to define the minimum and maximum angles that this item may rotate on the pitch.

In **Figure 10.73**, notice that the green rotational disc around Lower-Arm becomes shaded, showing you the rotational limits on that axis. The unshaded portion is the allowed range of rotation.

7. Click `Upper-Arm` in the Layout Viewport and the Motion Options panel will update appropriately.

8. Repeat Step 5 for `Upper-Arm`.

9. Type **–90** in the Min input field and **100** in the Max input field.

Once again, you've defined the minimum and maximum rotational angles for the Pitch axis and Layout displays the shaded rotational circle (**Figure 10.74**).

10. Click `Arm-Goal` in the Layout Viewport.

11. Select the Modify tab, and then click Move in the Translate tool group of the toolbar or press $\boxed{t}$.

12. Drag `Arm-Goal` around the Viewport.

Attempt to move it in a 180-degree arc around the `IK-Chain Null` object and hyperextend the Lower-Arm bone. You'll find you can't make the items rotate beyond the rotational limits you set for each of them (**Figures 10.75** and **10.76**).

✔ Tip

■ Rotational limits aren't just for IK. You can set rotational limits for any item in Layout to Constrain Movement for regular targeting, parenting, and manual rotation.

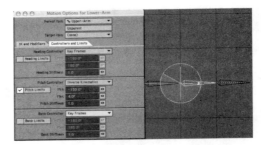

Figure 10.73 You can set the minimum and maximum rotation limits by typing in the numeric field or by using the mini-slider.

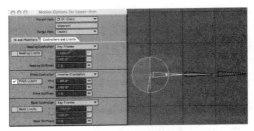

Figure 10.74 Layout shades the rotation handles to show just how far you can rotate your item.

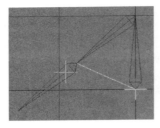

Figure 10.75 Drag the goal up and back until you hit the maximum limits.

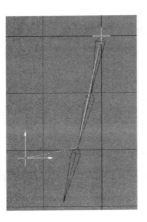

Figure 10.76 Drag the goal down and back until you hit the minimum limits.

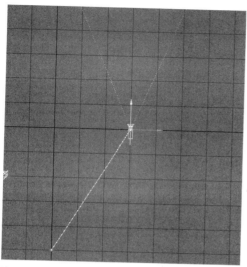

Figure 10.77 Create a keyframe for the camera at frame 30.

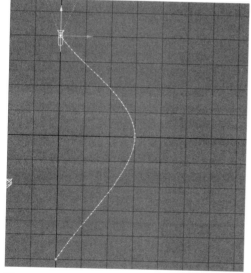

Figure 10.78 Create a keyframe for the camera at frame 60 to complete the motion path.

Using the Motion Options

You may have noticed there are a few different options in the Pitch Controller pull-down menu. We just covered Inverse Kinematics, and Key Frames is the default motion behavior. This simply tells the item to use your keyframe data for the rotation on that channel. The other two options—Align to Path and Point at Target—fulfill some special animation needs.

To use Align to Path:

1. Click the camera in the Layout Viewport.

2. From the View pull-down menu, choose the Top (XZ) View.

3. Go to frame 30 of the scene.

4. Select the Modify tab, and then click Move or press ⏺ and drag the camera to 0m on the Z axis and 3m on the X axis (**Figure 10.77**).

5. Go to frame 60 of the scene.

6. Drag the camera to 4m on the Z axis and 0m on the X axis (**Figure 10.78**).

   You should now have a nicely curved motion path.

continues on next page

7. Click the play button below the frame slider to preview the animation.

The camera continually faces the same direction as it moves along its path (**Figure 10.79**). Suppose this motion path moved through a tunnel. You'd be seeing the tunnel wall for the majority of the animation! To fix this you can use the Align to Path rotational controller.

8. Select the Setup tab, and then click Motion Options in the Motions tool group of the toolbar or press m to open the Motion Options panel.

9. Select the Controllers and Limits tab.

10. From the Heading Controller pull-down menu, choose Align to Path (**Figure 10.80**).

The camera now rotates to look down the path it's traveling (**Figure 10.81**).

✔ Tip

■ Align to Path works relative to the positive Z axis of your object. Whatever portion of the object was modeled to face the positive Z axis will be used to point down the path. For example, if you used Align to Path on a car modeled with the hood facing the positive X axis, it would travel down the motion path sideways.

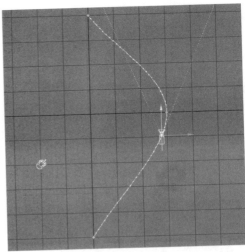

Figure 10.79 As the camera moves along the path its heading remains 0 degrees on the Heading axis.

Figure 10.80 The Align to Path rotation controller makes the item "look down" the motion path on the Heading axis.

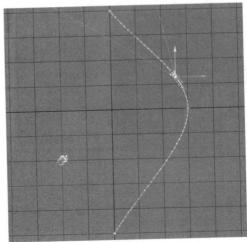

Figure 10.81 The camera now rotates as it moves along the motion path.

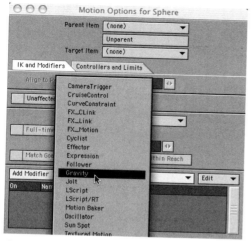

Figure 10.82 Add the Gravity motion modifier to the sphere.

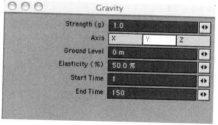

Figure 10.83 Adjust the sphere's elasticity to 50 percent so the bounce will dissipate over time and set the End Time to match that of your scene.

✔ Tip

- In addition to the motion modifiers included with LightWave 3D, there are scores of them available for download from the Internet and for purchase from third-party developers. For a complete list and description of the motion modifiers included with LightWave 3D, please refer to the LightWave 3D User's Manual.

Working with Motion Modifiers

Earlier, we used a channel modifier to augment the Y axis motion curve of an object. Channel modifiers are limited to functioning on a single channel, meaning if you want to affect all axes of an item's motion you need to apply a channel modifier to each one, which can be very time consuming. Fortunately, there's a special type of modifier—a Motion Modifier—that simultaneously works on all axes of an item's motion.

As a simple example, we'll use the bouncing ball again.

To use motion modifiers:

1. Create and load a sphere into Layout.
2. Set the frame slider end-frame to 150.
3. Select the Modify tab, and then click Move in the Translate tool group of the toolbar or press ⊤ and drag the sphere to 2m on the Y axis.
4. Select the Setup tab, and then click Motion Options in the Motions tool group of the toolbar or press ⓜ to open the Motion Options panel.
5. From the Add Modifier pull-down menu, choose Gravity (**Figure 10.82**).

   You should now see Gravity in the hierarchical list below the Add Modifier menu.
6. Double-click Gravity in the list to open the Gravity properties panel.
7. Change the Elasticity (%) value to 50 and the End Time to 150, so it matches the length of the animation (**Figure 10.83**).
8. Close the Gravity properties panel.
9. Click the play button below the frame slider to preview the animation.

   The motion modifier takes over the animation chore for you and the sphere falls to the ground, bouncing lower each time, until it comes to rest.

Working with Coordinate Systems

Sometimes an item will appear to move abnormally as you animate it. One such instance is when an item is in *gimbal lock*. This occurs when two or more of an item's rotational axes become aligned and cannot be broken. For example, if you rotate an item on its Bank axis, it appears to be rotating on its Heading axis, and vice versa. This happens all too frequently when animating characters.

Layout addresses this problem by offering you the following alternate coordinate systems:

World: The item's rotational orientation is always in relation to the Layout grid.

Parent: The item's rotational orientation is always in relation to that of its parent item. This is the default coordinate system applied to each new item you add to a Layout scene.

Local: The item's rotation orientation is always in relation to itself.

You can change the coordinate system for each item, giving you maximum flexibility in controlling their movement behavior. The following example shows how we learned to stop worrying and love gimbal lock.

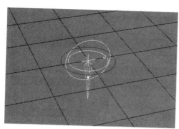

Figure 10.84 Rotate Leg 90 degrees on the Pitch axis.

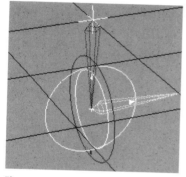

Figure 10.85 Rotate Foot –90 degrees on the Pitch axis and the Bank and Heading axes have become one. Rotating one will rotate the other. This is gimbal lock.

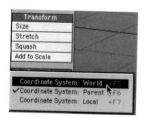

Figure 10.86 Switch the Leg bone to the World coordinate system.

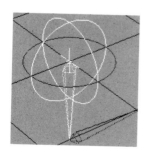

Figure 10.87 The rotational rings are now back in their proper orientation.

To change coordinate systems:

1. Select the Items tab to display new options in the toolbar.

2. Click Null in the Add tool group of the toolbar, and name the new object Gimbal-Lock.

3. Press = to add a bone to Gimbal-Lock, and name it Leg.

4. Select the Modify tab, and then click Rotate in the Rotate tool group of the toolbar or press y and rotate Leg to 90 on the Pitch axis (**Figure 10.84**).

5. Press = to add a child bone to Leg, and name it Foot.

6. Rotate Foot to –90 on the Pitch axis.

    You should already see the problem: The red (H) and blue (B) rotational rings are aligned on each bone (**Figure 10.85**).

7. Click Leg in the Layout Viewport.

8. Right-click and drag Leg in the Layout Viewport to rotate it on the Bank axis.

    It rotates left to right as if it were the Heading axis. This is gimbal lock.

9. From the Coord System pull-down menu in the General tool group of the toolbar, choose Coordinate System: World (**Figure 10.86**).

    The rotational rings snap back into orientation with the world (**Figure 10.87**).

10. Repeat Step 8.

    This time Leg rotates about the Bank axis properly.

There are other situations in which you may wish to use an alternate coordinate system for your animation, too. For example, if you wanted to reorient which way is up for an item so you could animate it at an angle. Choosing the Local coordinate system and reorienting the item's rotational axis accomplishes this.

To use the Local coordinate system:

1. From the Coord System pull-down menu in the General tool group of the toolbar, choose Coordinate System: Parent.

2. Click the camera to select it in the Layout Viewport.

3. From the View pull-down menu, choose the Right (ZY) view.

4. Click Rotate in the Rotate tool group of the toolbar or press $\boxed{y}$.

5. Rotate the camera by 25 degrees on the Pitch axis (**Figure 10.88**).

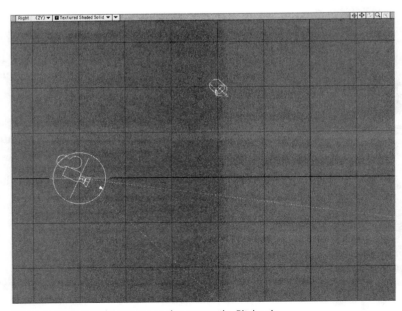

Figure 10.88 Rotate the camera 25 degrees on the Pitch axis.

WORKING WITH COORDINATE SYSTEMS

Figure 10.89 Switch the camera to the Local coordinate system.

6. Click Move in the Translate tool group of the toolbar or press $\boxed{t}$.

7. From the Coord System pull-down menu in the General tool group of the toolbar, choose Coordinate System: Local (**Figure 10.89**).

The X, Y, and Z axes are all realigned by 25 degrees along the Pitch axis, effectively redefining their directions (**Figure 10.90**).

8. Click the green tool handle and move the camera along the Y axis.

Movement on the Y axis is no longer up and down in relation to the world. It's at an angle along the world Y and Z coordinates.

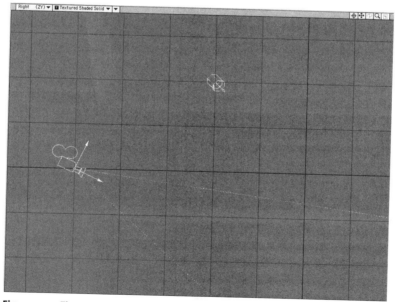

Figure 10.90 The movement axes are now based on the new orientation of the camera.

WORKING WITH COORDINATE SYSTEMS

CREATING SPECIAL EFFECTS

During the course of your work, at some time you're bound to need an explosion, falling snow or rain, smoke, or even the ability to make your rendered images negative. LightWave has an assortment of special effects tools that can make stylistic changes to your rendered images or create environments, smoke, flowing water, sparks, glowing objects, and the like.

This chapter gives you a basic understanding of LightWave's special effects tools, where to find them, and when to employ them.

Changing the Backdrop

The *backdrop* is what Layout renders when there are no objects or effects at a given location on the screen. By default, Layout uses the black backdrop color, but you can change it to suit your needs.

To change the backdrop color:

1. Select Backdrop Options from the Window pull-down in the toolbar or press Ctrl+F5 to open the Backdrop tab of the Effects panel (**Figure 11.1**).

2. Click and drag the red Backdrop Color component to the right until it reads 140 (**Figure 11.2**).

   Repeat for the green and blue components, which will leave you with a gray backdrop (**Figure 11.3**).

   or

   Click the color swatch to the right of the color values to open the color picker (**Figure 11.4**), then click the color well to choose a backdrop color and click OK or press Enter.

✔ Tip

■ If you prefer to have a gradient backdrop, click the Gradient Backdrop button, then choose the colors for the gradient.

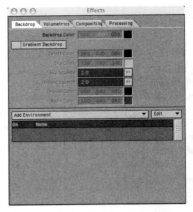

Figure 11.1 In the Backdrop tab of the Effects panel, you can apply effects related to the render backdrop.

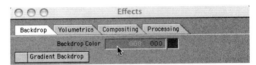

Figure 11.2 You can click directly on the color components and drag them to adjust their values.

Figure 11.3 Set the green and blue color components to 140 as well.

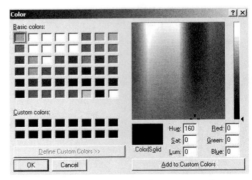

Figure 11.4 Click the color swatch next to a color control to open the color picker.

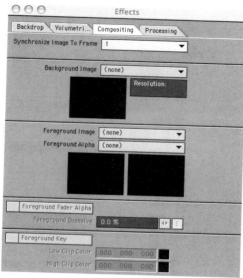

Figure 11.5 In the Compositing tab, you can set the backdrop and foreground images for your scene.

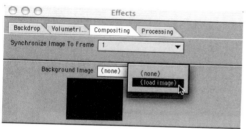

Figure 11.6 You can load an image directly through the Image pull-down menus in Layout so you don't have to open the Image Editor each time.

Figure 11.7 You can use any of the supported image file types as a backdrop image.

Using a backdrop image

You can add realism to your scene by replacing the backdrop color with an image. This is especially useful when you're creating scenes in which your objects appear to interact with a real environment, for example, a character walking through a room or a car driving down a road.

To use a backdrop image:

1. Select Compositing Options from the Window pull-down in the toolbar or press [Ctrl]+[F7] to open the Compositing tab of the Effects panel (**Figure 11.5**).

2. From the Background Image pull-down menu, select "(load image)" (**Figure 11.6**).

3. When the Load Image dialog appears, click an image from your hard drive that you would like to place in the background (**Figure 11.7**).

continues on next page

CHANGING THE BACKDROP

4. Click Open to load the backdrop image and close the dialog.

The resolution of the image you selected is displayed in the info window, and a thumbnail is displayed below the pull-down menu (**Figure 11.8**).

✔ Tip

■ You can use an image sequence or movie file as a backdrop image, as well.

Using a backdrop environment

Rather than using a solid backdrop color or a backdrop image, you may choose to use a backdrop environment. There are currently three different environment tools included with LightWave.

◆ **Texture Environment:** This environment tool uses the Texture Editor, which gives you the flexibility of using textures, gradients, and procedural textures to create an environment. The Texture Editor is covered in detail in Chapter 12, "Surfaces and Textures."

◆ **Image World:** This environment tool uses high dynamic range images (HDRI) both as the backdrop and as a source of illumination. Image World is covered in Chapter 13, "Rendering Your Scene."

◆ **SkyTracer2:** This environment tool can create both daytime and nighttime skies. It's indispensable for adding outdoor environments to your scenes.

To add a backdrop environment:

1. Select Backdrop Options from the Window pull-down in the toolbar or press Ctrl+F5 to open the Backdrop tab of the Effects panel.

2. From the Add Environment pull-down menu, select an environment tool (**Figure 11.9**).

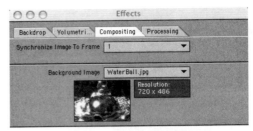

Figure 11.8 A thumbnail of the image and its size information are displayed below the Backdrop Image pull-down menu.

Figure 11.9 Select SkyTracer2 from the Add Environment pull-down menu.

CHANGING THE BACKDROP

Figure 11.10 You can preview some the render-oriented effects in Viper.

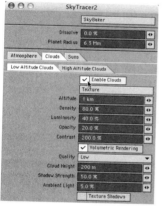

Figure 11.11 You can create a large selection of different cloud types with SkyTracer2. The clouds are off by default and must be enabled.

Figure 11.12 Viper updates, showing changes as you make them.

Using SkyTracer2

An excellent way to create either a still or animated sky quickly and easily is to use SkyTracer2. You can create skies with billowing clouds like on Earth, or you can modify the atmosphere parameters to create skies on alien worlds. You can even adjust the sun or moon over time to create time-lapse effects. You should note, however that SkyTracer2's atmospheric and cloud effects are based on real physics, so render speed depends on the complexity of the sky you create.

To create a simple sky:

1. Follow the preceding procedure, "To add a backdrop environment," and choose SkyTracer2.

2. Select the Render tab to display new options, and then click Viper in the Utilities tool group of the toolbar to open the Versatile Interactive Preview Renderer (**Figure 11.10**).

3. In the Effects panel, double-click SkyTracer2 in the list below the Add Environment pull-down menu to open the SkyTracer2 properties panel.

4. Select the Clouds tab, and then click the Low Altitude Clouds tab and check the Enable Clouds check box (**Figure 11.11**).

5. Watch the Viper panel to see the clouds added to your sky (**Figure 11.12**).

continues on next page

CHANGING THE BACKDROP

6. In the SkyTracer2 properties panel, click the High Altitude Clouds tab, and check the Enable Clouds check box again.

In Viper you'll see a light layer of clouds added above the ones that were already there (**Figure 11.13**).

7. Close the SkyTracer2 and Viper panels.

8. Press F9 to generate a preview render of your sky (**Figure 11.14**).

✔ Tip

■ There are many different parameters you can use to alter the look of your sky, and covering all of them is well beyond the scope of this book. Refer to the LightWave 3D User's Manual to learn what the various parameters do to a SkyTracer2 sky.

Figure 11.13 Now that you've set up separate layers of clouds at two different altitudes, you can see the high altitude cloud layers in Viper.

Figure 11.14 Viper does an excellent job of previewing your effects, usually identical to how the effect will look in your final render.

CHANGING THE BACKDROP

Creating Particle Effects

Particle effects are used to simulate things like dust, sparks, or water spray that require a multitude of tiny individual objects or particles. To create these effects in your scene, use the Particle tools.

The particles themselves are non-rendering points. For them to show up in your scenes, they must be associated with either a partigon (a particle polygon type) or hypervoxels (covered later in this chapter).

Particle FX has four separate components:

◆ **Emitter:** This tool makes the object it's applied to emit particles.

◆ **Collision:** This tool causes particles from an Emitter to collide with the object that it's applied to. For example, you would use this to make particles fill a cup object.

◆ **Gravity:** This tool simulates gravity, affecting either the entire scene or only those particles that fall within its influence range. Without gravity, your particles simply move in one direction at a constant speed.

◆ **Wind:** This tool simulates gusts of wind blowing particles from an Emitter. For example, wind could catch snow particles, blowing flurries across the scene.

The following procedures walk you through creating a simple particle animation.

To create a particle emitter:

1. Select the Items tab to display new toolbar options.

2. Click Add Null in the toolbar to open the Null Object Name dialog.

3. Name the Null object Emitter and then click OK or press Enter.

4. Click the Item Properties button below the frame slider or press p to open the Item Properties panel for Emitter.

5. Select the Dynamics tab, and then select Emitter from the Add Dynamic pull-down menu.

6. Double click Emitter 3 Particles in the list to open the Emitter properties.

7. Move the Item properties panel to the side so you can see Emitter in the Layout viewport (**Figure 11.15**).

8. In the frame slider's end frame input field, type 150, then press Enter to extend the length of the scene.

9. Click the play button below the frame slider.

10. In the Generator Size X input field, type 200mm, then press Enter to size the emitter on that axis (**Figure 11.16**).

11. Repeat Step 10 for the Y and Z input fields to resize Emitter to be a small box (**Figure 11.17**).

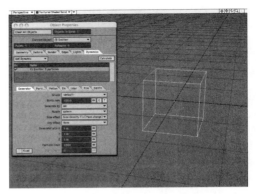

Figure 11.15 You can keep the Item Properties panel open so you can see the results of adjusting parameters in the Layout Viewport(s).

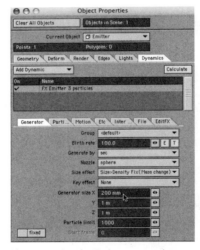

Figure 11.16 In the Emitter properties, set up the general attributes and motions of your particles. Resizing the emitter allows you to define the beginning size of the particle group.

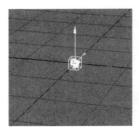

Figure 11.17 Resize the emitter until it's a small box.

CREATING PARTICLE EFFECTS

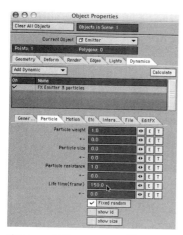

Figure 11.18 You can control how long each particle is displayed after it's emitted.

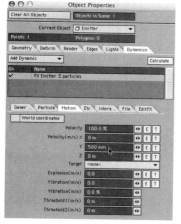

Figure 11.19 A positive value makes the particles travel along the positive axis, while a negative value makes them travel along the negative axis.

Figure 11.20 The Explosion parameter causes the particles to spread out.

12. Select the Particle tab to display the Particle options.

13. In the Life time(frame) input field, type 150, so each particle will last 150 frames (**Figure 11.18**).

14. Select the Motion tab to access the Motion options for Emitter.

15. In the Vector(m/s) Y input field, type 500mm, then press [Enter] (**Figure 11.19**). This gives the particles a little upward motion.

16. In the Explosion(m/s) input field, type 2, then press [Enter]. This makes the particles spread out as they move upward (**Figure 11.20**).

CREATING PARTICLE EFFECTS

301

To add gravity:

1. Follow Steps 1–4 in the previous procedure, "To create a particle emitter," naming the Null object Gravity.

2. From the Add Dynamics pull-down
   menu, select Gravity.

3. Double-click Gravity in the list to open
   the FX_Gravity properties.

4. Move the Item properties panel to the
   side so you can see Gravity in the Layout
   viewport.

5. From the Falloff Mode pull-down menu,
   select OFF, so the gravity affects the
   whole scene (**Figure 11.21**).

6. In the Gravity(m/s^2) Y input field,
   type –1, then press Enter, so that gravity
   will pull the particles downward after
   they're emitted (**Figure 11.22**).

To add a collision plane:

1. Follow Steps 1–4 from the "To create a
   particle emitter" procedure, naming the
   Null object Collision.

2. From the Add Dynamics pull-down
   menu, select Collision.

3. Double-click Collision in the list to
   open the Collision properties.

4. Move the Item properties panel to the
   side so you can see Collision in the
   Layout viewport.

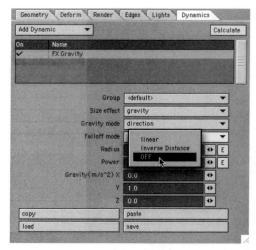

Figure 11.21 Set the Falloff Mode to Off and all emitters in the group will be affected by the gravity. Leave it at Linear and the gravity will affect only the particles that pass into its influence area.

Figure 11.22 A negative value in the Gravity(m/s^2) field makes the particles fall, while a positive value makes them rise.

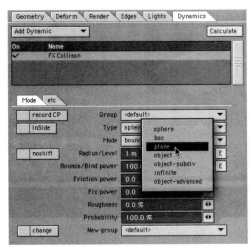

Figure 11.23 Use Collision to make particles interact with objects in the scene. Choose the plane collision type to simulate a flat surface, such as a tabletop.

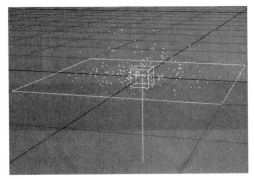

Figure 11.24 The particles can't travel through the plane.

5. From the Type pull-down menu, select Plane (**Figure 11.23**).

6. In the Radius/Level input field, type 0, then press [Enter] to lower the collision plane to the origin of Collision (currently at 0 m on the Y axis).

The particles stop when they hit the plane (**Figure 11.24**).

✔ Tip

■ You'll notice as you perform Step 6 above that the word *Bounce* appears on the collision plane. This tells you that the collision mode is currently set to Bounce. This label is updated if you change the mode, so you always know the collision mode, whether the Collision properties panel is open or not.

To add wind:

1. Follow Steps 1–4 from the "To create a particle emitter" procedure, naming the Null object Wind.

2. From the Add Dymamics pull-down menu, select Wind.

3. Click the pause button below the frame slider.

4. Drag the frame slider to frame 0 of the animation.

5. Select the Modify tab in Layout, and then click Stretch from the Transform tool group in the toolbar.

6. Right-click and drag the mouse upward to stretch Wind to 3.5 on the Y axis.

7. Create a keyframe for Wind at frame 0.

8. Click the play button below the frame slider.

9. Double-click Wind in the list to open the FX_Wind properties.

continues on next page

CREATING PARTICLE EFFECTS

10. Move the Item properties panel to the side so you can see Wind in the Layout viewport.

11. From the Wind mode pull-down menu, select "rotation(y)" (**Figure 11.25**).

12. Type 300mm in the Radius input field and press Enter to change the Wind effect radius (**Figure 11.26**).

13. Type 3000 in the Spiral Amount input field and press Enter to make the particles swirl around (**Figure 11.27**).

✔ Tips

- You can animate the position and size of the effect for each Particle tool by animating the scale and position of the items they're attached to.

- The effect combinations possible with Particle are virtually endless. Review the parameters for each Particle tool in the LightWave 3D User's Manual and seek out tutorials online at www.newtek.com, www.luxology.net, and www.flay.com.

- Use the FX_Linker (select the Utilities tab in the Layout interface and select it from the Additional pull-down menu in the Plugins tool group) to replace the individual particles with objects that have motions. This is good for creating flocks of birds, swarms of bees, rolling rocks, or even falling snowflakes.

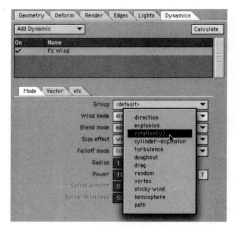

Figure 11.25 Use Wind to create wind effects. The Rotation(y) mode makes the particles swirl around the Y axis.

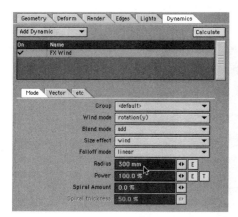

Figure 11.26 Change the wind's influence area by changing its radius.

Figure 11.27 The higher the spiral amount, the more the particles will swirl about.

CREATING PARTICLE EFFECTS

Figure 11.28 The object as it looks before basic fog is applied.

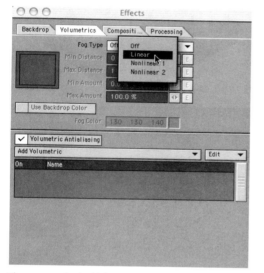

Figure 11.29 In the Volumetrics tab, apply effects like fog and HyperVoxels. The linear mode causes the fog to fall straight off. Nonlinear 1 and Nonlinear 2 create nonuniform fog effects.

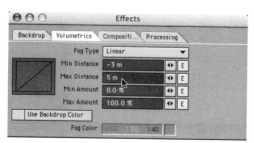

Figure 11.30 The Min and Max Distances are the beginning and end positions of your fog.

Using Fog in Your Scenes

Sometimes you may want to create a fog effect in your scenes, so objects fade away the farther they are from the camera. LightWave's fog parameters allow you to specify the type, beginning and end limits, and color used to fade out objects as they move further from the camera. However, fog does not affect the backdrop, so it won't create a realistic-looking fog. In the following procedure, we leave the backdrop color as the default black to illustrate this point.

To apply basic fog:

1. Select the Items tab, and then click Object from the Load tool group in the toolbar or press ⊞ to open the Load Object dialog.

2. From your hard drive, select an object to load and click Open.

3. Press F9 to render your object (**Figure 11.28**).

4. After your frame is rendered, click Abort or press Esc to close the Render Status window.

5. Select Volumetric and Fog Options from the Window pull-down menu in the toolbar or press Ctrl+F6 to open the Volumetrics tab of the Effects panel.

6. From the Fog Type pull-down menu, select Linear (**Figure 11.29**).

   The fog controls now become active.

8. In the Min Distance input field, type –3m, and then press Enter to set the beginning of the fog (**Figure 11.30**).

continues on next page

9. In the Max Distance input field, type 5m, and then press (Enter) to set the end of the fog.

10. Press (F9) to perform a test render (**Figure 11.31**).

✔ Tip

- You can preview the fog effect in the Layout viewports in one of two ways. The first is to enable the Show Fog Circles option in the display tab of the Layout preferences panel. This will draw two circles representing the minimum and maximum distances for the fog. The second is to switch to the camera view and enable the OpenGL Fog option in the display tab of the layout preferences panel.

If you want a more realistic fog effect, use the Ground Fog volumetric tool. This creates a thick, wispy fog that affects the backdrop as well as the objects in your scene. Instead of specifying a distance from the camera, you set the height of the fog effect as if it were resting on the ground.

To apply ground fog:

1. Repeat Steps 1–6 of the previous procedure, "To apply basic fog."

2. From the Add Volumetric pull-down menu, select Ground Fog (**Figure 11.32**).

3. Double-click "Bottom: –4.000000 Top: 0.000000" in the list below the pull-down menu to open the Ground Fog properties panel (**Figure 11.33**).

Figure 11.31 This is the object after applying basic fog. Notice that the backdrop isn't affected, but the object has been tinted with the fog color.

Figure 11.32 Use the Add Volumetric pull-down menu to add volumetric effects.

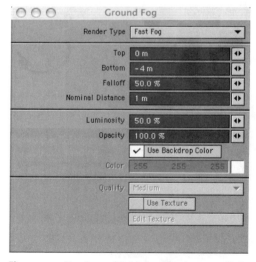

Figure 11.33 Use Ground Fog to create a more realistic effect.

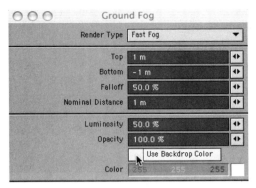

Figure 11.34 The Use Backdrop Color option makes the fog match the current backdrop color.

Figure 11.35 The object as it looks after applying Ground Fog.

4. In the Top input field, type 1m, and press [Enter] to set the top boundary of the fog effect.

5. In the Bottom input field, type –1m, and press [Enter] to set the bottom boundary of the fog effect.

6. Uncheck the Use Backdrop Color check box (**Figure 11.34**).

7. Press [F9] to perform a test render (**Figure 11.35**).

Ground Fog Types

You have two choices in the Render Type pull-down menu of the Ground Fog properties panel.

◆ **Fast Fog:** This is a quick-rendering fog whose thickness doesn't vary. Think of it as the volumetric version of basic fog, and use it when you want a fast but somewhat realistic fog effect.

◆ **Raymarcher:** This fog type calculates physically accurate fog. You can use the Texture Editor to combine gradients, images, and procedurals to break up the look of the fog and animate the wisps over time. This is computationally intensive and will lengthen your render times.

Making Your Objects Glow

In the real world you sometimes see a halo effect around luminous items, as the light they emit is scattered by the atmosphere around them. Anything from the LED in your bedside clock to a car's taillights may exhibit this, and LightWave provides a post-process effect that simulates it. Because this is a post-process effect, however, it isn't a true volumetric glow, just a 2D glow composited on top of the rendered image.

To make a surface glow

1. Select the Items tab, and then click Object from the Load tool group in the toolbar or press +.

2. When the Load Object dialog appears, select an object to load and click Open.

3. Click Surface Editor in the toolbar or press Ctrl+F3 to open the Surface Editor (**Figure 11.36**).

4. In the surface list, select the surface that you want to glow (**Figure 11.37**).

5. Select the Advanced tab to display the advanced surface properties (see Chapter 12).

6. In the Glow Intensity input field, type the percentage of the overall glow effect that you want this surface to use.

   For the example, we use 100% (**Figure 11.38**).

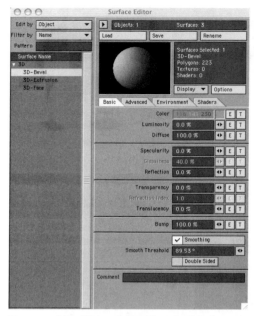

Figure 11.36 Modify how your objects look in the Surface Editor.

Figure 11.37 Choose the surface you want to work with from the list.

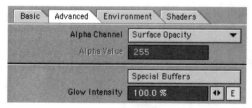

Figure 11.38 The Glow Intensity field lets you specify how much of the global glow value is applied to each surface in your object.

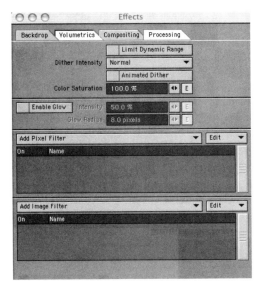

Figure 11.39 Configure post-render effects in the Processing tab.

Figure 11.40 Changing the parameters here will affect every surface with a glow intensity in the scene.

Figure 11.41 Here's your glow effect.

7. Close the Surface Editor.

8. Select Image Processing from the Window pull-down menu in the toolbar or press ⌈Ctrl⌉+⌈F8⌉ to open the Processing tab of the Effects panel (**Figure 11.39**).

9. Check the Enable Glow check box and type 200 in the Intensity input field and 24 in the Glow Radius input field (**Figure 11.40**).

Remember that the surface glow intensity is relative to the global glow intensity. If the global glow is 60 percent and the surface glow is 25 percent, then the actual glow intensity of the surface will be 15 percent.

10. Press ⌈Enter⌉ to accept the values, and close the panel.

The Intensity input field sets the global glow intensity and the Glow Radius input field determines how many pixels beyond the surface edge the glow will be drawn.

11. Press ⌈F9⌉ to render a preview of the glow effect (**Figure 11.41**).

✔ Tips

- You can use the Graph Editor to animate the glow intensity and radius.

- You can enter values greater than 100 percent in most of Layout's input fields to heighten effects.

MAKING YOUR OBJECTS GLOW

309

Applying Image Filters

Image filters are used to process each frame of your scene as it's finished. You can apply these filters to manipulate the rendered image and create specialized effects or to enhance the final look.

To apply an image filter:

1. Select Object from the Load tool group in the toolbar or press ⊞.

2. When the Load Object dialog appears, select an object to load and click Open.

3. Select Image Processing from the Window pull-down menu in the toolbar or press ⌃Ctrl⌃+⌃F8⌃ to open the Processing tab of the Effects panel.

4. From the Add Image Filter pull-down menu, choose an image filter to apply.

   We used Negative for the example (**Figure 11.42**).

5. Press ⌃F9⌃ to render a preview of the effect (**Figure 11.43**).

✔ Tip

■ Several image filters are included with LightWave, and you'll find many others available for free on the Web. You can search for them at www.flay.com using the LightWave plug-in search engine.

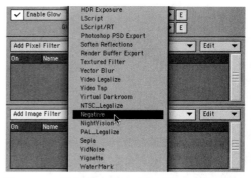

Figure 11.42 LightWave 3D comes with a number of image filters to choose from.

Figure 11.43 The 3D logo rendered with the Negative image filter.

APPLYING IMAGE FILTERS

Using HyperVoxels

HyperVoxels is LightWave's volumetric rendering engine, which you can use to create smoke, cloud, dust, and liquid effects. It creates a three-dimensional volume around a position in space, such as a point on an object, a null object, or a particle from a particle emitter. The main benefit of using HyperVoxels is that these effects are done in full 3D space, so you can move the camera around and through them. HyperVoxels has three modes of operation:

♦ **Surface:** This mode will create a smooth sphere that can be surfaced and textured. Individual HyperVoxels surfaces, whether individual objects or a Particle emitter, can be blended together to create liquid effects.

♦ **Volume:** This mode will create a volumetric cloud. You can apply Hyper-Textures to the surface to create wisps and even animated turbulence. This is the most computationally intensive of the three modes because it uses physically accurate volumetric calculations. Only use it when you need to move into or around the effect or when you need the added realism in your scene.

♦ **Sprite:** This mode isn't truly volumetric. It takes a slice of the center of the volumetric effect from the camera's perspective and draws it in 2D, saving greatly on render calculations. This mode is best suited for creating steam, dust, missile contrails, and anything else that requires a stream of smoke.

Volumetric rendering is computationally intensive and can significantly lengthen the amount of time it takes your scene to render. We recommend that you use the Volume mode only when Sprite mode won't do. You'll find that you can use the Sprite mode for the majority of your effects.

HyperVoxels and the nature of volumetric rendering could fill an entire book themselves. The following procedures will get you up and running, but you'll want to explore the various parameters to see how they affect the final result. Refer to the LightWave 3D User's Manual and some of the fine HyperVoxels related tutorials at sites such as www.newtek.com, www.Luxology.net, and www.flay.com for more information.

To create a liquid effect:

1. Select the Items tab, and then click Add Null from the Add tool group in the toolbar.

2. When the Null Object Name dialog appears, name the object Clump-1.

3. Repeat Steps 1 and 2, naming the second object Clump-2.

4. In the frame slider's end frame input field, type 30 to change the length of the animation.

5. Select the Modify tab, and then click Move in the Translate tool group of the toolbar and drag Clump-1 to −1m on the X axis.

6. Drag Clump-2 to 1m on the X axis. Your scene should look like **Figure 11.44**.

7. Drag the frame slider to frame 30.

8. Drag Clump-2 to 0m on the X axis and create a keyframe.

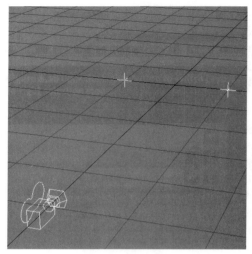

Figure 11.44 Your scene should contain two Null objects, spaced 2 meters apart.

Figure 11.45 You'll find HyperVoxels in the same location as Ground Fog.

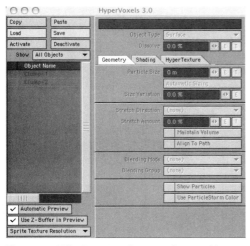

Figure 11.46 The HyperVoxels properties panel is divided into Geometry properties, Shading properties, and HyperTexture properties, so you'll know where to find options relating to your current task.

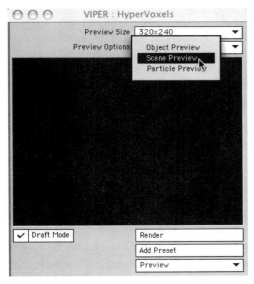

Figure 11.47 Choose Scene Preview from the Preview Options menu in Viper.

9. Select Volumetric and Fog Options from the Window pull-down menu in the toolbar or press [Ctrl]+[F6] to open the Volumetrics tab of the Effects panel.

10. From the Add Volumetric pull-down menu, select HyperVoxels (**Figure 11.45**).

11. Double-click HyperVoxels 3.0 in the list below the pull-down menu to open the HyperVoxels properties panel (**Figure 11.46**).

12. Click the Render tab, then click Viper in the Utilities tool group of the toolbar to open the Versatile Interactive Preview Renderer.

13. From the Preview Options pull-down menu in Viper, select Scene Preview so you'll see both of the Null objects in the HyperVoxels preview (**Figure 11.47**).

   ▲ Scene Preview mode tells Viper to render everything in the scene that's associated with this effect.

   ▲ Object Preview mode tells it to render only the object currently selected in HyperVoxels.

   ▲ Particle Preview mode renders each individual particle.

continues on next page

USING HYPERVOXELS

14. In the HyperVoxels properties panel, double-click `Clump-1` in the item list to activate it.

Viper renders a smooth HyperVoxels surface around `Clump-1` from the camera's point of view (**Figure 11.48**).

15. In the Geometry tab, change the Particle Size to 1.5m.

The HyperVoxels surface grows in the Viper window (**Figure 11.49**).

16. From the Blending Mode pull-down menu, select Additive (**Figure 11.50**).

▲ Additive blending mode makes surfaces clump together.

▲ Negative blending mode makes surfaces "push into" each other (like poking a cube of Jell-O).

▲ Effector blending mode makes a surface cause other surfaces it comes into contact with grow.

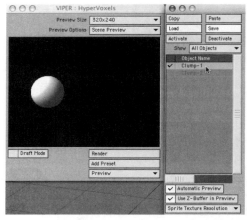

Figure 11.48 Double-click items in the list to apply HyperVoxels to them. Viper updates to show you the surface that will be rendered around Clump-1.

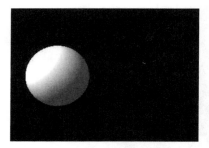

Figure 11.49 Particle Size governs how large a volume is drawn around each point.

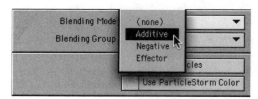

Figure 11.50 Choose Additive from the Blending Mode pull-down menu.

Figure 11.51 You can create different blending groups so that you can specify which HyperVoxels surfaces should interact with one another.

Figure 11.52 When naming your blend groups, use descriptive names so you won't forget which HyperVoxels they're associated with.

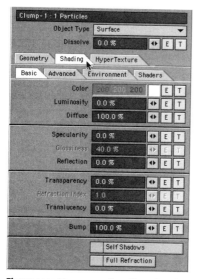

Figure 11.53 You can surface HyperVoxels just as you do regular objects.

Figure 11.54 Make the surface of Clump-1 red.

17. From the Blending Group pull-down menu, select "(new Group)" (**Figure 11.51**).

18. When the Blend Group Name dialog appears, type Clumpy, then press Enter or click OK (**Figure 11.52**).

19. Select the Shading tab to display the HyperVoxels surface shading options (**Figure 11.53**).

20. Click the red component in the Color field and drag right until it reads 255.

21. Click the green and blue components, but drag them left to 0 (**Figure 11.54**).

22. Repeat Steps 14–16 for Clump-2.

23. From the Blending Group pull-down menu, select Clumpy.

continues on next page

USING HYPERVOXELS

24. Select the Shading tab and drag the blue component right to 255 and the red and green left to 0.

When you're finished Viper should look like **Figure 11.55**.

25. In Viper, select Make Preview from the Preview pull-down menu (**Figure 11.56**) to generate a moving preview of your HyperVoxels animation.

Unlike the main Layout Preview, the Viper preview automatically uses the frame slider's start and end frames.

26. When the preview is finished generating, click the play button to preview your clumping sphere animation (**Figure 11.57**).

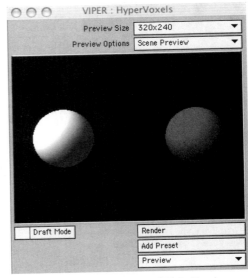

Figure 11.55 You now have one red HyperVoxels surface and one blue HyperVoxels surface.

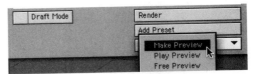

Figure 11.56 You can make a preview in Viper just as you would in the main Layout Viewport. This is an excellent way to preview effects without having to do a full render, which can take more time.

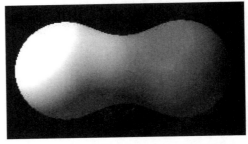

Figure 11.57 Your two HyperVoxels surfaces clump together, blending their surface colors where they touch.

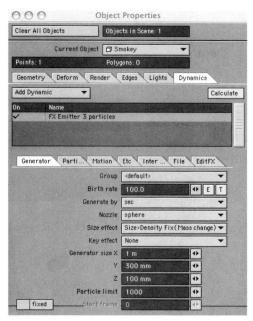

Figure 11.58 Create a thin rectangle as the base shape for the smoke emitter.

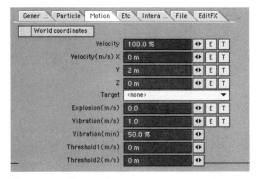

Figure 11.59 Change the motion parameters of your Smokey emitter to match those in this figure.

To create a smoke effect:

1. Select the Items tab, and then click Add Null from the Add tool group in the toolbar.

2. When the Null Object Name dialog appears, name the object Smokey.

3. Click Item Properties below the frame slider or press p to open the Item Properties panel for Smokey.

4. Select the Dynamics tab, and then choose Emitter from the Add Dynamics pull-down menu.

5. Double-click Emitter 3 Particles in the list to open the Emitter properties.

6. Change the Generator Size Y to 300mm and change Generator Size Z to 100mm (**Figure 11.58**).

7. Select the Motion tab to access the particle motion properties.

8. Change the Vector(m/s) Y to 2m so that the particles move upward and then change Vibration(m/s) to 1.0, and Vibration(min) to 50%, which will make the motion of the particles appear random (**Figure 11.59**).

9. Close the Item Properties panels.

continues on next page

USING HYPERVOXELS

10. Select the Modify tab, and then click Move in the Translate tool group of the toolbar, and drag the camera to 700mm on the Y axis.

    Your scene should look like **Figure 11.60**.

11. Repeat Steps 9–12 from the previous exercise "To create a liquid effect."

12. In the HyperVoxels panel, double-click Smokey in the items list to activate it.

13. From the Object Type pull-down menu, select Sprite (**Figure 11.61**).

14. In the Particle Size input field of the Geometry tab, type 250mm.

    Viper updates the HyperVoxels sprites to the new size (**Figure 11.62**).

15. Select the HyperTexture tab in the HyperVoxels panel to display the texture options.

16. In the Frequencies input field, type 1 to lower the number of Crumple frequencies and smooth out the effect.

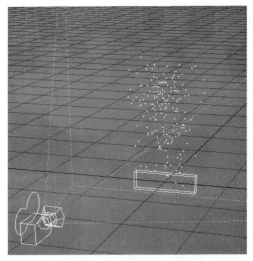

Figure 11.60 Your camera should be slightly elevated so it has a full view of the entire particle animation.

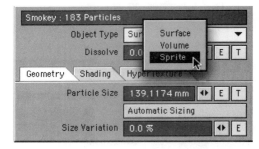

Figure 11.61 Set the HyperVoxels render mode to Sprite.

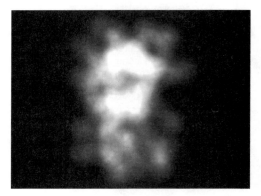

Figure 11.62 Make the sprites that are drawn around each particle 250mm in size.

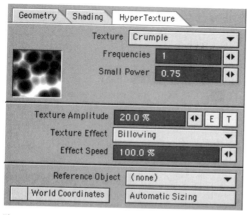

Figure 11.63 In the HyperTexture tab, you can use texture effects to create nice rolling-smoke effects or make the HyperVoxels volume dissolve over time.

17. In the Texture Amplitude input field, type 20 to lessen the texture's affect on the sprites, then press (Enter).

18. From the Texture Effect pull-down menu, select Billowing to give your smoke a bit of a rolling effect (**Figure 11.63**).

19. In Viper, select Make Preview from the Preview pull-down menu.

20. After the preview is finished generating, click the play button to see your smoke animation (**Figure 11.64**).

21. In the HyperVoxels panel, select Volume from the Object Type pull-down menu. Repeat Steps 20 and 21 to make a new preview and view it (**Figure 11.65**).

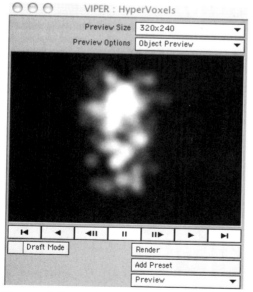

Figure 11.64 Your sprite smoke animation.

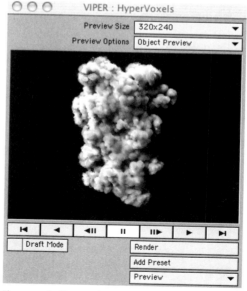

Figure 11.65 Change the HyperVoxels type to Volume and generate another preview. This version looks more like a giant column of smoke and has a lot of detail, but it takes significantly longer to render.

USING HYPERVOXELS

SURFACES
AND TEXTURES

Unless you're making a movie about plastic models, nothing we've made in Modeler so far should be used in your projects. This may sound a bit discouraging, but the flat, gray look of all the geometry in this book is merely a starting point. And now that you've mastered the basics, you can add style and texture to your geometry. You can go for an ultrarealistic look, matching every little detail to its real-world counterpart, or a very stylized look, with all the detail determined by you. In either case, those details are achieved through surfaces and textures.

In fact, you've already seen surfacing in use. All geometry created in Modeler initially has a generic or default surface applied. A multitude of parameters in LightWave let you customize the surfaces of your objects. With a little practice, adjusting these settings will not only result in a predictable look and feel for your surface, but also give you an unlimited range of possibilities.

In this chapter, you'll learn how to create surface groups and apply basic, as well as some advanced, surface attributes. Using image maps, procedural textures, and gradients, you'll give your surfaces details that will make them look like they're made from real substances. Finally, you'll learn how to use LightWave's Viper and Presets windows to make surfacing even easier and more interactive.

Creating Surfaces in Modeler

A surface is simply a group of polygons that share the same attributes. Identified by a name, these groups and their values are saved with the object's geometry when you save the object in either Layout or Modeler. Before we can start setting any of the surface's properties, we have to determine which polygons are to be grouped together and what they should be named.

You may have noticed that Layout doesn't offer you any way to directly select either points or polygons. This is a problem when you're creating surfaces, because you need to be able to say, "These polygons belong to this group, but those belong to another group." Without selecting geometry, this is impossible. So you'll have to go to Modeler to name the surface, specify which polygons belong to which surface groups, and define basic group attributes.

A LightWave object can have a single surface or a whole group of surfaces applied to its geometry. There is one limitation, however: Only one surface can be applied per polygon. The number of surfaces you use depends on how many different materials you want your object to look like it was made from. You can give your object a lot of subtle variances and a lot of detail by adding numerous surfaces, or you can keep it simple and only have a few surfaces. It all depends on the style and look of your animation.

In the following exercises, we'll show you how to surface a sphere to look like an eyeball. First, create a simple sphere similar to **Figure 12.1** (see Chapter 3, "Creating Geometry," and Chapter 4, "Editing Geometry," for a refresher). Be sure to save this object as Eyeball.lwo (it will be referenced as such in the following procedures).

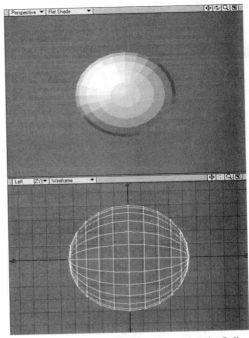

Figure 12.1 Make a sphere in Modeler using the Ball tool and rotate it 90 degrees in the Left view. Make it 500mm in the X, Y, and Z axis.

Figure 12.2 The Change Surface dialog assigns surfaces to polygons. Name the surface Eyeball.

Next, assign each of the object's polygons a surface name corresponding to the different parts of the eyeball: the white of the eye, the pupil, and the iris. Start by making the object's base surface. This is like applying a base coat of paint to every polygon in the layer: It ensures every polygon has at least one defined texture, rather than simply using the default.

To create a surface for all the polygons in Modeler:

1. Load Eyeball.lwo into Modeler.

2. Click the Surface button in the bottom portion of the interface or press ⓠ to open the Change Surface dialog.

3. Type Eyeball in the Name field and uncheck the Make Default check box (**Figure 12.2**).

4. Click OK to create the surface and assign the default values listed in this dialog.

5. Press ⓢ or choose Save Object from the File pull-down menu to save the object.

   Like most of the tools in Modeler, the Surface tool affects the entire layer if nothing is selected. Because we didn't have any of the object's polygons selected when we created the surface, the Eyeball surface was applied to our entire object. And we kept the simple, default values for the surface attributes in the Change Surface dialog, so you probably didn't see much of a change.

✔ Tip

■ After you're more familiar with the surface attributes, you can use the Change Surface dialog to better define your surfaces initially.

CREATING SURFACES IN MODELER

Next we'll define the two other surfaces of the model: the iris and pupil.

To create a surface for a group of polygons:

1. Load Eyeball.lwo into Modeler.

2. Click the Polygons button on the bottom toolbar (**Figure 12.3**) or press [Ctrl]+[h] to switch Modeler into polygon-selection mode.

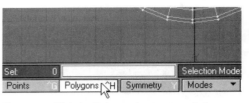

Figure 12.3 Click the Polygons button to switch Modeler into polygon-selection mode.

3. In the Top view, right-click and draw a lasso around the first two rows of polygons (**Figure 12.4**).

   This will be your pupil surface.

4. Click the Surface button located in the bottom portion of the interface or press [q] to open the Change Surface dialog.

5. Type Pupil in the Name field.

6. Click OK to create the Pupil surface and assign it the preliminary values listed in this dialog.

7. Click the polygons in the center of the eye to deselect them (**Figure 12.5**).

8. Repeat Steps 4–6, but name the surface Iris instead of Pupil.

9. Press [s] or choose Save Object from the File pull-down menu.

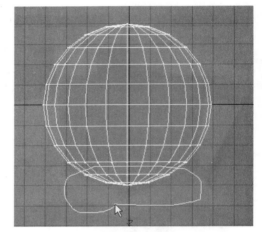

Figure 12.4 Use the right mouse button to draw a lasso and select the first two rows of polygons.

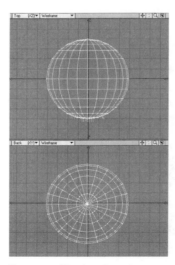

Figure 12.5 Deselect the polygons in the center of the eye.

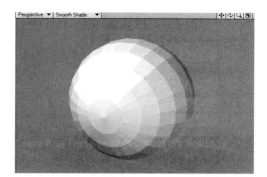

Figure 12.6 We need to spruce up the surfaces of this model.

Working with Surfaces

So far, the surfaces for your eyeball object use a flat, gray, boring, default texture (**Figure 12.6**). Needless to say, no matter what problems your character may have, its eyes shouldn't look like this! So now you'll need to set some of the surface's characteristics to make your object look more like a real eye. Without getting hyperrealistic, there are a few settings you can easily change that will make it seem a little more lifelike. These parameters can be adjusted in one of LightWave's dedicated windows, the Surface Editor.

The Surface Editor

You'll find most of the controls and attributes you need to adjust your objects' surfaces in the Surface Editor. You can open it in either Modeler or Layout—both will allow you to change the object's surfaces. However, you'll want to use LightWave's renderer to preview the surfaces you're adjusting, and since Modeler doesn't have this capability, we'll access the Surface Editor from Layout. After you get more accustomed to how the editor works and you need fewer previews, you'll be able to use the one found in Modeler more frequently.

Let's take a look at the Surface Editor interface (**Figure 12.7**).

◆ **Surface management (1):** The number of objects and surfaces loaded in the scene are displayed here. We can also load and save premade surfaces from a file.

◆ **Surface preview (2):** The surface preview area contains a thumbnail rendering of the currently selected surface, as well as a window displaying statistical information about the surface.

◆ **Surface list (3):** The surface list displays the name of every object in the scene. Click the expansion arrow next to an object's name to reveal a list of the surfaces belonging to that object.

◆ **Surface properties tabs (4):** Each of these tabs contains various controls that adjust the surface's parameters. You'll explore their properties over the course of this chapter.

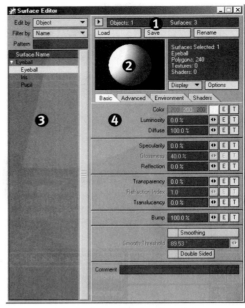

Figure 12.7 The Surface Editor lets you change many aspects of a surface.

Figure 12.8 The left sphere has the Default surface applied to it. The right sphere has its Luminosity attribute set at 100 percent.

Figure 12.9 The left sphere has the Default surface applied to it. The right sphere has its Specularity attribute set at 100 percent. Notice the highlight.

Basic Surface Attributes

When you're surfacing, you'll spend most of your time adjusting the controls in the Basic tab. These cover everything from a surface's color and level of transparency to how shiny it can get. The 12 basic surface attributes in this tab can be combined to create a huge assortment of looks for your surface. Let's take a look at what each does.

◆ **Color:** This controls the base color of the surface. You can define a color either by dragging the red, green, and blue (RGB) values, or by clicking the color swatch and selecting a color in your system's color picker.

◆ **Luminosity:** This makes a surface look illuminated or self-lit (**Figure 12.8**). It's particularly useful when surfacing light bulbs or glowing liquids, whose surface is lit by itself, not the surrounding lights. However, unless you plan to use LightWave's Radiosity rendering feature, the illuminated surface will have no affect on any of the other surrounding surfaces.

◆ **Diffuse:** This controls how a surface absorbs light. Light absorbs less from a surface with a low Diffuse setting, resulting in a darker surface. This is typically used in conjunction with textures to create darker details on a surface, such as scratches or dirt.

◆ **Specularity:** This adjusts how much a surface reflects light (**Figure 12.9**). Typically, a surface with a high Specularity setting has a highlight, reflecting the color of the light on the surface. It's important to note that, unlike Reflection in Layout, a surface with specular highlights will not aid in reflecting its surroundings. Specularity can be used for glass, diamonds, floors, and so forth.

◆ **Glossiness:** Naturally, the Glossiness parameter affects how much gloss or shine your surface has. To use this parameter, you first need to set specularity. The Glossiness value specifically controls the size of the highlights on specular surfaces. The larger the value, the glossier the object's surface will be, thus the smaller the highlight (**Figure 12.10**).

Figure 12.10 The left sphere has a Glossiness value of 25 percent, while the right sphere's is set at 100 percent.

◆ **Reflection:** As the name suggests, this value determines how much of the surrounding environment is visible in a surface (**Figure 12.11**). A high value creates a mirror effect, while low values reflect very little. To see these reflections, you must use either ray tracing or the tricks found in the Environment tab.

◆ **Transparency:** You can make an object's surface transparent, revealing the surfaces behind the object, by adjusting the Transparency setting (**Figure 12.12**). Use it for liquids, glass, and gas effects.

Figure 12.11 The left sphere has the Default surface applied to it. The right sphere has its Reflectivity attribute set at 75 percent. Notice how its surface reflects the background.

◆ **Refraction Index:** Light bends as it travels through semitransparent objects like glass and water, causing everything seen through them to warp (**Figure 12.13**). The Refraction Index controls the amount of distortion that occurs in this effect. Typically, water has a value of 1.333 and glass 1.5, while air has a value of 1.0003. Note: This field will only affect an object that is transparent if Ray-Traced Refraction is toggled on in the rendering panel. Refer to the LightWave 3D User's Manual for a table listing several common materials and their Refraction Index values.

Figure 12.12 The left sphere has the Default surface applied to it. The right sphere has its Transparency attribute set at 90 percent.

◆ **Translucency:** Translucent surfaces mimic how light travels through thin materials. A good example is an old-fashioned window shade: A light illuminates one side, passes through the surface, and transfers colors, shading, and shadows

Figure 12.13 By adjusting the Refraction Index, we can change how light bends as it travels through the transparent sphere. Here, the Refraction Index is set to 0.75.

Figure 12.14 The window shade's surface has a Translucency setting of 75 percent. It transfers the shadows to the other side of the polygon to create a silhouette.

Figure 12.15 A bump map can be used to fake surface details.

Figure 12.16 The Smoothing attribute smoothes out the shading on surfaces.

to the other side of the geometry, creating a classic silhouette effect (**Figure 12.14**). Other uses for this effect include skin, membranes, leaves, lampshades, and curtains.

◆ **Bump maps:** Using various texturing methods (described later in this chapter), LightWave can create the illusion of bumps on a surface (**Figure 12.15**). You can use this to re-create a wide range of surface irregularities such as craters, stucco, grooves, and rust. Remember, though, that bump maps are merely shading tricks, and no actual geometry is ever created or modified.

◆ **Smoothing** and **Smooth Threshold:** Turn this effect on to give the illusion of smoothness to the faceted geometry of a surface (**Figure 12.16**). The angle created by any two adjoining polygons is compared with the value set in the Smooth Threshold control. If the angle isn't greater than this value, LightWave will adjust the polygons' shading to make it look smooth. Like bump mapping, no additional geometry is ever created or modified.

◆ **Double Sided:** By default, polygons in LightWave are single-sided. That is, they only get drawn on one side of the surface (see Chapter 4, "Editing Geometry"). This check box instructs LightWave to override that default and draw both sides of a surface. The surface properties are merely copied to the other side of the surface.

Adjusting surface attributes

Most of the 12 surface attributes in the Basic tab use a standard group of controls to adjust the strength of their effect on a surface (**Figure 12.17**).

Figure 12.17 Each of the attributes has numerous controls to adjust its effect on the surface.

◆ **Value:** Whether it's a percentage or absolute number, most of the attributes in the Basic tab have a value that tells LightWave how much to use. To change it, either type directly in the field or use the control's mini-slider arrows to increase or decrease the value already set. Many of these fields allow both over-driven values (greater than 100 percent) and negative values.

◆ **Envelopes (E):** Click this button to open the Graph Editor and animate the attribute's strength over time.

◆ **Textures (T):** Click this button to open the Texture Editor. Textures let you add subtle details to many attributes by using images, procedurals, and gradients to control the effect.

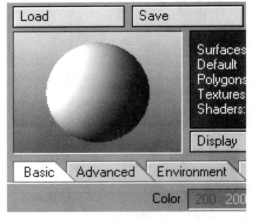

Figure 12.18 The surface preview window shows what the surface currently looks like.

The Surface Editor provides a few simple ways to immediately adjust these values and get real-time feedback. The first is the surface preview window (**Figure 12.18**), located in the section above the controls. This window displays a sphere (or cube, if you want) that previews the surface. Naturally, it can't show exactly how the surface will be drawn when it's rendered, but it should give you a good idea of what effect your adjustments have on your surface. The second way to get feedback is through the OpenGL Viewport. When you change most of the surface parameters in the editor, the surface is automatically updated in the Viewport.. The third way to preview a surface is in LightWave's Viper window, discussed later in this chapter.

Let's get surfacing!

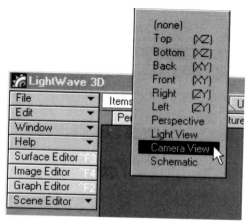

Figure 12.19 Select Camera View to change the Viewport's current view.

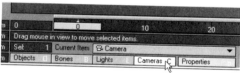

Figure 12.20 Switch Layout to camera mode by pressing the button at the bottom of the screen.

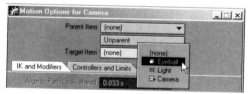

Figure 12.21 Select Eyeball from the Target Item pull-down menu in the Motion Options panel.

To set up the Surface Editor:

1. Load Eyeball.lwo into Layout.

2. From the Viewport's view type pull-down menu, choose Camera View (**Figure 12.19**) or press ⑥.

3. Click the Cameras button at the bottom of the interface (**Figure 12.20**) or press ⓒ to switch Layout into camera mode.

4. Click Motion Options from the Window pull-down menu or press ⓜ to open the Motion Options dialog.

5. From the Target Item pull-down menu, choose Eyeball (**Figure 12.21**).

    Targeting the eyeball object will make it easier to maneuver the camera's view by always pointing at the object.

6. Click Surface Editor in the toolbar or press Ctrl+F3 to open the Surface Editor.

7. Click the Modify tab, then click Move in the toolbar and drag the camera to a position on the screen that allows you to see both the Surface Editor and the eyeball object.

8. From the File pull-down menu, select Save > Save Scene As or press ⓢ to open the Save Scene As dialog.

9. Name the scene Eyeball_setup.lws and click OK.

BASIC SURFACE ATTRIBUTES

With your work space all set up, the next step is to adjust the surface's parameters. First you'll adjust the surface's colors. Then you'll add some gloss to simulate wetness on the surface of the eye. Finally, you'll smooth it all out so it's less faceted.

To modify the color of a surface:

1. Follow the preceding procedure to set up the interface for surfacing.

    The first surface in your object should already be selected in the surface list. (If not, click Eyeball in the surface list.)

2. In the Color field, click the red color component and drag to the right to increase the value to 255 (**Figure 12.22**).

3. Repeat Step 2 for the blue and green components of the control.

    These values, when combined, will create a white surface.

4. Click Pupil in the surface list.

5. Click the color swatch at the end of the Color control to open the color picker (**Figure 12.23**).

6. Click the black color swatch and click OK to close the Color Picker.

7. Repeat Steps 5 and 6 for the Iris surface, giving it one of the shades of green from the color picker.

8. Press F9 to render a preview (**Figure 12.24**).

9. From the File pull-down menu, choose Save > Save Current Object.

    This step saves the object with the new surfacing information; simply pressing s only saves the screen, it will not automatically save the new information into the object.

Figure 12.22 Change the red color value to 255.

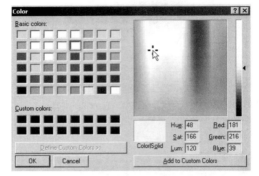

Figure 12.23 Use your system's color picker to create a color.

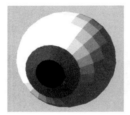

Figure 12.24 A quick render shows what we have so far.

✔ Tip

- Right-clicking on a surface color swatch adjusts the brightness of the color. You can sort the surface list in several different ways. Use the Edit By, Filter By, and Pattern controls in the top-left corner of the Surface Editor to reorder the surfaces and their relationships with their objects. This is particularly useful when your scene has hundreds of surfaces.

Figure 12.25 Group-select the three surfaces from the surface list.

Figure 12.26 Turn on Smoothing to smooth out all three surfaces.

Figure 12.27 Set the Specularity attribute to 50 percent.

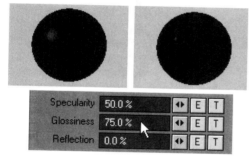

Figure 12.28 Set the Glossiness attribute to 75 percent.

Figure 12.29 Render the frame to see what we have so far.

With the colors of the surfaces set, you can move on to smoothing out the shading and making the eye look wet. Since you need to do this for all three surfaces, you'll use the surface list's group-select feature.

To modify an attribute for multiple surfaces:

1. Load Eyeball_setup.lws into Layout.

2. Click Surface Editor in the toolbar or press Ctrl+F3 to open the Surface Editor.

3. In the surface list, Ctrl-click or Shift-click all the surfaces in the object to select them all (**Figure 12.25**).

4. Check the Smoothing check box to turn on the attribute for all three surfaces (**Figure 12.26**).

5. In the Specularity field, use the numeric input or mini-slider arrows to set the value to 50 percent (**Figure 12.27**).

   This will create a specular highlight on each of the surfaces, reflecting the existing lights.

6. In the Glossiness field, set the value to 75 percent.

   This decreases the size of the highlight (**Figure 12.28**).

7. From the File pull-down menu, choose Save > Save Current Object to save the changes to the object.

8. Press F9 to render a preview (**Figure 12.29**).

✔ Tip

- You can copy and paste surface attributes by right-clicking the surface name in the surface list.

BASIC SURFACE ATTRIBUTES

Creating a Texture

Texturing is a further method of surfacing. In surfacing you set certain visual properties of geometry, and in texturing you add details that make the geometry look like it really is made from that material, whether rock, wood, sand, or whatever your model calls for. Adding bumps to a surface, determining how light will affect the appearance of a surface, or adding texture takes your model's surfaces to a completely new level.

So far, all of your surfaces have been straightforward examples that show what very basic surfacing can do. But we've only just begun to touch the surface (pardon the pun) of what LightWave's surfacing can do.

The problem with basic surfacing is that it lacks any real variation. All these surfaces are perfectly smooth, with perfect paint jobs in a perfectly clean environment (**Figure 12.30**). You need to give your surface detail, add some texture, and make it look more realistic (**Figure 12.31**). This can be done with textures.

Textures are basically qualifiers: They increase or decrease the effect an attribute has on a surface's pixel. The amount of texture is based on yet another parameter, such as data from an image file, a mathematical formula, or a simple range of predefined values. Which one you choose depends on the specific needs of the texture.

Figure 12.30 A bland and boring surface.

Figure 12.31 Same surface, with a few textures added.

CREATING A TEXTURE

For example, one of the most popular uses of texturing is to add dirt or dust to a surface to give it some age. You may remember that the surface attribute that produces this kind of effect is Diffuse. If you were to simply adjust the Diffuse value in the Surface Editor, you'd be able to make the entire surface look darker and dirtier, but what surface has a perfect layer of dirt on it? With a texture, you can give some of the surface's pixels a high amount of diffusion, and others barely any at all. Each pixel's Diffuse value is determined by the texture.

There are three basic forms of texturing in LightWave: image maps, procedural textures, and gradients. But regardless of what type you choose, or what you're adding the texturing details to, all texturing is performed in the same place: the Texture Editor.

✔ Tips

- Any attribute with a T button next to its controls can make use of LightWave's texturing capabilities.

- When a surface parameter's T button is highlighted, that means it already has a texture. Simply click the button to edit the texture's parameters.

- To easily remove a texture from an attribute, simply [Shift]-click its T button. Once the button is no longer highlighted, the texture is removed. But be warned: This action can't be undone. So if you remove a texture and then change your mind, you can only go back to an earlier version of your object or start over.

Texture Editor

Just as the Surface Editor contains all the
controls you need to adjust the surfaces in a
scene, the Texture Editor has nearly everything you'll need to make even the most
complex of textures (**Figure 12.32**). One of
the Texture Editor's most powerful features
is its ability to layer several textures together
to create a single texture. You create and
organize these layers in the left half of the
Texture Editor interface. The controls for
the various types of effects you can make
are in the right side of the editor.

At the very top of the editor's controls are
the layer options. They not only control
the layer's type, but how strong its effect will
be on the attribute. As a layer becomes less
and less opaque, the layers underneath it
become more visible, thus changing the overall strength of the layer. The Layer Opacity
setting, like many value fields in LightWave,
not only supports the typical range of 0–100
percent, but also both overdriven and negative values.

As you change the type of a texture, the
remaining space on the editor changes as
well. Some texture types require a great many
controls. Other types have far fewer controls
and can easily fit in the interface. Regardless,
in the space directly below the Layer options
you'll find the controls that affect not only
the texture, but its placement.

The first type of surface texturing we'll look
into is one of the easiest and most used: the
image map.

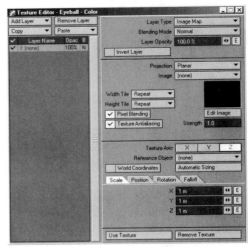

Figure 12.32 The Texture Editor lets you add details to
your attributes.

Figure 12.33 An image can be placed directly on a surface.

Image maps

As the name implies, an image map uses an image to add details to an object's surface (see Chapter 5 for more on image maps). It can be anything from a picture you took with a digital camera to something you drew in a paint program, just as long as the image was saved in one of the file formats LightWave supports. (For more information and a complete list of the supported file formats, please refer to the manual.)

When an image map is added to a surface attribute as a texture, it uses the pixel values as a reference for the attribute's strength. Because the reference data for an image map is an image, each pixel in the image becomes a reference point. The brighter a pixel is, the greater its value, and thus the stronger the effect will be. A pixel value of 255 will translate to 100 percent, and a pixel value of 0 will naturally be 0 percent.

Because LightWave only needs the pixel's value and not all its color information, all that's really necessary is a grayscale image. If you give a color image to a texture, it's simply converted to grayscale internally. The one exception is in the Color attribute. If it's given a color image, it will draw the complete color depth of the image on the surface (**Figure 12.33**). This is because the Color attribute supports the three color values in the image.

For the next part of the eyeball example, you're going to give the iris a lot more detail. You've already given your eye's iris surface a color. Now you want to add typical line details to this color, without losing the color itself. You can do that by adding an image map to the Diffuse attribute of the surface, so that, depending on how you have it set up, any details in the image file can make your surface darker.

To add an image map to the Diffuse attribute:

1. Load Eyeball_setup.lws into Layout.

2. Click Surface Editor in the toolbar or press Ctrl+F3 to open the Surface Editor.

3. Click Iris in the surface list.

4. Click the Diffuse attribute's T button to open the Texture Editor (**Figure 12.34**).

5. From the Image pull-down menu, select (load image) to open the Load Object dialog and choose any image from your hard drive. We used the one in **Figure 12.35**.

6. From the Projection pull-down menu, choose a projection style.

   This determines how the image is placed on the surface (see the "Projections" sidebar). The default value, Planar, will work best for this example (**Figure 12.36**).

7. Use the Texture Axis buttons to select the axis on which you want the texture applied.

   For the Iris surface, we can leave in on the default, Z axis (**Figure 12.37**).

8. Click the Automatic Sizing button to have LightWave automatically calculate the texture's scale to fit the surface.

9. Click Use Texture to close the Texture Editor.

10. Press F9 to render the frame (**Figure 12.38**).

11. From the File pull-down menu, choose Save > Save Current Object.

✔ Tip

■ We made a grayscale image for our example's texture in Adobe Photoshop. You can replace it with any similar image you find or create.

Figure 12.34 Clicking the T button will open the Texture Editor.

Figure 12.35 Load an image from your hard drive.

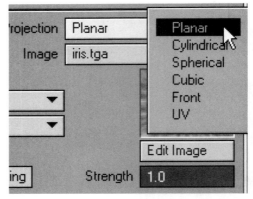

Figure 12.36 Use the default Planar projection to map the image along an axis of a surface.

Figure 12.37 Select the axis to project it along. For this example, we'll stay with the default, Z axis.

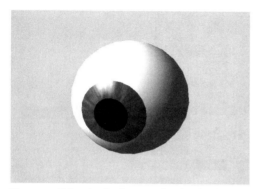

Figure 12.38 Render the frame and notice the details of the image affecting the Diffuse channel of the iris surface.

As you can see, the texture darkened parts of the iris based on the texture we provided. This method will work for any surface attribute that supports textures. Because of the number of controls and adjustments available to both surfaces and textures, there are always several ways you can create the same effect.

In fact, you can draw the complete iris image, color and all, and apply it to the surface's Color attribute instead of to Diffuse. The result would be the same. However, the way we did it is more flexible, because you can simply adjust the texture's Layer Opacity value to increase or decrease the effect, rather than having to go back into your paint program. Speed and flexibility should always be considered.

Some of the best artists can create images to fit almost every texturing need. Others are less proficient and can use a little more help in this area. That's when we start using procedural textures.

Projections

A projection type describes the shape an image's projection on a particular surface. There are several available, each with its own advantages and disadvantages. Which type of projection you use usually depends on the shape of the surface: flat, round, or irregular.

♦ **Planar:** This is a flat projection, like projecting an image on a movie screen.

♦ **Cylindrical:** This wraps a texture around curved geometry, like putting a label around a soup can.

♦ **Spherical:** Like cylindrical projection, this wraps a texture around a curved surface, but this time a sphere. The poles of the surface pinch the texture, like on a globe.

♦ **Cubic:** This projects the same texture on all six sides of a surface (top, bottom, left, right, front, and back), creating a complete volume, like wrapping a present.

♦ **Front:** This uses the camera as the projection axis. As the camera moves and rotates, the texture is always rendered flat and facing the camera.

♦ **UV:** This is the most flexible and complex projection type. It requires the model to have the UV vertex maps set in Modeler (see Chapter 5 for more on VMaps).

Procedural textures

There are several textures in the real world that can be defined by complex mathematical algorithms. It sounds hard to believe, that natural objects could be drawn using nothing more than a calculator—and actually, they can't. Their brain-bending formulae require years of algebra, geometry, trigonometry, and calculus (basically every college math class!) to understand. Fortunately for us, their actual function is way outside the scope of this book, and we just need to tell you how to use them.

Lucky for us artist types, 3D-programming wizards have made it easy for us and written 32 of the more popular algorithms into LightWave, as *procedurals* (**Figure 12.39**). While not everything can be solved through math (although some mathematicians disagree), those that can be usually find their way into a complex, layered texture. These procedurals include things like clouds, wood, bricks, and ripples. All we have to do is set some of the texture's determining parameters, and the computer will do the rest.

The trick to understanding each of the procedurals is to first understand their controls. We change the equation's variables by adjusting various values and switch controls found in the editor. For example, one of the simplest procedurals to understand initially is the Brick texture. The artist provides parameters like the color of the brick, the width of the mortar, and the area the bricks need to cover. LightWave then figures out the rest, drawing rows and rows of bricks according the set values (**Figure 12.40**).

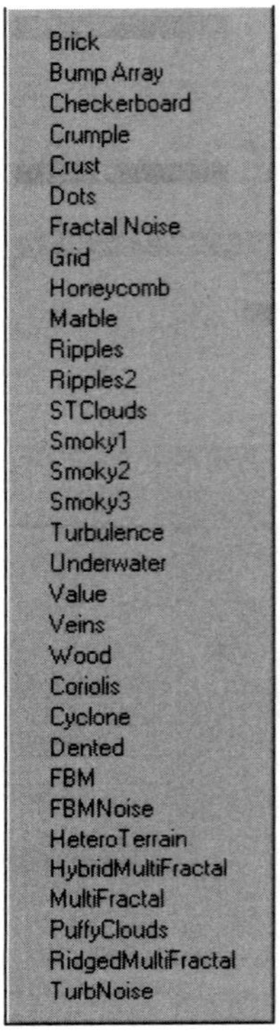

Brick
Bump Array
Checkerboard
Crumple
Crust
Dots
Fractal Noise
Grid
Honeycomb
Marble
Ripples
Ripples2
STClouds
Smoky1
Smoky2
Smoky3
Turbulence
Underwater
Value
Veins
Wood
Coriolis
Cyclone
Dented
FBM
FBMNoise
HeteroTerrain
HybridMultiFractal
MultiFractal
PuffyClouds
RidgedMultiFractal
TurbNoise

Figure 12.39 There are 32 procedural textures included with LightWave.

Figure 12.40 The Brick procedural lets you quickly add a brick wall.

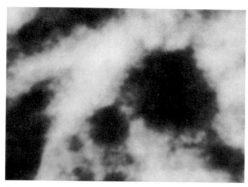

Figure 12.41 A complex procedural texture rendered close up still looks good.

Figure 12.42 The image starts to look ugly when you get closer.

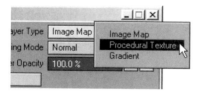

Figure 12.43 Change the Layer Type from Image Map to Procedural Texture.

An important benefit of procedural textures is that because they're solved as each frame is rendered, their resolution is infinite. Unlike an image, if the camera gets close to a procedural texture, the details are still well defined (**Figure 12.41**). This is not true, however, if the camera travels further away from the camera. Textures that use procedural maps tend to "swim," creating unwanted artifacts and ruining the shot.

An image is defined by its resolution, so as you move closer, the image appears more and more jagged, actually showing its pixels close up (**Figure 12.42**). Naturally, we can minimize this by using the Pixel Blending and Texture Antialiasing options, but the differences are still pretty strong.

No surface found in nature is ever really one unvarying color. For example, the Eyeball surface in our object is currently a consistent white. We're going to add a very subtle effect in order to break it up a bit.

To add a procedural texture:

1. Load Eyeball_setup.lws into Layout.

2. Click Surface Editor in the toolbar or press Ctrl + F3 to open the Surface Editor.

3. Click Eyeball in the surface list.

4. Click the Diffuse attribute's T button.

5. When the Texture Editor opens, choose Procedural Texture from the Layer Type pull-down menu (**Figure 12.43**).

continues on next page

CREATING A TEXTURE

6. From the Procedural Type pull-down menu, choose Crumple (**Figure 12.44**).

7. Type 200 in the Texture Value field, 4 in the Frequencies field, and 0.75 in the Small Power field (**Figure 12.45**).

8. Click Automatic Sizing to have LightWave automatically calculate the texture's scale to fit the surface.

Watch the surface preview window to see how these changes affect the surface (**Figure 12.46**).

9. Type 50 in the Layer Opacity field and click Use Texture to close the editor.

Notice that we've reduced the effect's strength (**Figure 12.47**).

10. From the File pull-down menu in the toolbar, choose Save > Save Current Object to save the new surfacing attributes to the object.

11. Press F9 to render the frame.

✔ Tips

■ Most procedurals are either a good starting point, or a modifier for an existing texture. You'll rarely ever see professionals use procedurals alone to create an effect.

■ As you adjust the procedural's values, the texture preview window displays a two-dimensional solution of the texture's algorithm, showing you what changes your adjustments are making. You may have noticed that a procedural texture doesn't give you the option to set a projection axis. That's because all procedurals are applied to a 3D space, rather than a single axis.

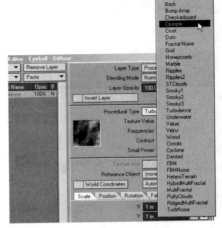

Figure 12.44 Select Crumple from the Procedural Type pull-down menu.

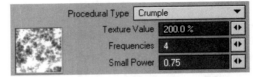

Figure 12.45 Enter these values into the Crumple texture's parameters.

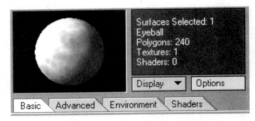

Figure 12.46 The surface preview window displays what these changes did.

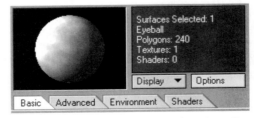

Figure 12.47 Reducing the layer's opacity reduces the overall strength of the texture layer.

CREATING A TEXTURE

Figure 12.48 A simple gradient going from one color to another.

Figure 12.49 A complex gradient involving several colors.

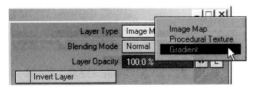

Figure 12.50 Change the Layer Type to Gradient.

Gradients

Typically, a gradient is two colors gradually blending from one to another (**Figure 12.48**). LightWave gradients can go one step further and blend to and from multiple colors, creating a very complex gradient (**Figure 12.49**). LightWave can use these blends in any of the attributes that support textures.

To create a gradient:

1. Follow Steps 1–3 in the "To add a procedural texture" procedure.

2. Click the Color attribute's T button.

3. When the Texture Editor opens, choose Gradient from the Layer Type pull-down menu (**Figure 12.50**).

   The large vertical white bar shows a preview of the proposed gradient. The horizontal bars indicate a value (or color) already entered. In order to have a gradient you need at least two colors.

   continues on next page

4. Click somewhere in the gradient preview to create another bar (**Figure 12.51**).

5. Drag the adjustment handles on the left side of the bar to move it to the bottom of the gradient (**Figure 12.52**).

   or

   Enter the numeric value in the Parameter field (**Figure 12.53**). A value of 1.0 is the end of the gradient.

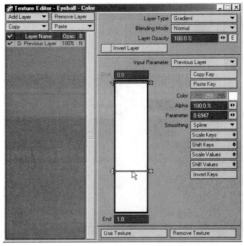

Figure 12.51 Click somewhere in the gradient window to create another value bar.

Figure 12.52 Drag the left portion of the bar to move it up and down the gradient.

Figure 12.53 Enter the position of the bar directly in the Parameter field.

CREATING A TEXTURE

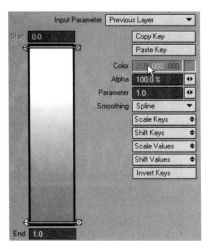

Figure 12.54 Change the color of the bar.

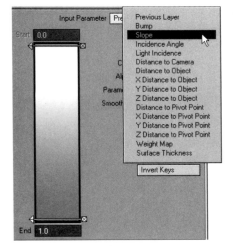

Figure 12.55 Change the Input Parameter to Slope.

6. Use the swatch or drag to adjust the second bar's color value. Make this color bar red.

The gradient preview is updated when the value is entered (**Figure 12.54**).

7. From the Input Parameter pull-down menu, choose Slope to use the range of colors depending on the slope of the geometry (**Figure 12.55**).

This step determines how the gradient is to be used.

8. Press F9 to render the preview (**Figure 12.56**).

You don't need to save the object because you won't be using this version in any further examples.

Figure 12.56 Render the image. Notice that the color of the surface changes according to the both the gradient and the slope of the surface.

CREATING A TEXTURE

345

Texture layers

A more popular use for gradients is to feed their color values into another texture, like a procedural. Texture layers allow you to stack several textures together in order to create a large, complex texture. The texture layer at the top of the list takes precedence over those underneath. So layer order becomes very important when you start using multiple textures, especially if they're supposed to work with each other.

This example demonstrates one way to use a gradient and procedural together, creating a much more complex texture.

To use gradients and procedural textures together:

1. Follow Steps 1–3 in the "To add a procedural texture" procedure.

2. Click the Color attribute's T button.

3. When the Texture Editor opens with the first (and only layer) selected, choose Procedural Texture from the Layer Type pull-down menu.

4. From the Procedural pull-down menu, choose Marble.

5. Enter the following values for the Marble procedural (**Figure 12.57**):

   ▲ Frequencies: 5

   ▲ Turbulence: 1.25

   ▲ Vein Spacing: 0.75

   ▲ Vein Sharpness: 4.0

6. Click the Scale tab and change the X, Y, and Z values from 1.0 m to 150 mm (**Figure 12.58**).

   This will make the effect appear much smaller on the surface.

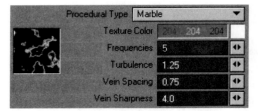

Figure 12.57 Enter these values into the Marble procedural texture.

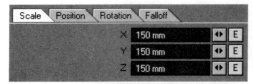

Figure 12.58 In the Scale tab, change the values of the axes to 150 mm.

Figure 12.59 Select Gradient from the Add Layer pull-down menu.

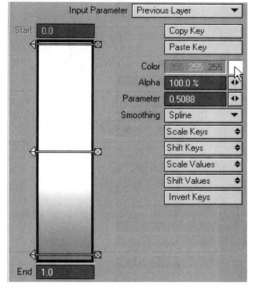

Figure 12.60 Change the center edit bar's color to white.

Figure 12.61 Move the bar to the exact middle of the gradient by entering 0.5 in its Parameter field.

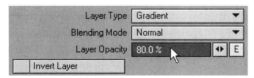

Figure 12.62 Change the Layer Opacity to 80 percent.

7. From the Add Layer pull-down menu, choose Gradient (**Figure 12.59**).

   This adds a second layer to your texture directly above the Marble texture.

8. Follow Steps 3–6 in the "To create a gradient" procedure to make a blend from white to red.

9. From the Input Parameter pull-down menu, choose Previous Layer to use the range of colors depending on the Marble layer.

10. Click somewhere in the middle of the gradient again to create a third value bar.

11. Use the color swatch or drag to make this bar's color white as well (**Figure 12.60**).

12. Type 0.5 in the Parameter field to position the bar precisely in the middle of the gradient (**Figure 12.61**).

13. Adjust the Layer Opacity to 80 percent to quickly reduce the strength of the gradient (**Figure 12.62**)

continues on next page

CREATING A TEXTURE

14. Switch to the marble layer by clicking on Marble from Layer Name list.

15. Select the Falloff tab to display new options below (**Figure 12.63**).

16. Type 100 in the Z parameter to use Texture Falloff to make the effect stronger in the back than the front

17. Click Use Texture to close the editor.

18. From the File pull-down menu in the toolbar, choose Save > Save Current Object to save the new surfacing attributes to the object.

19. Press [F9] to render the frame (**Figure 12.64**).

✔ Tips

- The most important value we set here was in the gradient's Input Parameter. Because the previous layer was our Marble texture, the gradient's color range was fed into that. This produces a nice gradient from the low and high values created by the Marble procedural.

- If you have multiple layers in your texture, you'll have to either adjust each of their Layer Opacity settings or create a more advanced layer system using alpha channels, blending modes, and gradients.

- You can change the order of the layers by simply clicking their names and dragging them up and down in the list.

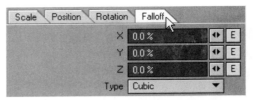

Figure 12.63 Click the Falloff tab to display falloff options for this texture.

Figure 12.64 Render the frame to see that the eyeball is now bloodshot.

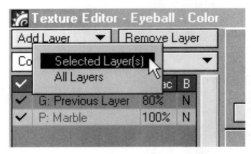

Figure 12.65 Choose Selected Layers from the Copy pull-down menu to copy the current layer.

CREATING A TEXTURE

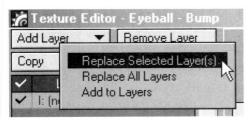

Figure 12.66 Select Replace Current Layer from the Paste pull-down menu.

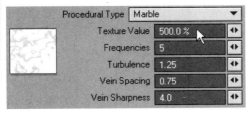

Figure 12.67 Change the Texture Value setting to 500 percent to increase its strength in the bump map.

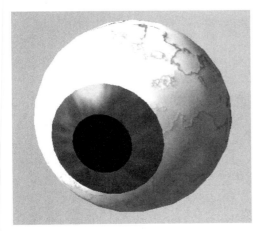

Figure 12.68 A render now shows that bloodshot eye with a little texture to it—bumpy veins.

Finally, you want to raise the veins we just made a little. You can do this by simply adding the same Marble effect to the Bump attribute. The values have to be the same as in the Color attribute in order for the effect to work. Luckily, it's very easy to do.

To copy a texture:

1. Follow Steps 1–3 in the "To add a procedural texture" procedure.

2. Click the Color attribute's T button.

3. When the Texture Editor opens, click Marble in the texture's layer list.

4. From the Copy pull-down menu, choose Selected Layer(s) (**Figure 12.65**).

5. Click Use Texture to close the Texture Editor.

6. Click the Bump attribute's T button to open its Texture Editor.

7. From the Paste pull-down menu, choose Replace Selected Layer(s) (**Figure 12.66**).

8. Type **500** in the Texture Value field (**Figure 12.67**) and click Use Texture to close the editor.

   This value controls the level of the bump map.

9. Save the object and press F9 to render the frame (**Figure 12.68**).

Animating Surface Attributes

One of the really powerful options available to LightWave's surfaces is the ability to animate the values over time. This is done by creating and editing keyframes in an envelope (see Chapter 10, "Advanced Animation Tools"). Only the values of the overall attribute can be animated, not the individual settings.

To add an envelope to a surface attribute:

1. Load Eyeball_setup.lws into Layout.

2. Click Surface Editor in the toolbar or press Ctrl+F3 to open the Surface Editor.

3. Click Eyeball in the surface list.

4. Click the Bump attribute's E (envelope) button (**Figure 12.69**).

5. Edit the envelope in the Graph Editor (**Figure 12.70**) by adding and adjusting its keyframes (see Chapter, 10 "Advanced Animation Tools").

6. Close the Graph Editor.

When it comes time to render the scene, the eyeball's bump map values (the bump height) will be animated according to the envelope set in the Graph Editor.

Figure 12.69 Click on the E button to animate the surface value in the Graph Editor.

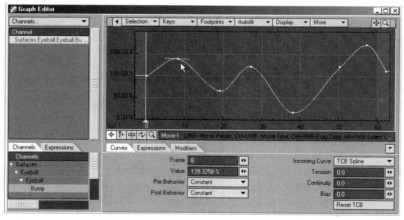

Figure 12.70 The Graph Editor lets you animate the attribute's value.

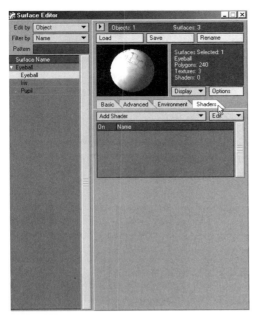

Figure 12.71 Click the Shaders tab to display the list of Shaders.

More Surface Property tabs

The surface parameters found in the Advanced and Environmental tabs pertain to very specific surfacing effects. Unless you're actually trying these settings out, it may be a while before you delve so deep into LightWave's surfacing techniques. These settings are beyond the scope of this book, but full descriptions can be found in the LightWave User's Manual.

Nevertheless, here are the basics. In the Advanced tab, you'll handle how the surface looks in alpha channels and special buffers, enable vertex colors and glow effects, and add special lighting effects. The Environmental tab lets you determine what gets reflected or refracted in a surface. You can use ray tracing, the backdrop, spherical maps, or a combination of these.

Shaders

The Shaders tab is the last one in the Surface Editor. A shader is a plug-in that extends LightWave's capabilities by generating a special effect on a surface. These special effects range from rendering your surface to look like a cartoon to handling complex lighting calculations. Several shaders are already supplied by NewTek, and plenty more can be found online or purchased from third-party developers. Some of them are really incredible.

In this exercise, you'll add one of the more stylized shaders. This is the one that makes a surface look like it belongs in a cartoon!

To add a shader:

1. Load Eyeball_setup.lws into Layout.

2. Click Surface Editor in the toolbar or press Ctrl + F3 to open the Surface Editor.

3. Click Eyeball in the surface list.

4. Select the Shaders tab to display the shader options (**Figure 12.71**).

continues on next page

5. From the Add Shader pull-down menu, choose Super Cel Shader (**Figure 12.72**).

In the surface preview window, notice how this shader affects the surface (**Figure 12.73**). This effect is typically used to help create a total of four flat-color shading zones.

6. To adjust the shader's parameters to your liking, double-click its name in the list of shaders applied to this surface.

If the Shader has an option window, it will open (**Figure 12.74**).

✔ Tip

■ The shaders listed in the Add Shader pull-down window vary depending on what plug-ins have been added to LightWave. If you installed LightWave normally, the Super Cel Shader plug-in should be there. Otherwise, please refer to the LightWave 3D User's Manual for how to add a plug-in to LightWave.

Figure 12.72 Select Super Cel Shader from the Add Shader pull-down menu.

Figure 12.73 The surface preview window shows the effect of this plug-in.

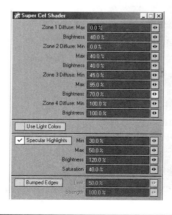

Figure 12.74 The Super Cel Shader's options window.

ANIMATING SURFACE ATTRIBUTES

Figure 12.75 Select Enable Viper from the Render tab.

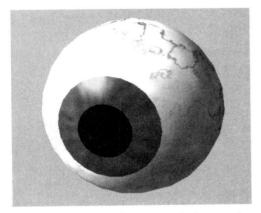

Figure 12.76 Render the frame to put the image and special data into Viper.

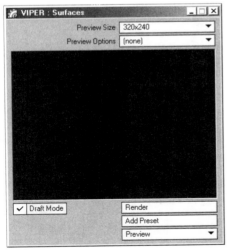

Figure 12.77 The Viper window can be used for surfaces, volumetric lights, and HyperVoxels.

Viper

The Versatile Interactive Previewing Renderer (Viper) can be used when rendering a full frame takes too long and the surface preview window doesn't show you enough of the surface. Rather than rerendering the whole frame, Viper automatically detects which surface is currently being edited and only redraws that particular part of the surface. This can drastically reduce the time it takes to preview a surface in a complex scene.

The Viper window has two real functions: It makes editing surfaces and effects more interactive, and it lets you quickly select surfaces.

To use Viper:

1. Load the Eyeball_setup.lws scene we saved in the "To set up the Surface Editor" procedure.

2. From the Render tab, choose Enable Viper (**Figure 12.75**).

3. Press F9 to render the current frame and put the image and special data into Viper (**Figure 12.76**).

4. Click Surface Editor in the toolbar or press Ctrl+F3 to open the Surface Editor.

5. Click the Viper button in the toolbar to open the Viper window (**Figure 12.77**).

continues on next page

VIPER

6. Click the Render button in the Viper window to have Layout use the internal data saved in Step 3 (**Figure 12.78**).

7. Click the Iris texture in the Viper window. It's now selected in the Surface Editor (**Figure 12.79**).

8. Edit the Color attribute's base color to dark red using either the swatch or drag method.

Watch the changes in the Viper window (**Figure 12.80**).

✔ Tips

■ Viper is also used for previewing both volumetric lights (see Chapter 8, "Lighting") and HyperVoxels (see Chapter 11, "Creating Special Effects").

■ For more accurate previews, turn off Draft Mode by clicking its check box, but for faster previews keep it checked.

■ A test render is not necessary for the Viper window to work properly with volumetrics.

Figure 12.78 Click Render to display the render data in the window.

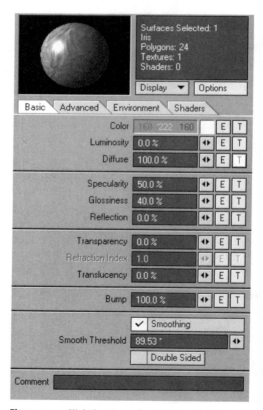

Figure 12.79 Click the Iris surface to select it in the Surface Editor.

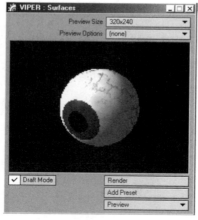

Figure 12.80 As you edit surface attributes in the Surface Editor, Viper updates its window to reflect the changes.

Presets

LightWave lets you save, load, and organize surfaces from a database, which is displayed and managed in the Surface Preset window. This feature allows you to save various surfaces to disc and recall them later.

To use the Preset window:

1. Follow the Steps 1–6 in the "To use Viper" procedure.

2. Click Presets from the Window pull-down menu to display the Surface Preset window.

3. Click Add Preset in the Viper window to save the Iris surface to the Surface Preset window (**Figure 12.81**).

4. Alter the Color attribute again to change the color of the Iris surface.

continues on next page

continues on next page

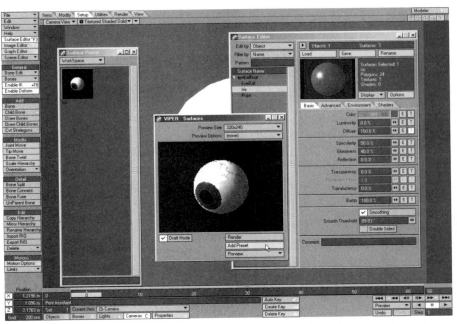

Figure 12.81 Click the Add Preset button in the Viper window to add the surface parameters to the Surface Preset database.

PRESETS

5. Double-click the picture of the eyeball (labeled Iris) in the Surface Preset window (**Figure 12.82**).

6. When the Load Confirmation window appears, click Yes to load the Surface Preset's values into the current surface.

✔ Tips

■ The database mentioned is simply a list of files located in the NewTek/Programs/ Presets directory. You can manipulate the contents of this database using your system's file-editing functions.

■ Manage the contents of the database by right-clicking the Preset window. You can choose to remove, rename, and organize into libraries all the presets in this window.

■ Be sure to check to the various Web sites for free, downloadable presets.

Figure 12.82 Double-click the Iris surface from Viper to load its settings into the current surface.

PRESETS

RENDERING YOUR SCENE

After you've modeled and surfaced your objects and finished animating the items in your scene, you'll want to output the results so that you can view them. This process is called *rendering*. Layout uses all of the information you've given it to render your scene—calculating item positions, surface attributes, item and surface interactions, and post-processing effects to create full-color images.

In this chapter, you'll learn how to configure the LightWave renderer for generating preview and final output renders of your scene, as well as how to optimize some of the individual items in your scene to save render time.

Considering Render Time

LightWave 3D is a ray-tracing renderer, meaning that it casts render rays from the camera, lights, and other items to calculate realistic reflections, shadows, and caustic and radiosity effects. For instance, if you have Ray Trace Reflections on, LightWave first casts render rays from the camera to determine what items are visible in the current frame. Then it casts rays from each of the lights in the scene to determine which items they illuminate. Finally it casts rays from object surfaces that have a reflectivity value greater than zero to determine what items in the scene should be reflected. It works the same for shadows, caustics, and refraction. Although ray tracing is excellent for creating realistic surfaces, it's also computationally intensive and adds to your render times.

How long Layout takes to render a frame from your scene depends on many factors, including the number of items, effects, and surfaces visible to the Layout camera, and what ray-tracing options are active. For instance, using true volumetric light and smoke effects takes longer to render than simply using a fractal procedural texture as a transparency map on a flat polygon for smoke or on a cone to simulate a volumetric light. Similarly, rendering using the radiosity settings for global illumination takes considerably longer than faking the effect with multiple lights in your scene.

You need to weigh the level of detail that you want against how long it will take to render the frame. In high-end movie projects, it is not unheard of to have a single frame of animation take more than 15 hours to render! There are many time-saving tricks that you can use to optimize your scene and reduce render time. Check out any of the magazines that cover LightWave, such as *NewTek Pro* and

Keyframe Magazine, or Internet sites, such as www.lightwave3d.com, www.luxology.net, and www.flay.com.

Although generating an OpenGL preview of your scene or doing a quick surface or volumetric test with Viper is a great timesaver, to properly preview effects such as surface specularity, reflection, refraction, image filters, or the combination of different environmental effects, you must perform an actual render. Still, there's no need to do a full-sized, fully anti-aliased render with all of the bells and whistles if you're checking the reflectivity of a surface, so you can create a preview at a lower resolution than the final output render, with less image anti-aliasing and the effects you don't need to see turned off. Preview renders are generally a single frame, but sometimes you'll want to render out a range of frames to an animation file to preview animated effects.

When you're completely finished with your scene and ready to show it to your client or friends, you need to render out a final version. The main difference between a preview render and a final output render is that on final output, you're rendering and saving a full-resolution image to a file. These images are generally saved as an animation file in a format such as Video for Windows or QuickTime or as sequentially numbered image files in whatever format you choose.

Configuring the Renderer

As we mentioned in Chapter 10, "Advanced Animation Tools," you set the final resolution of your image and the anti-aliasing level in the Camera Properties panel. When rendering, LightWave uses the currently selected Layout camera, so you might want to set up multiple cameras with different resolutions, and then switch between them for preview renders and final output. You set the non-camera render properties in the Render Options panel, specifying which frames to render, how to render them, whether you want to watch the render in progress, and if you want to use one of the built-in viewers to view each frame at full resolution as they're finished. We've broken the following example into several sections to make it easier to follow.

To set up a render:

1. Create or load a scene with some animation into Layout.

2. Select the Render tab, and then click Render Options in the toolbar (**Figure 13.1**).

3. When the Render Options panel appears, make sure that the Render First Frame and Render Last Frame fields contain the appropriate frame numbers for your animation (**Figure 13.2**).

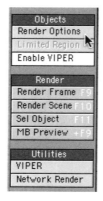

Figure 13.1 Choose Render Options to open the panel below.

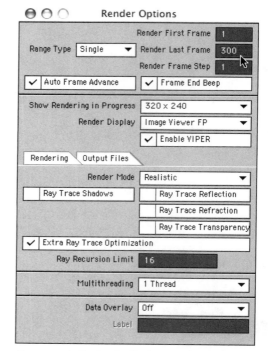

Figure 13.2 In the Render Options panel, you can specify a range of frames to render if you want to preview just a certain part of your animation, or render out the whole thing.

CONFIGURING THE RENDERER

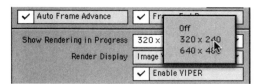

Figure 13.3 Use Show Rendering in Progress to watch your frame as it renders.

4. Double-check to make sure that the Render Frame Step field is set to 1 (the default setting) so that Layout will advance one frame each time it renders.

5. If you want to prevent your computer from beeping each time Layout finishes rendering a frame and advances to the next, deselect the Frame End Beep check box.

6. Leave Auto Frame Advance checked so that Layout will automatically advance to the next frame as it finishes each one.

7. From the Show Rendering in Progress pull-down menu, choose 320 × 240 (**Figure 13.3**).

8. Deselect the Enable Viper check box. Capturing render information for Viper can add to your render time.

CONFIGURING THE RENDERER

Now you need to specify a filename and location for your animation. You have a couple of different options when choosing how to output your finished scene. You can render out either a continuous animation file (for example, in Video for Windows or QuickTime) or a single frame or series of sequentially numbered frames. Doubtless, your choice will hinge upon the intended viewing medium and whether you need to import the frames into another application for compositing or further image processing.

To save out an animation file:

1. Follow the preceding procedure, "To set up a render."

2. Select the Output Files tab in the middle of the Render Options panel to display more image file options (**Figure 13.4**).

3. Check the Save Animation check box to open the Animation File dialog.

4. Select a file location and name for your animation file, and click Save (**Figure 13.5**).

5. From the Type pull-down menu in the Render Options panel, choose a suitable animation format for your system (**Figure 13.6**).

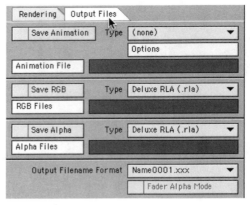

Figure 13.4 The Output Files tab contains all of your image and animation file-saving options.

Figure 13.5 Saving an animation outputs an animated movie file.

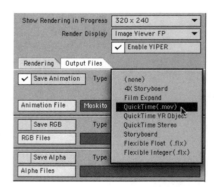

Figure 13.6 You can render out different types of QuickTime and Video for Windows movie files.

CONFIGURING THE RENDERER

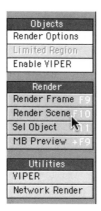

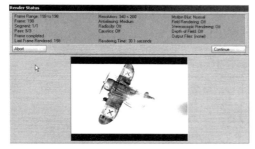

Figure 13.7 The Render Scene option is located in the toolbar under the Render tab.

Figure 13.8 The Render Status window lets you save time by aborting the render if you spot a problem. However, if enabled, it can add to your overall render time.

6. Click the Options button to open the interface for the format you chose, and choose an appropriate codec.

7. Close the Render Options panel.

8. Click Render Scene in the toolbar or press F10 to render the frame range you specified in the previous set of steps (**Figure 13.7**).

LightWave now renders your scene and saves each frame to the animation file that you specified.

✔ Tips

■ At the beginning of a render, if you have a Render Display selected in the Render Options panel, LightWave notifies you and asks if you want to disable it. When rendering entire sequences, it's a good idea to disable the Render Display, which is used primarily for previewing.

■ As it renders, LightWave displays a Render Status window with information about the scene. If you choose Show Rendering in Progress, the status window includes a panel of the size you specified showing you the current frame as it is rendered (**Figure 13.8**). When LightWave is finished rendering your scene, it automatically closes the Render Status window and returns you to the Layout interface.

CONFIGURING THE RENDERER

In addition to saving an animation file, you can save out a sequence of individual frames. This is useful when you're going to output to film or want to import the images into another application for further modification. When saving to individual image files, you must specify a base name that is shared by all the files, an Output Filename Format (how LightWave appends the frame numbers to the base name), and the desired image file format.

To save out sequential frames:

1. Follow the first procedure in this chapter, "To set up a render."

2. In the Render Options panel, deselect the Save Animation check box.

3. Check the Save RGB check box to open the Save dialog; then select a file location and base name for your animation file and click OK.

4. From the Type pull-down menu, choose a suitable image file format (**Figure 13.9**).

5. From the Output Filename Format pull-down menu, choose a file-naming method.

   We used Name001.xxx (**Figure 13.10**).

6. Click Render Scene in the toolbar or press F10 to render the frame range you specified.

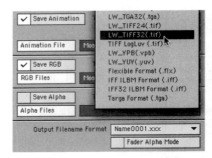

Figure 13.9 LightWave supports all the major image file formats.

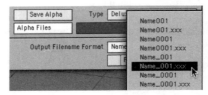

Figure 13.10 You can specify in what format LightWave appends the frame number to the base name of your image files.

CONFIGURING THE RENDERER

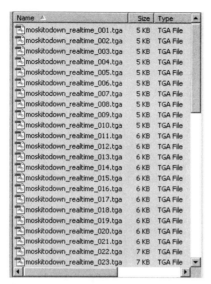

Figure 13.11 LightWave saves an individual image file for each frame in your scene to the directory that you specified.

7. When LightWave is finished rendering your scene, use a file browser to open the directory where you saved the images (**Figure 13.11**).

LightWave renders out an individual file for each frame of the animation, appending to it the specified frame number and file extension.

✔ Tips

■ To do a preview render of the current frame without saving a file, click Render Frame in the toolbar or press ⎡F9⎤ to render the current frame. Be sure you have a Render Display active in the Render Options panel so that you can view the image when LightWave is finished.

■ If your work requires you to render out separate alpha channels for your images, you can check the Save Alpha check box, located below the Save RGB option. Configure it the same way as the Save RGB option to make it save out individual alpha images in the specified format to the specified location. Choosing a 32 bit saver in the Save RGB options creates an image with an embedded alpha channel.

Exploring Render Modes

Now that you know how to render an animation, let's take a look at some of Layout's different render modes. LightWave has three render modes: Wireframe, Quickshade, and Realistic. The Wireframe render mode renders objects as wireframe representations. The Quickshade mode renders objects using only their base color, luminosity, and diffuse surface attributes, ignoring all others. The Realistic mode is LightWave's default render mode, and renders all of an object's surface attributes. The ray-tracing options are available only in Realistic mode. Let's take a closer look at the modes.

To use the Wireframe render mode:

1. Create or load a simple scene into Layout.

2. Click Render Options in the toolbar to open the Render Options panel.

3. From the Render Display pull-down menu, select Image Viewer (**Figure 13.12**).

4. Select the Rendering tab in the middle of the panel to display new options, and choose Wireframe from the Render Mode pull-down menu (**Figure 13.13**).

5. Click Render Frame in the toolbar or press F9 to initiate a test render.

6. When the render is finished, click Abort or press Esc to close the Render Status window.

   When the render is done, Layout displays the finished frame in the image viewer window (**Figure 13.14**).

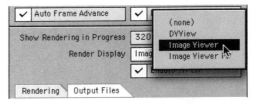

Figure 13.12 Use the image viewer when doing test renders.

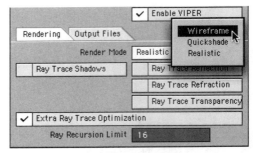

Figure 13.13 Set the rendering mode to Wireframe.

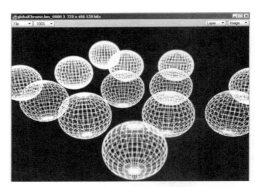

Figure 13.14 Frames rendered using the Wireframe mode look like raw wireframe models.

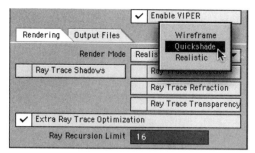

Figure 13.15 Set the rendering mode to Quickshade.

Figure 13.16 In Quickshade mode, objects are rendered using the most basic surface attributes to speed up render time. It's great for creating animatics.

✔ Tips

- You can leave the image viewer open between renders, and it will store all of the images as layers. You can switch between the layers using the Layer pull-down menu in the upper-left corner. This is handy for viewing differences as you make changes.

- The image viewer can display the RGB image or the alpha channel of the image depending on which mode you choose in the pull-down menu to the right of the Layer menu.

- You can zoom in on your rendered image using the image viewer's Zoom Level pull-down menu, in the upper-left corner next to the File menu. Once zoomed in, you can scroll around the image using the cursor keys.

- To save an image directly from the image viewer, select Save RGB from the File pull-down menu, and then choose an image file format.

To use the Quickshade render mode:

1. Follow Steps 1–3 in the previous procedure.

2. Select the Rendering tab in the Render Options panel, and choose Quickshade from the Render Mode pull-down menu (**Figure 13.15**).

3. Click Render Frame in the toolbar or press [F9] to initiate a test render.

4. When the render is finished, click Abort or press [Esc] to close the Render Status window.

   When the render is done, Layout displays the finished frame in the image viewer window (**Figure 13.16**).

To use the Realistic render mode:

1. Follow Steps 1–3 in the first procedure in this section, "To use the Wireframe render mode."

2. Select the Rendering tab and choose Realistic from the Render Mode pull-down menu (**Figure 13.17**).

3. Click Render Frame in the toolbar or press F9 to initiate a test render.

4. When the render is finished, click Abort or press Esc to close the Render Status window.

   When the render is done, Layout displays the finished frame in the image viewer window (**Figure 13.18**).

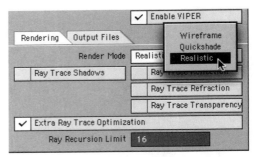

Figure 13.17 Set the rendering mode to Realistic.

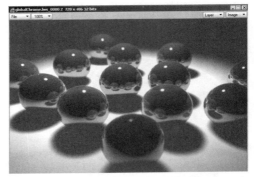

Figure 13.18 In Realistic mode, all properties of the objects and scene are taken into account during the render.

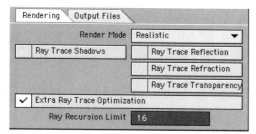

Figure 13.19 The ray-trace options can increase both realism and render time.

Using Ray Trace Options

LightWave has a few ray-trace options that you can set to optimize your scene. You can use all of these options in tandem or individually, depending on the demands of your scene. Obviously, the more ray tracing you have, the longer your scene takes to render. When working, you want to save as much time as possible, so you can find good tutorials on the Web and in various magazines for simulating ray tracing effects to cut down on render times. To access the ray-trace options, click the Rendering tab in the Render Options panel (**Figure 13.19**):

◆ **Ray Trace Shadows:** This option tells the renderer to create the shadows of any lights with a ray-traced type of shadow.

◆ **Ray Trace Reflection:** This option tells the renderer to use ray tracing to create reflections in surfaces.

◆ **Ray Trace Refraction:** This option tells the renderer to use ray tracing to create refraction effects.

◆ **Ray Trace Transparency:** This is a special option used to render volumetric effects behind transparent surfaces. For instance, without this option, active volumetric lights and HyperVoxels would not appear through the glass of a window surface.

continues on next page

USING RAY TRACE OPTIONS

◆ **Extra Ray Trace Optimization:** By default, LightWave uses a fast and efficient ray-tracing method to calculate effects. But sometimes you want a little extra detail in your ray-traced effects. This option tells LightWave to use a more sophisticated ray-tracing method that confines rays to a tighter area, adding more realism to the effect. This option can speed up the rendering of scenes with a lot of ray tracing, but might slow down scenes that have a lot of geometry and little ray tracing.

◆ **Ray Recursion Limit:** This option sets the number of bounces that a ray makes when determining different ray-tracing effects. For example, if you have two mirrors facing one another, you would see what seemed like an endless corridor of mirrors as they reflected one another. In rendering this scene, there needs to be a limit to the number of reflections; otherwise, the renderer would get stuck in an infinite loop. If you set the Ray Recursion Limit to 4, then each mirror would only reflect the other (and itself) four times and so on. Higher ray-recursion levels can lead to longer render times, so it isn't advisable to raise this value unless you need that added punch of realism.

✔ Tip

■ If you're working on a multi-CPU machine, you can shorten your render times by using the Multithreading pull-down menu to divide the work among a user-definable number of CPUs. Sometimes setting the Thread number to twice the number of physical CPUs you have in your machine will shorten render times even further. Experiment with the Multithreading setting to find out what works best with your machine.

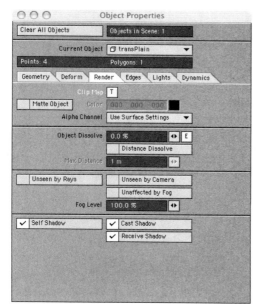

Figure 13.20 You can modify the render properties of an object in the Object Properties panel. Click the Render tab to display the first set of options.

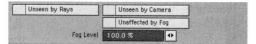

Figure 13.21 You can specify what gets ray traced and what doesn't for each object.

Using Object Render Options

In addition to setting the general render options, you can modify some render properties for each individual object. Access these options through the Object Properties panel (**Figure 13.20**), where you'll find two tabs with render options: Render and Edges.

Ray-trace options

These four render options allow you to control how the ray-tracing engine interacts with your object (**Figure 13.21**):

◆ **Unseen by Rays:** With this option active the surfaces of your object are not included in any ray-tracing calculations. For instance, a sphere with a reflective surface no longer reflects.

◆ **Unseen by Camera:** With this option active, your object is not rendered, but is still included in any ray-tracing calculations, meaning that its ray-traced shadows still renders and it still shows up as a reflection in other objects.

◆ **Unaffected by Fog:** With this option active, your object is not included when rendering fog, meaning that it shows up 100 percent in the final image.

◆ **Fog Level:** Unlike Unaffected by Fog, which totally omits the object from any fog rendering, this option lets you determine how much the object is affected by the fog in the scene, and thus how much it shows up in the final image.

Shadow options

The Object shadow render options allow you to control how LightWave deals with the shadows an object casts and those that fall on it from other objects in the scene (**Figure 13.22**).

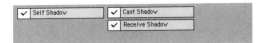

Figure 13.22 You can control how each object in the scene interacts with shadows.

◆ **Self Shadow:** This option determines whether or not an object casts shadows on itself.

◆ **Cast Shadow:** This option determines whether or not an object casts shadows on other objects.

◆ **Receive Shadow:** This option determines whether or not other objects can cast shadows upon an object.

Edge options

LightWave also provides options for rendering polygon and object edges. These come in handy when you want to render a line around the edges of your object or its surfaces. Click the Edges tab to display these options (**Figure 13.23**).

◆ **Polygon Size:** This control determines whether LightWave renders each polygon at its original size or a fraction of its size (**Figure 13.24**). You can animate this parameter over time with an envelope to create the effect of polygons growing to form the object.

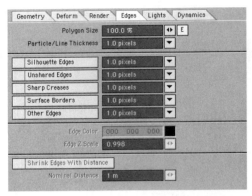

Figure 13.23 Click the Edges tab to display a new set of options. The object edge options when used in conjunction with the BESM surface shader are great for creating cartoon-style renders.

Figure 13.24 The polygon size has been set to 85 percent for this object.

Figure 13.25 These particles are 5 pixels wide.

Figure 13.26 Silhouette Edges traces the outline of your object.

Figure 13.27 Sharp Creases draws a line wherever there is a crease.

◆ **Particle/Line Thickness:** This option determines how big LightWave renders particles, single-point, and two-point polygons (**Figure 13.25**).

◆ **Silhouette Edges:** This option renders the outer edge or outline of the object in the specified color and thickness (**Figure 13.26**).

◆ **Unshared Edges:** This option renders an edge in the specified color and size where two surfaces meet but do not share an edge.

◆ **Sharp Creases:** This option renders an edge in the specified color and size wherever there's a crease between two polygons (**Figure 13.27**).

continues on next page

USING OBJECT RENDER OPTIONS

◆ **Surface Borders:** This option renders an edge in the specified color and size wherever two surfaces meet (**Figure 13.28**).

◆ **Other Edges:** This option renders an edge in the specified color and size around each polygon in the object.

◆ **Edge Color:** This control determines what color the rendered edges will be.

◆ **Edge Z Scale:** This option determines the Z-depth of the object's edges. This is an advanced feature that you won't need to change 99 percent of the time.

◆ **Shrink Edges with Distance:** This option tells the renderer to scale the size of the edges as the object moves away from the Layout camera (**Figure 13.29**). Without this option, as the object gets smaller the edge lines don't, so they could easily become bigger than the object and obscure it.

◆ **Nominal Distance:** This option specifies at what distance from the camera the edges are 100 percent of their specified size.

Figure 13.28 Surface Borders draws a line between each of the surfaces.

Figure 13.29 The object edges are drawn smaller the farther the object moves from the camera.

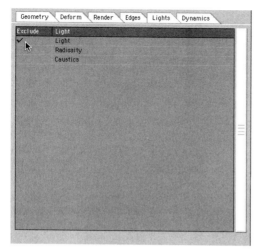

Figure 13.30 The light exclusion list is in the Object Properties panel. Click in the Exclude column to tell the light to ignore the current object.

Figure 13.31 Who turned the lights out?

Light exclusion

You can also exclude an object from being effected by various lights in your scene. This is a powerful feature, allowing you to prevent light spill, where a light meant to illuminate a different part of the scene also hits another object.

In Chapter 8, "Lighting," you learned to use the object exclusion list in the Light Properties panel to exclude multiple objects from a single light. However, if you want to exclude a single object from multiple lights, it is quicker to use the light exclusion list in the Object Properties panel. As you'll see, the end result is the same with both procedures, but you should know how to do them both.

The light exclusion list displays the name of every light in the scene and also has options for excluding the object from radiosity and caustics. Excluding an object from these latter two can greatly reduce unnecessary render calculations and shorten your render times.

To exclude an object from a light:

1. Press [+] to open and select an object to load into Layout.

2. Click Properties or press [p] to open the Object Properties panel.

3. Select the Lights tab to open the light exclusion list, and click in the Exclude column next to the entry for the default light (**Figure 13.30**).

   Your object goes dark without a light source to illuminate it (**Figure 13.31**).

Working with High Dynamic Range Imagery

LightWave's render engine supports both input and output of up to 32 bits of floating-point data per color channel, which makes it ideal for working with high dynamic range imagery, or HDRI. HDRI is a relatively new technology, in which special image maps are used as a form of global illumination. Basically, you use the image to light your scene. There are several HDRI images included with the LightWave content, and SkyTracer2 can save your sky creations out as spherical HDRI maps for later use. An excellent resource for HDRI maps and technical information is on the Internet at www.debevec.org. Like radiosity, HDRI is render-intensive, so for the following exercise, we recommend using a relatively low camera resolution.

To light a scene using HDRI:

1. Create or load a scene into Layout.

   A simple object or group of objects works great for this exercise.

2. Click the default light in the Layout Viewport.

3. Click the Properties button or press [p] to open the Light Properties panel.

4. In the Light Intensity field, type **10** and press [Enter] to accept the new value (**Figure 13.32**).

5. Click the Global Illumination button to open the Global Illumination panel (**Figure 13.33**).

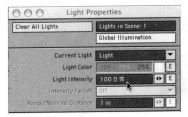

Figure 13.32 Adjust light intensity in the Light Properties panel.

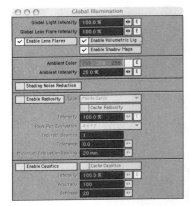

Figure 13.33 The Global Illumination panel contains the radiosity settings.

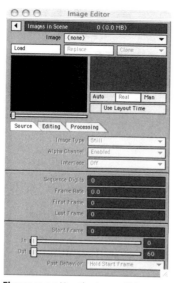

Figure 13.34 Use the Image Editor to load the HDRI image into Layout.

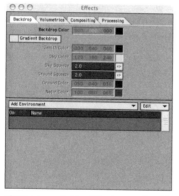

Figure 13.35 In the Effects panel, add the HDRI lighting environment.

Figure 13.36 Image World uses the HDRI image to replace LightWave's default backdrop.

6. In the Ambient Intensity field, type 25 and press [Enter] to accept the change.

7. Click the Enable Radiosity check box.

8. From the Type pull-down menu, choose Backdrop Only so that the renderer uses the HDRI image as the source of illumination.

9. In the Intensity field, type 50 and press [Enter] to accept the change.

10. From the Rays Per Evaluation pull-down menu, select 3 × 9.

11. Click the Image Editor button in the toolbar or press [Ctrl]+[F1] to open the Image Editor (**Figure 13.34**).

12. Click the Load button and navigate to Images/hdri; then double-click building_probe.hdr to load it into Layout.

13. Click the Scene tab at the top of the interface to display new options in the toolbar, and then click Backdrop or press [Ctrl]+[F5] to open the Backdrop Effects panel (**Figure 13.35**).

14. From the Add Environment pull-down menu, select Image World (**Figure 13.36**).

continues on next page

15. Double-click the Image World entry in the environment list to open its properties (**Figure 13.37**).

16. From the Light Probe Image pull-down menu, select `building_probe.hdr`.

17. In the Brightness field, type 35 and press Enter to accept the change.

18. Press Enter again to render the scene.

You end up with a scene in which the objects are completely illuminated by the `building_probe.hdr` image (**Figure 13.38**).

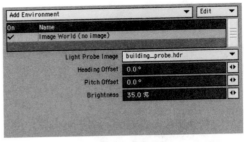

Figure 13.37 Double-click the Image World entry.

✔ Tip

■ Your results might differ somewhat from the example shown here. Try modifying the various settings and rerendering to gain an understanding of how each setting impacts the final look of your scene.

■ The Shading Noise Reduction option, as well as higher anti-aliasing settings, helps to reduce grain and produce smoother images.

Figure 13.38 Now the objects are illuminated by the HDRI map.

INDEX

A

Absolute Size dialog, 191
Absolute Size tool, 190
Accuracy parameter, Caustics effect, 230
Add Edges tool, 107–108
Add function, Boolean operations, 118
Add Key tool, Graph Editor interface, 259
Add Partigon button, 8
Add Points tool, 104
Affect Diffuse option, lights parameter, 218
Affect Specular option, lights parameter, 218
Align to Path option, 285–286
animation
    axis movement disabling, 153
    info numeric fields, 154
    keyframes, 163
        deleting, 166
        manually creating, 164–165
    manipulating items with mouse, 148–152
    preview
        creating, 168–169
        shuttle controls, 167
    surfaces, 350–352
    time, 158
        change frame number, 160
        frame rate, 161–162
        frame slider label change, 160–161
        setting start and end frames, 159
    tools, 155–157, 249
        channel modifiers, 268–270
        coordinate systems, 288–291
        handles, 152
        Inverse Kinematics, 276–284
        keyframe automation, 250–253
        managing keyframes, 254–267
        motion modifiers, 287
        motion options, 285–286
        parenting items, 272–275
        targeting objects, 271
anti-aliasing, cameras, 242–244
Area Light command (Lights menu), 214
area lights, 208, 214
attributes, surfaces, 327–333
Auto Key option, 163, 250–253

B

Back view type, 24
backdrops, special effects
    color change, 294
    environment, 296
    SkyTracer2, 297–298
    using image, 295–296
Background Color option, 41
bend displacement tool, 187–188
Bend tool, 96–97
Bevel tool, 113
Bias control, Curves Properties, 264
Blend Group Name dialog, 315
Blur Length parameter, 247
Bone Weight Shade drawing mode, 30
Bone Weights, 136
Bone X-Ray drawing mode, 30
bones
    adding to objects, 198–200
    adjusting falloff, 201
    joint compensation, 202–203
    muscle flexing, 204
    skelegons
        editing, 80
        series using curves, 79
        Skelegon tool, 77–78
    use from other objects, 205
Bones properties panel, 202
Boolean operations, geometry editing, 116–120

Bottom view type, 24
Bounding Box
   drawing mode, 26
   Threshold option, 40
bump maps surface attributes, 329

C

Camera Name dialog, 233
Camera Properties panel, 235
Camera view type, 25
cameras, 231
   anti-aliasing, 242–244
   depth of field
      focal distance, 245
      Lens F-Stop, 246
   image resolution, 235
   lens customization, 239–241
   management, 232
      adding to scene, 233
      removing, 234
   motion rendering
      field rendering, 248
      motion blur, 247
   pixel aspect ratio, 236
   render time reduction
      Limited Region, 238
      Resolution Multiplier, 237
Cast Shadow option, 372
Caustics effect, Global Illumination panel, 230
Center current item tool, 31
Change Surface dialog , 124, 323
Channel bin, Graph Editor interface, 254
Channel list, Graph Editor interface, 254
channels
   adding to Channel bin, 257–258
   editing, 255–256
   modifiers, 268–270
Clear All Objects button, Object Properties
      panel, 173
Clear Camera dialog, 234
clipboard actions, 90
collision planes, particle effects, 299, 302–303
color
   backdrop special effects, 294
   light parameters, 216
   modifying surface, 332
   shadows, 224
color maps, 144–145
Color surface attributes, 327
Color Wireframe drawing mode, 27
Command hierarchical list, 7

commands
   Edit menu
      Display Options, 33
      Edit Keyboard Shortcuts, 10
      Edit Menu Layout, 6
   File menu
      Export, 18
      Load Object, 13
      Save, 15
      Save Object, 17
   Hub menu, Send Object to Layout, 13
   Layout menu, Quad, 44
   Lights menu
      Area Light, 214
      Distant Light, 209
      Linear Light, 213
      Point Light, 211
      Spotlight, 212
   Option menu, General Options, 21
   Preset menu, Default, 9
   Preview menu, Make Preview, 180
   Scene Editor menu, Open, 12
Configure Keys panel, 10
Configure Menus panel, 6
content directories, 19–21
Continuity control, Curves Properties, 264
coordinate systems
   changing, 288–289
   Local, 290–291
Create Endomorph dialog, 142
Create Motion Key dialog, 164
Create UV Texture Map dialog, 125
Create Vertex Color Map dialog, 145
Create Weight Map dialog, 136
Cubic projection types, 339
Current Item menu, Layout interface, 3
Current Object menu
   Modeler interface, 4
   Object Properties panel, 173
curves, 70. *See also* spline patches
   creating from points, 71
   Make Spline Patch panel, 75–76
   Sketch tool, 71
   Spline Draw tool, 73–74
Curves Properties, Graph Editor interface, 254, 264
customizing
   camera lens, 239–241
   interfaces, 6–8
      creating tabs, 8–9
      reset interface default, 9
   objects, 174–175
   OpenGL Viewports options, 37–38
Cylindrical projection types, 339

D

Default command (Preset menu), 9
defaults, keyboard short cuts, 11
deforming geometry, 183–186
Delete Motion Key dialog, 166
depth of fields
    focal distance, 245
    Lens F-Stop, 246
dialogs
    Absolute Size, 191
    Blend Group Name, 315
    Camera Name, 233
    Change Surface, 124, 323
    Clear Camera, 234
    Create Endomorph, 142
    Create Motion Key, 164
    Create UV Texture Map, 125
    Create Vertex Color Map, 145
    Create Weight Map, 136
    Delete Motion Key, 166
    General Options, 21
    Go to Frame, 160
    Light Name, 210, 211
    Load Image, 295
    Load Object, 16
    Load Scene, 15
    Make Preview, 168
    Null Object, 174
    Null Object Name, 149, 176, 215
    Open File, 13
    Properties (Hub), 14
    Rename Group, 9
    Save File, 18
    Save Scene As, 15
    Set Vertex Map Value, 138
    Subdivide Polygons, 183
Diffuse surface attributes, 327, 338–339
directories, content, 19–21
discontinuous UVs, 131
discussion boards, xii
displacement maps, 183–186
displacement tools, 187–188
Display Options command (Edit menu), 33
Distant Light command (Lights menu), 209
distant lights, 208–210
Dope Track, Layout interface, 3
Double Sided surface attributes, 329
Drag tool, 92
DragNet tool, 93–94
Dynamic Update option, 39

E

Edge Color option, 374
Edge options, rendering, 372–374
Edge Z Scale option, 374
edges
    anti-aliasing images, 243–244
    modifying tools
        adding, 107–108
        extend polygon edge, 106–107
        reduction, 108–109
        removing, 109–110
Edit Font List panel, 63
Edit Keyboard Shortcuts command (Edit menu), 10
Edit menu commands
    Display Options, 33
    Edit Keyboard Shortcuts, 10
    Edit Menu Layout, 6
Edit Menu Layout command (Edit menu), 6
Edit modes, Layout interface, 3
Edit Skelegon tool, 80
emitter tool, particle effects, 299–301
Enhanced High anti-aliasing setting, 242
Enhanced Low anti-aliasing setting, 242
envelopes control, surface attributes, 330
environments, backdrop special effects, 296
Export command (File menu), 18
exporting files, 18
Extender Plus tool, 106–107
Extra Ray Trace Optimization option, 370
Extrude tool, 111–112

F

falloff values, bones, 201
Fast Fog type, 307
Faster Highlights option, 38
File menu commands
    Export, 18
    Load Object, 13
    Save, 15
    Save Object, 17
files
    exporting, 18
    Layout interface, 15–17
    Modeler interface, 17
Flat Shade drawing mode, 28
Flay website, xii
focal distances, depth of fields, 245
Fog Level option, rendering, 371
fog special effects, 305–307

INDEX

fonts, adding to Modeler interface, 63
Forward Kinematics (FK), 276
four-point polygons, 51
Frame control, Curves Properties, 264
frame rates (fps), 161–162
frame slider, 159
    change frame number, 160
    frame rate, 161–162
    label change, 160–161
    Layout interface, 3
    setting start and end frames, 159
    time options, 161
Front Face Wireframe drawing mode, 27
Front projection types, 339
Front view type, 24

G

General Options command (Option menu), 21
General Options dialog, 21
geometry
    altering Modeler interface, 44–46
    deforming, 183–186
    editing
        Add Points tool, 104
        bending, 96–97
        Boolean operations, 116–120
        clipboard actions, 90
        edge modification, 106–110
        extending, 111–115
        layers, 82–85
        Merge Points command, 102–103
        Merge Polygons command, 105
        moving, 91–94
        rotating, 95–96
        scaling, 98–99
        selection methods, 86–89
        Spline Guide tool, 100–102
        Split command, 104–105
        tapering, 100
        twisting, 97
        Unweld Points command, 103
        Weld Points command, 103
    Info panels, 56–57
    normals, 55
    organic modeling
        curves and spline patches, 70–76
        SubPatches, 66–70
    points. *See also* points
        creating, 47–48
        Numeric panel, 49
        series, 49
    polygons, 50–51. *See also* polygons
        creating, 52

Pen tool, 53
    shared points, 54
primitives, 59
    creating segments, 62
    making box, 60
    Numeric panel, 61
skelegons
    editing, 80
    series using curves, 79
    Skelegon tool, 77–78
Statistics panel, 58
text
    adding font to Modeler interface, 63
    creating, 64
    Text tool Numeric panel, 65
global display options, Viewports, 39–42
Global Illumination panel
    Caustics effect, 230
    Radiosity effect, 228–229
Glossiness surface attributes, 328
glowing objects, special effects, 308–309
Go to Frame dialog, 160
gradients
    layered textures, 346–349
    textures, 343–345
Graph Editor interface
    editing motions, 259–267
    keyframe management, 254–258
gravity, particle effects, 299, 302
ground fog special effects, 306–307

H

HDRI (High Dynamic Range Imagery), light
    rendering, 376–378
Hub
    configuring, 14
    send object to Layout interface, 13
Hub menu commands, Send Object to
    Layout, 13
HyperVoxels properties panel, 314
HyperVoxels special effects, 311
    liquid effects, 312–316
    smoke effects, 317–319

I

image maps, textures, 337–339
Image World environment tool, 296
images
    anti-aliasing, 242–244
    backdrop special effects, 295–296
    pixel aspect ratio, 236
    resolution, 235
    special effects filters, 310

importing files, 18
in-betweens, 147
Incoming Curve control, Curves Properties, 264
Info display, Modeler interface, 5
Info numeric fields
    animation, 154
    Layout interface, 3
Info panels, 56–57
Intensity Falloff, shadows, 220–221
Intensity parameter, Caustics effect, 230
interfaces
    customizing, 6–8
        creating tabs, 8–9
        reset interface default, 9
    keyboard shortcuts, 10–11
    Layout, 2–3
    Modeler, 4–5
Intersect function, Boolean operations, 117
Inverse Kinematics (IK), 276
    creating chain, 277–280
    Keep Goal Within Reach option, 281–282
    Match Goal Orientation option, 282–283
    rotational constraints, 283–284
Invert Selection command, 88

J-K

joint compensation, bones, 202–203

Keep Goal Within Reach option, Inverse
        Kinematics (IK), 281–282
keyboard shortcuts, 10–11
Keyframe Magazine, xii
Keyframe tools, Layout interface, 3
keyframes, 147, 163
    automation, 250–253
    deleting, 166
    management
        editing motions, 259–267
        Graph Editor interface, 254–258
    manually creating, 164–165

L

Lathe tool, 113–114
Layer bank, Modeler interface, 4
layers, 82–85
    clipboard actions, 90
    textures, 346–349
Layout interface, 2–3
    content directory, 20–21
    customizing, 6–8
        creating tabs, 8–9

reset interface default, 9
disabling Auto Key feature, 163
files, 15–17
mouse button menus, 5
object sent from Hub, 13
Viewports
    global display options, 39–41
    grid configuration, 35
    modifying, 33
Layout menu commands, Quad, 44
Left view type, 24
lens, cameras, 239–241
Lens F-Stop, depth of fields, 246
Lens Flare Options for Light panel, 226
Level-of-Detail Replacement Properties
        panel, 179
Level-of-Detail tool, 177–179
Light Name dialog, 210
Light Properties panel, 216
Light view type, 25
lights, 207
    adding
        area light, 214
        distant light, 209–210
        linear light, 213
        point light, 211
        spotlight, 212–213
        target object, 215
    Global Illumination panel
        Caustics effect, 230
        Radiosity effect, 228–229
    HDRI (High Dynamic Range Imagery), 376–378
    parameters
        Affect Diffuse, 218
        Affect Specular, 218
        color, 216
        intensity, 217
        OpenGL toggle, 219
    rendering exclusion, 375
    shadows
        Intensity Falloff, 220–221
        ray-traced, 222
        shadow map, 223–224
    special effects, 225
        Lens Flare, 226
        volumetric lights, 227
    types, 208
Lights menu commands
    Area Light, 214
    Distant Light, 209
    Linear Light, 213
    Point Light, 211
    Spotlight, 212

LightWave 3D
   companion website, xii
   Windows *versus* Macintosh, x–xi
Limited Region option, camera rendering, 238
Linear Light command (Lights menu), 213
linear lights, 208, 213
liquid effects, HyperVoxels special effects, 312–316
Load Image dialog, 295
Load Object command (File menu), 13
Load Object dialog, 16
Load Scene dialog, 15
Local coordinate systems, 288, 290–291
Luminosity surface attributes, 327
Luxology website, xii

M

Magnet tool, 93–94
Make Preview command (Preview menu), 180
Make Preview dialog, 168
Make Spline Patch panel, 75–76
Match Goal Orientation option, Inverse
   Kinematics (IK), 282–283
Max OpenGL Lights option, 37
memory, Segment Memory setting, 239
Menu hierarchical list, 6
Merge Points command, 102–103
Merge Polygons command, 105
Message window
   Layout interface, 3
   Modeler interface, 5
Meta-geometry modeling, 66
Metaball controls, 182
Minimize/Maximize view tool, 31
Modeler interface, 4–5
   changing settings, 44–46
   content directory, 21
   files, 17
   mouse button menus, 5
   Viewports
      global display options, 41–42
      grid configuration, 36
      modifying, 34
Modes menu, Modeler interface, 5
morph maps, 141–143
morphing objects
   continue using envelope, 194–195
   EndoMorph Mixer, 196–197
   geometry set up, 189–191
   Morph Amount value, 193–194
   target objects invisible, 192
Motion graph, Graph Editor interface, 254
Motion Options panel, 271
MotionMixer, x

motions
   blurs, 247
   channel modifiers, 268–270
   Graph Editor interface, 259–267
   modifiers, 287
   pictures, 158
   Post Behavior, 265–267
   rendering
      field rendering, 248
      motion blur, 247
Move Key tool, Graph Editor interface, 259
Move tool, 91–92
Movie view tool, 31
multiple surfaces, 333
multiple UV manipulators, 145
muscle flexing, bones, 204

N

N-gon polygons, 51
NewTek Pro, xii
NewTek website, x
Nominal Distance option, 374
normals, polygons, 55
NTSC video, 158
Null Object dialog, 174
Null Object Name dialog, 149, 176, 215
null objects, 172, 176
Numeric panel
   points, 49
   primitives, 61
   Text tool, 65

O

Object Properties panel, 173
Object Replacement tools, 176–179
objects, 172
   bones
      adding to objects, 198–200
      adjusting falloff, 201
      joint compensation, 202–203
      muscle flexing, 204
      use from other objects, 205
   changing subdivision surfaces, 181–182
   customizing, 174–175
   deforming geometry, 183–186
   displacement tools, 187–188
   generating preview, 180
   glowing, 308–309
   importing/exporting, 18
   Level-of-Detail tool, 177–179
   light targeting, 215
   morphing

continue using envelope, 194–195
EndoMorph Mixer, 196–197
geometry set up, 189–191
Morph Amount value, 193–194
target objects invisible, 192
Object Properties panel, 173
replacement, 176
skelegons, 206
Objects in Scene field, Object Properties
panel, 173
one-point polygons, 50
Open command (Scene Editor menu), 12
Open File dialog, 13
OpenGL Pixel Blending option, 38
OpenGL Reflections option, 38
OpenGL Texture Resolution option, 37
OpenGL Textures option, 37
OpenGL Transparency option, 38
OpenGL Viewports, 23. *See also* Viewports
Layout interface, 2
Modeler interface, 4
Option menu commands, General Options, 21
organic modeling
curves and spline patches, 70–76
SubPatches, 66–70
Other Edges option, 374
Overlay Color option, 41

P

PAL video, 158
parameters, lights
Affect Specular, 218
color, 216
intensity, 217
OpenGL toggle, 219
Parent coordinate systems, 288
parenting items, animation, 272–275
particle effects, 299
collision plane, 302–303
creating particle emitter, 300–301
gravity, 302
wind, 303–304
Particle/Line Thickness option, 373
parts, assigning points/polygons, 57
Pen tool, 53
Perspective Amount option, 41
Perspective view type, 24
pixels, aspect ratio, 236
Planar projection types, 339
Point at Target option, 285
Point Info panel, 56–57
Point Light command (Lights menu), 211

points
creating, 47–48
lights, 208, 211
Merge Points command, 102–103
Numeric panel, 49
selection sets, 57
series, 49
Unweld Points command, 103
Weld Points command, 103
Points and Polygons field, Object Properties
panel, 173
Polygon Info panel, 56–57
Polygon Size option, 372
polygons, 50–51
Add Points tool, 104
creating, 52
edge modifying tools
adding, 107–108
extend polygon edge, 106–107
reduction, 108–109
removing, 109–110
extending, 111–115
hiding, 89
Merge Polygons command, 105
Pen tool, 53
shared points, 54
skelegons
adding to objects, 206
editing, 80
series using curves, 79
Skelegon tool, 77–78
Split command, 104–105
surfaces
advanced properties, 351
animating over time, 350–352
attributes, 327–333
creating, 322–324
Preset window, 355–356
Surface Editor, 325–326
textures, 334–349
Viper (Versatile Interactive Previewing
Renderer), 353–354
Post Behavior control
Curves Properties, 264
setting for motion, 265–267
Pre Behavior control, Curves Properties, 264
Preset menu commands, Default, 9
Preset window, surfaces, 355–356
Preview menu commands, Make Preview, 180
primitives, 59
creating segments, 62
making box, 60
Numeric panel, 61

procedurals
    layered textures, 346–349
    textures, 340–342
Progress monitor, Modeler interface, 5
projection types, 339
Properties dialog (Hub), 14

Q-R

Quad command (Layout menu), 44
Quickshade rendering mode, 367

Radiosity effect, Global Illumination
        panel, 228–229
Rail Extrude tool, 114–115
Ray Recursion Limit option, 370
Ray-trace options, 369–371
    renderer, 358
    shadows, 222
Raymarcher fog type, 307
Realistic rendering mode, 368
Receive Shadow option, 372
Reduce Edges tool, 108–109
Reflection surface attributes, 328
Refraction Index surface attributes, 328
Remove Edges tool, 109–110
Rename Group dialog, 9
Rename Skelegon tool, 80
Render Options panel, 243, 360
Render Status window, 363
rendering, 357
    configuring
        save out animation file, 362–363
        sequential frames, 364–365
        set up, 360–361
    Edge options, 372–374
    HDRI (High Dynamic Range Imagery), 376–378
    light exclusion, 375
    modes
        Quickshade, 367
        Realistic, 368
        Wireframe, 366–367
    Ray-trace options, 369–371
    Shadow options, 372
    times, 358–359
        Limited Region, 238
        Resolution Multiplier, 237
Reset View Position tool, 32
Reset View Rotation tool, 32
Reset View Zoom tool, 32
Resolution Multiplier option, camera
        rending, 237
resources, xii
Right view type, 24

Roll Keys tool, Graph Editor interface, 259
Rotate Skelegon tool, 80
Rotate view tool, 31, 95–96
rotation, Inverse Kinematics (IK), 283–284

S

Save command (File menu), 15
Save File dialog, 18
Save Object command (File menu), 17
Save Scene As dialog, 15
Scale Key tool, Graph Editor interface, 259
Scene Editor, 12
Scene Editor menu commands, Open, 12
scenes, rendering, 357
    configuring, 360–365
    Edge options, 372–374
    HDRI (High Dynamic Range Imagery), 376–378
    light exclusion, 375
    modes, 366–368
    Ray-trace options, 369–371
    Shadow options, 372
    times, 237–238, 358–359
Schematic view type, 25
Segment Memory setting, frame rendering, 239
Selected Connected command, 87
selection methods
    hiding polygons, 89
    Invert Selections command, 88
    Selected Connected command, 87
    test object, 86–87
Selection Modes, Modeler interface, 5
Self Shadow option, 372
Send Object to Layout command (Hub
        menu), 13
Set Skelegon Weight tool, 80
Set Vertex Map Value dialog, 138
Shaded Solid drawing mode, 29
shaders, surfaces, 351–352
Shadow options, rendering, 372
shadows
    Intensity Falloff, 220–221
    ray-traced, 222
    shadow map, 223–224
Sharp Creases option, 373
Show Backdrop option, 42
Show Cages option, 42
Show Fog Circles option, 40
Show Grid option, 42
Show Guides option, 41
Show Handles option, 40
Show IK Chains option, 40
Show Motion Path option, 40
Show Normals option, 42

Show Point Selection option, 42
Show Points option, 41
Show Polygon Selection option, 42
Show SubPatch Cages option, 41
Show Surfaces option, 41
Show Target Lines option, 41
Show Texture Editor Layer option, 38
Shrink Edges with Distance option, 374
Shuttle controls
    animation preview, 167
    Layout interface, 3
Silhouette Edges option, 373
Size tool, 98, 156
Skelegon tool, 77–78
Skelegon Tree tool, 80
skelegons
    adding to objects, 206
    editing, 80
    series using curves, 79
    Skelegon tool, 77–78
Sketch drawing mode, 28
Sketch tool, creating curves, 72
SkyTracer2 environment tool, 296-298
smoke effects, HyperVoxels special
        effects, 317–319
Smooth Threshold surface attributes, 329
Smoothing surface attributes, 329
Snap tool, 92
soft-body dynamics, x
Softness parameter, Caustics effect, 230
special effects, 293
    backdrop
        color change, 294
        environment, 296
        SkyTracer2, 297–298
        using image, 295–296
    fog, 305–307
    glowing objects, 308–309
    HyperVoxels, 311
        liquid effects, 312–316
        smoke effects, 317–319
    image filters, 310
    lights, 208, 225
        Lens Flare, 226
        volumetric lights, 227
    particle effects, 299
        collision plane, 302–303
        creating particle emitter, 300–301
        gravity, 302
        wind, 303–304
Specularity surface attributes, 327
Spherical projection types, 339
Spherize tool, 190

Spline Draw tool, creating curve, 73–74
Spline Guide tool, 100–102
spline patches, 70–76. See also curves
Split command, 104–105
Split Skelegon tool, 80
Spotlight command (Lights menu), 212
spotlights, 208, 212-213
Spreadsheet Scene Manager, x
Sprite mode, HyperVoxels special effects, 311
Squash tool, animation tools, 157
Statistics panel, 58
Stretch tool, 99, 156
Subdivide Polygons dialog, 183
subdivision surfaces, 66, 181–182
SubPatch Weights, 132
    adjusting, 133–134
    Weight Shade mode, 135
SubPatches modeling, 66–70
Subtract function, Boolean operations, 118
Surface Borders option, 374
Surface Editor, 325–326, 331
Surface mode, HyperVoxels special effects, 311
surfaces
    advanced properties, 351
    animating over time, 350–352
    attributes, 327–333
    creating, 322
        all polygons, 323
        groups of polygons, 324
    Preset window, 355–356
    Surface Editor, 325–326
    textures, 334–335
        gradients, 343–345
        image map, 337–339
        layers, 346–349
        procedurals, 340–342
        Texture Editor, 336
    Viper (Versatile Interactive Previewing
        Renderer), 353–354
Swap Layers command, 120

T

tabs
    Layout interface, 2
    Modeler interface, 4
Taper Constrain tool, 100
target objects
    adding lights, 215
    animation tools, 271
telephoto lens, 241–242
Tension control, Curves Properties, 264

text
  adding font to Modeler interface, 63
  creating, 64
  Text tool Numeric panel, 65
Text tool, 65
Texture control, surface attributes, 330
Texture Editor, 336
Texture Environment tool, 296
Texture Guide, 145
Texture Resolution option, 41
Textured Shaded Solid drawing mode, 29
Textured Shaded Solid Wireframe drawing
      mode, 29
textures, 334–335
  gradients, 343–345
  image map, 337–339
  layers, 346–349
  procedurals, 340–342
  Texture Editor, 336
three-point polygons, 50
Tool Falloffs, 137–140
tool handles, animation, 152
toolbars
  Layout interface, 2
  Modeler interface, 4
tools
  animation, 155–157, 249
    channel modifiers, 268–270
    coordinate systems, 288–291
    handles, 152
    Inverse Kinematics, 276–284
    keyframe automation, 250–253
    managing keyframes, 254–267
    motion modifiers, 287
    motion options, 285–286
    parenting items, 272–275
    targeting objects, 271
  Viewports, 31–32
Top view type, 24
Translucency surface attributes, 328–329
Transparency surface attributes, 328
tutorials, xii
tweeners, 147
tweens, 147
Twist tool, 97
two-point polygons, 50

U

Unaffected by Fog option, rendering, 371
Union function, Boolean operations, 117
Unseen by Camera option, rendering, 371
Unseen by Rays option, rendering, 371
Unshared Edges option, 373

Unweld Points command, 103
UV projection types, 339
UV texture maps, 122
  creating, 125
  edit coordinates, 130–131
  interface set up, 128–129
  surface set up, 126–127
  test polygon, 123–124
UV Texture view type, 25

V

Value control
  Curves Properties, 264
  surface attributes, 330
Versatile Interactive Previewing Renderer
      (Viper), 353–354
vertex maps (VMap), 69, 121
  color maps, 144–145
  morph maps, 141–143
  UV texture maps, 122
    creating, 125
    edit coordinates, 130–131
    interface set up, 128–129
    surface set up, 126–127
    test polygon, 123–124
  weight maps
    Bone Weights, 136
    SubPatch Weights, 132–136
    Tool Falloffs, 137–140
Vertex Paint, 145
vertex shading, 144
Vertices drawing mode, 26
video games, color maps, 144
Viewports, 23
  customizing OpenGL options, 37–38
  drawing modes, 26–30
  global display options, 39–42
  grid configuration, 35–36
  modifying, 33–34
  tools, 31–32
  types, 24–25
views, modifying, 32
Viper (Versatile Interactive Previewing
      Renderer), 297, 353–354
VMap (vertex map), 69, 121
  color maps, 144–145
  Modeler interface edit modes, 5
  morph maps, 141–143
  UV texture maps, 122
    creating, 125
    edit coordinates, 130–131
    interface set up, 128–129
    surface set up, 126–127

INDEX

test polygon, 123–124
weight maps
    Bone Weights, 136
    SubPatch Weights, 132–136
    Tool Falloffs, 137–140
Volume mode, HyperVoxels special effects, 311
volumetric lights, special effects, 227
Volumetric Options for Light panel, 227

W

Web sites
    Flay, xii
    LightWave 3D companion, xii
    Luxology, xii
weight maps
    Bone Weights, 136
    SubPatch Weights, 132
        adjusting, 133–134
        Weight Shade mode, 135
    Tool Falloffs, 137–140
Weight Shade drawing mode, 30
Weld Points command, 103
wide angle lens, 241–242
wind, particle effects, 299, 303–304
Wireframe
    drawing mode, 27
    rendering mode, 366–367
    Shade drawing mode, 28
World coordinate systems, 288

X-Y-Z

Zoom Box tool, Graph Editor interface, 259
Zoom view tool, 31